ON SILVER WINGS

This colour portrait of Desmond, recreated on a commemorative plate, began the search. (Ibbotson family album)

ON SILVER WINGS

A SPITFIRE ACE REDISCOVERED

JAMES B. WRIGHT

Cover illustrations: Front: Desmond Ibbotson (Ibbotson family archive), Spitfire MK IXe MK356 (Wikimedia Commons/Tony Hisgett); *Back:* Desmond Ibbotson (Ibbotson family archive).

First published 2025

The History Press
97 St George's Place, Cheltenham,
Gloucestershire, GL50 3QB
www.thehistorypress.co.uk

© James B. Wright, 2025

The right of James B. Wright to be identified as the Author of this work has been asserted in accordance with the Copyright, Designs and Patents Act 1988.

All rights reserved. No part of this book may be reprinted or reproduced or utilised in any form or by any electronic, mechanical or other means, now known or hereafter invented, including photocopying and recording, or in any information storage or retrieval system, without the permission in writing from the Publishers.

British Library Cataloguing in Publication Data.
A catalogue record for this book is available from the British Library.

ISBN 978 1 80399 920 3

Typesetting and origination by The History Press
Printed and bound in Great Britain by TJ Books, Padstow, Cornwall

The History Press proudly supports

Trees for Life

www.treesforlife.org.uk

EU Authorised Representative: Easy Access System Europe
Mustamäe tee 50, 10621 Tallinn, Estonia
gpst.request@easproject.com

For June, our family, and in memory of
Sqn Ldr Mark Long of the BBMF

Contents

Acknowledgements   9

PART 1: The Unofficial Eyewitness: A Chance Meeting and New Questions

    An Introduction   15
1   The Unknown Eyewitness   25

PART 2: What Happened to Desmond: The Man, the Ace and the Woman He Taught to Fly

2   From Yorkshire to New Zealand and Back   29
3   No. 4 Elementary Flying Training School   35
4   No. 8 Service Flying Training School   38
5   53 Operational Training Unit   43
6   129 Squadron   49
7   54 Squadron   55
8   54 Squadron – French Rhubarbs and Scottish Hail   69
9   112 Squadron – The Western Desert   89
10   112 Squadron – The Great Retreat   99
11   601 Squadron – El Alamein and Escape   111
12   601 Squadron – The Advance to Tunis   124

13	The Interlude Between Tours	140
14	Central Gunnery School	142
15	103 Maintenance Unit – Test and Delivery Duties	148
16	601 Squadron – Spitfires Over Anzio	163
17	601 Squadron – Final Victories	180
18	601 Squadron and the WAAFs	195
19	No. 5 Refresher Flying Unit	211
20	5 RFU – Final Flight	217

PART 3: The Aftermath: The Family and Two Burial Sites for One Man

21	The Aftermath	227
22	Sarah Remembers Desmond – The Way to the Stars	231
23	Sarah Visits Desmond's Grave	234
24	Muriel Remembers Desmond's Death	239
25	The Re-Excavation of Desmond's Spitfire	257
26	Digging for the Truth	263
27	Desmond's Story Emerges	269
28	Desmond is Laid to Rest	273
29	The Knowns and Unknowns	285

Notes	293
Glossary	309
Bibliography	313
Index	317

Acknowledgements

I first began researching this story over twenty years ago, and I am very grateful to a wide number and variety of people whose contribution deserves recognition. Muriel's husband, Jim, unwittingly started the whole thing off when he kindly agreed to my interviewing him in the autumn of 2003 about his army days in Italy when he took part in the landings at Salerno, crossing a beach under enemy fire some sixty years earlier. Jim was an ideal interviewee because of the clarity and detail with which he remembered his experiences. A true gentleman, he was always patient with my questions and interesting to talk to. Like many others, Jim served his country faithfully and faced the same dangers as those alongside him who did not come home. After a long life, he died in 2004.

Muriel, understandably, never forgot her brother and made sure her children knew about their Uncle Desmond, the Spitfire pilot. It is thanks to them – Muriel, John, David, Judy and Barbara – who, along with Molly's daughter, Jayne, all very kindly helped me understand Desmond and research his life. Without their kindness, generosity, support and assistance as a family, none of this would have been possible. After a long and happy marriage to Jim, Muriel died in 2012.

Similarly, I'd like to give a special thank you to Patsy's son Rob, who very kindly allowed me to discuss his mum's memoir and reproduce some of that material to give another, previously unheard, side to Desmond's story and a glimpse of a life he could have enjoyed if he had made it home. Patsy died in 2015.

In addition, I am grateful for the unstinting help, advice, encouragement, patience, humour and forbearance of my (now sadly deceased) parents, my wife, June, and stepdaughters, Caz and Jose, who together did so much in the background that enabled me to complete this work.

Then there are the veterans and their families. Ray Sherk, one of Desmond's fellow Spitfire pilots, both in training and on No. 129 Squadron, who lived in Ontario, Canada, kindly replied to my letters and sent me a rare photo he took of Norm Peat, Jimmy Whalen and Desmond with a Spitfire. Of these four friends, only Ray survived the war. He clarified an inaccuracy in the official records too regarding his time on 601 Squadron in the desert. Ray continued to fly until the age of 91 and died in 2016 aged 94.

Jamie Ivers put me in touch with 601 Squadron's biographer, Tom Moulson, who also kindly helped with background information and answered some thorny questions on Desmond's alleged meeting with Rommel. I am indebted to Rob Brown, who runs the 112 Squadron tribute website – an impressively detailed database – through which I have been able to request help in verifying information from that period of the war. Through contact with his son, G. Howe, D.J. Howe, a Canadian flight sergeant who joined 112 Squadron as a pilot, was able to put names to a previously unidentified group photo. 'Tex' Phillips's daughter, Sarah, kindly passed my questions on to her father, who flew with Billy Drake and Desmond in the summer of 1942. Sadly, her father died not long after, at the age of 93. To have had the chance to communicate with some of Desmond's wartime friends has been much appreciated.

Gp Capt Steve Lloyd of the Ministry of Defence Air Historical Branch, based at Bentley Priory, provided unique information on Perugia airfield in the early stages of my research and a summary of Desmond's career from sources not readily available to me at the time.

Sue Raftree of the Joint Casualty Clearing Centre, part of the RAF Personnel Management Agency at Imjin Barracks (since renamed the Joint Casualty and Compassionate Centre Commemorations team, and informally known as the 'MoD War Detectives') in Gloucestershire, helped with background information on the identification process when Desmond's remains were found.

David Hirst and cameraman Martin of Yorkshire Television very kindly allowed me to tag along with them in Italy for the memorial services.

Acknowledgements

Leo Venieri and Marco Maiani of Romagna Air Finders helped me to learn more about the team's work. I thank them for their very kind assistance and their dedicated work in recovering and preserving the memory of many young airmen from all sides who lost their lives in the war.

John Purtell, a Foreign and Commonwealth Office official based at the British Embassy in Rome, very kindly translated for me, both out in Italy when questioning the eyewitnesses and later when translating letters to the witnesses and passages from an Italian book regarding Perugia airfield. Much would still be a mystery, were it not for his efforts.

Thanks to Bruno Cavallucci, Antonio Cavallucci and Eugenio Pennacchi because without them, there would be no chance of ever having an idea about what happened in November 1944. When the ceremonies ended, at the edge of that field in Umbria, this kind and humble gentleman, Eugenio, finally told Desmond's family his story about that final flight and the recovery efforts he was part of at the time.

Thank you to the staff of The National Archives, Royal Air Force Museum Hendon, Imperial War Museum (Department of Documents and Department of Photographs) and the Liddell Hart Centre for Military Archives at King's College London, who all kindly fielded my numerous queries with much patience and efficiency.

Oreste Martini kindly flew Bruno, Eugenio and me over the crash site at low level and over the Rivotorto cemetery. He was proud to have flown with his small display team, 'Walter's Bad', over the cemetery on the day Desmond was reburied. He and his colleague Claudio Munalli, the secretary of Perugia Aeroclub, kindly provided contemporary photos of St Egidio airfield and a book about the airfield's history. Claudio's father, Luigi, was actually a sergeant in the Italian Air Force based at the airfield when the Allies captured it and was given special dispensation to work with the British at the airfield for the time they were there.

More recently, as research led to writing, meeting Shelley Harris, Helen Fields and Diccon Bewes in 2012 at West Dean near Chichester in West Sussex proved both inspirational and motivational. Seeing them go on from early success to release more titles and flourish, sometimes in the face of very difficult challenges along the way, has kept me going and given me many happy memories too. I'd also like to express my deep gratitude for Stephanie Butland and her professional oversight and expertise in managing both me and my writing, through various rewrites to completion. To conclude the journey to the finished article has taken the very kind assistance and expertise of Amy Rigg and the fantastic team at The History Press to bring this book to life.

Lastly my thanks goes to Desmond and Patsy, because his logbooks and memorabilia (now in the Yorkshire Air Museum) and her memoirs (now in the RAF Museum) are precious artefacts through which we understand what happened. Desmond's logbooks evolved into a diary which, with typical understatement, reveal the enjoyment, frustration, fun, courage, hope and danger he experienced. Like so many others, Desmond did not live to see the end of the war itself. It is, therefore, to the young men and women of that generation that the final thanks of all must go. I hope this story does them justice.

Every effort has been made to ascertain copyright throughout, but in the event of any omission, please contact the author, care of the publisher.

PART I

The Unofficial Eyewitness

A Chance Meeting and New Questions

An Introduction

Hotel Giotto
Assisi, Umbria, Italy, 8 June 2007

The press conference ended. People, some in uniform, others in smart civilian clothes, shuffled and pardoned their way past each other and fought their way to refreshment: a cooling drink from the bar or a waft of air from the gentle, cool breeze drifting up the side of the valley, over the medieval rooftops.

A small cluster of people remained inside the function room for the time being, gathered round those who were involved in the story and the journalists who wanted more details from them.

I wanted to talk to one of them myself – the official eyewitness. I had travelled a long way, from the north of England to central Italy, to attend the press conference that would precede the ceremony of reinterment for Desmond Ibbotson scheduled for the following day. I had journeyed into Desmond's life and death and grown to admire him enormously. What had started out as researching a few additional facts to add to the family's knowledge and understanding of what their relative had done had turned into a personal quest to find the truth behind his untimely death and reveal the full extent of his daring exploits.

Desmond had lived the kind of life I had only imagined or seen pictured in comics when I was a boy – characters who faced their 'death or glory' destinies with resolute determination, often in the face of overwhelming odds. Duty called and decent men did as they must.

As Churchill said in 1940, 'We will defend our island, whatever the cost may be.'[1] That same man, Desmond Ibbotson, whose ceremony I had come to attend, had been a Spitfire pilot and a decorated ace in November 1944.

In my view, Desmond Ibbotson was much more than a comic strip hero; he had, in fact, been one of the best fighter pilots of his generation until he had been killed flying a Spitfire in November 1944. His sister Muriel, four years his junior, had grown up with him until she was almost 14. Then he joined the RAF and was later posted overseas. She did not see him after the spring of 1942 and was certain he had died in an accident – the records said so, and he had a marked grave that the family had visited in the years since.

These were the established facts that formed the basis of Muriel's family story. Strangely, Desmond was not the reason I initially met Muriel. Four years before flying to Italy, in 2003, I had gone round to her house to interview her husband, Jim, about his experiences from the landings at Salerno through to the prelude to the Battle of Monte Cassino. As I made to leave at the end of our last meeting, Muriel arrived home. I asked her whose face was on the picture-plate that hung on the white wallpapered wall of their front lounge. Muriel replied that it was her brother, Desmond, a Spitfire pilot who had been killed on a test flight. The sense of mystery about the death of a Spitfire pilot and my deep interest in RAF history drew me in. I wanted to find out more about what had happened. Desmond had never been forgotten by his family. Aside from the picture, Muriel had named her eldest son after him: John Desmond. Now, at this afternoon's press conference, Desmond's nephew had sat at the long table on a small stage with officials from the British Embassy in Rome.

Fourteen months earlier, a story about Desmond had hit the national press, both in the UK and Italy. Now he was hitting the headlines for a second time. Desmond had been in the papers a couple of times when he was alive, and he had enjoyed the recognition. Despite the upset the recent media attention had brought, we all agreed he would have loved to have been here and heard us talking about him. I would have given my eye-teeth to have shared a bottle of whisky with him and hear his stories about his time flying Spitfires over Yorkshire, France, Libya, Tunisia,

An Introduction

Egypt and Italy. I had been in touch with some of the pilots he had flown with, and all it had done was fire me up to hear more.

It was in this very hotel, the Hotel Giotto, almost certainly this very room, nearly sixty-three years to the day that Desmond had been partying with his fellow pilots, drinking and carousing late into the night, dancing to a swing band until last orders, then drunkenly swaying down the newly liberated streets of Assisi singing a well-known anthem of the Third Reich – Horst Wessel's 'The Flag Raised High' – and laughing like drains. So, when the reporters in the conference asked John what kind of man Desmond was, I wanted to call out from the back row, like someone interrupting a wedding ceremony, and tell them what I knew.

'He was a dashing Spitfire ace, an accomplished pilot, but he was also someone who loved fast cars and had an eye for the ladies,' John informed the audience. All of which was true if leaning towards a caricature straight out of those 1970s comics. There was more to Desmond's life and death than had previously been reported though.

As the meeting closed, I headed for the official eyewitness. He was a distinguished-looking gentleman, around 70 years of age, with a full head of silver hair neatly clipped at the sides and brushed back. He was clean shaven and wore an expensive-looking dark suit with a light-pink shirt that was open at the neck. To one side of him were a couple of British Foreign and Commonwealth Office officials, one of whom, Francesca, was also a fluent Italian speaker. She introduced us – his name was Bruno – and he agreed we could talk outside later.

Out on the veranda, I joined the Yorkshire Television crew I had met the previous evening. They were interviewing a stout Italian gentleman called Leo Venieri who had been one of the four panel members on stage and who had led the team of aviation archaeologists who had found Desmond's remains. David, the reporter, put me to use holding a fold-out reflector screen while Martin, the cameraman, began filming David interviewing Leo. I did as I was told until the interview was over.

As we were packing away and making polite chit-chat, I fell into conversation with a young English-speaking Italian man called Dario, who I guessed to be in his late twenties or early thirties, with long dark hair and slender features. He also had an interest in the story, and he agreed to translate for me, so I approached Leo and asked if I could interview him.

I introduced myself and explained that I was researching Desmond's story. I thanked Leo for his email informing me that Bruno would be attending the event today as the official eyewitness and asked if he could join us at some stage. He agreed, and I hastily drew up a list of questions for Bruno. Dario and his girlfriend, who sat diagonally across from me, were making a documentary about the story. Dario leant back against the railing, took a long draw on a Camel Light cigarette and, in a well-practised exhalation, cocked his head back slightly and directed the smoke upwards.

After asking Leo a few questions, I turned to the details of the crash itself. How had it happened? What did the eyewitness see? He answered them in a proficient but considered manner. Part way through, Bruno appeared to one side of Leo. He drew up a chair and listened to Leo's introduction.

The officer who had led the press conference, Cdr Shawn Steeds, the naval and air attaché based in Rome, had mentioned Bruno but only to a limited extent. Bruno was only 7 years old at the time. He had been standing in the kitchen of his house when he heard an explosion outside. I asked Bruno more about what had happened. Although only very young, he remembered it vividly. He described what he thought had been a bomb going off and had been too frightened to go outside. As he talked, I took notes and went over some of the same questions I had asked Leo separately just a few moments before, in an effort to judge the consistency of their answers and see if Bruno would reveal any other morsels of information – something that would explain not just the 'what' but the 'how' and perhaps even the 'why' Desmond had been killed.

With the interviews over, a short time later, I drove David and Martin to the crash site. John and his brother, Dave, and sister, Judy – the other members of Desmond's family attending – were going to be there, and they wanted to film the family's reaction to visiting the spot where Desmond's Spitfire came down.

We made our way through the narrow streets of the old town, emerged in a small cavalcade from one of the old stone-walled gateways over the street, onto the main highway and snaked our way down the hill to the valley floor once more. I had failed to find the place earlier. Now, with an embassy official in the lead, there would be no trouble.

An Introduction

Heading parallel to the north side of the railway line and round the hairpin, visible only at the last minute, is a small junction. We turned right, following the road under a railway bridge, and turned left at the junction immediately on exiting from under the bridge. Parallel to the railway once more and past a factory was another, hidden, junction. This road was narrower still. Only wide enough for one vehicle and, with fields on either side, I understood now why I had not found it. This little lane meandered off round field boundaries, past isolated farmhouses and dirt tracks for another 2 miles or so before hitting a straight stretch. The road was now hidden from view by a field of tall sunflowers to one side and, behind a tree line, level fields full of ripening wheat on the other. Only a local would have known this area, or indeed have had any reason to come down here at all.

Our little convoy slowed and began to park up. Opposite the slight embankment that bordered the field of sunflowers, and between a gap in the old trees lining the opposite side of the road, was the memorial. One or two of the locals had been tending the site, making sure all was ready for the ceremony the next day. As we arrived, they took the cover off the stone and stepped back from the flower bed at the front.

There, in a little white gravel bay offset from the road, at a point where the ditch was crossed by a concrete land drain, was a large stone. It looked about the same size and rough shape as an aeroplane's tail-fin. On its polished, white marble-like face was black engraving and a black and white photo of Desmond in an oval surround. I recognised it immediately; I had seen the image in Muriel's photo album several years before. It was a full-faced, sepia-toned portrait of him in RAF battle-dress, laughing. It had been taken on the afternoon of 8 November 1942, following his safe return to his squadron. Written records suggested Desmond had been shot down while on a patrol, possibly seeking to kill the very man it was said he had escaped from – Erwin Rommel, the legendary Desert Fox. Desmond had survived a crash-landing, escaped from the Germans and walked home – just like that. No wonder he was laughing about it – he couldn't believe it himself. Two years later he had been killed, here in Italy, in another Spitfire crash.

This was it then. The actual field in which Desmond's Spitfire had come down. It was noticeably silent, peaceful in the approaching summer evening. Everyone had retreated into their own thoughts and was taking in the scene. A minute or two went by, then John stepped forward and leant out to touch the picture to the left side of the stone face. I surreptitiously took a photo, conscious of the fact this was the first time anyone from Desmond's family had actually been here. Everyone believed he had been buried in 1944 in the Rivotorto military cemetery that lay a few miles to the north-east. So, when Leo's team of archaeologists found Desmond's remains in this field, inside the remnants of his Spitfire, it begged the question: just who was buried in the grave marked with Desmond's name?

David and Martin slipped quietly into news mode again. Martin raised his TV camera onto his shoulder and began recording some footage while David waited for the right moment to approach the family. I walked to a position about 50m away and tried to work out which way Desmond's Spitfire had been flying to end up in this particular field, and where it was in relation to the nearest village, Castelnuovo. When I looked again, I noticed Martin now had a digital camera in his hand. He stood in the road, taking photos. One of them would be on a newspaper's front page the next day.

I climbed the small embankment and stood in front of the regimented rows of sunflowers facing Desmond's memorial. The sunflowers were each 6ft tall and had, in unison, tracked the sun across the sky through the day. Now every one of their large dark faces stared silently and directly towards the west as the day's end approached. Every inch of land had been used in cultivating this densely packed crop, and I stood unsteadily at the top of the 3ft-high slope trying to keep my balance on the loose soil. Assisi was still visible in the distance. I recalled the photos Romagna Air Finders (RoAF) had taken from the actual excavation site, and everything now fell into place. The background and orientation of the photos made sense at last. They had not been digging between the military cemetery and the Assisi ridge, as I had first thought; they had been digging over to the west and a few miles further south.

I looked back to the stone and saw Desmond's relatives – John, Dave, Liz and Judy – in a group embrace. They were no doubt thinking not only about Desmond, but of their mum, Muriel, who had been unable to make the long journey. After half an hour or so, we all returned to the Hotel Giotto. In the hotel foyer we made informal plans for the evening. I had already agreed to meet up again with Dario and Leo that evening. Dario had asked for some help in understanding what Desmond had been doing in Assisi before his accident. I returned to my hotel in Santa Maria degli Angeli briefly before setting out again to meet Dario and Leo at their hotel by the railway station at 7.30 p.m. On arriving, though, I found they had left a note at reception to say they planned to go to the crash site separately and would meet me there. I set off again in fear of missing them altogether.

There were no other cars at the crash site when I arrived, and it was still pleasantly warm. This time, I stood in the road for a moment. The silence emphasised the fact I was alone here. I checked my watch and cursed under my breath. It was 7.35 p.m. now. I resigned myself to the fact I had missed Dario and Leo, or perhaps they had decided not to come at all. I looked across the fields. The only sounds were a dog barking in the distance and the odd ripple of birdsong drifting from the trees. I sighed and decided instead to use the time here as best I could to make a few notes and take photos.

I took out my camera and positioned it so the sun was just visible behind the memorial. The way the memorial stone had been placed, facing towards the lane, meant the sun would now set directly behind it every day. I recalled Laurence Binyon's famous line from the poem 'For the Fallen', which is recited every Remembrance Sunday: 'At the going down of the sun, and in the morning, we will remember them.' At this time of year, looking east towards the field of sunflowers, it appeared as though each of them were lined up on parade in front of the memorial.

After a few minutes I replaced the camera and unfolded my notepad. Finding it was difficult to write properly kneeling down with the pad balanced on one knee, I put the pad on the ground, knelt on the gravel facing the memorial and started making notes, trying to picture the field as it might have been way back in November 1944. A car pulled up in the lane. It must have looked as though I was praying. I expected it was just Dario and Leo arriving at last so did not look up initially.

I heard a car door close and glanced behind to see someone slowly walking across the tree-lined road towards the memorial. As the figure drew closer to me, I looked up to see an elderly man wearing a checked shirt and brown trousers fastened with a belt standing there, hands behind his back watching me curiously. He had not been at the press conference that afternoon. From his casual appearance and gentle, inquisitive demeanour, I took him to be a resident from one of the farmhouses that were dotted around the area. He looked at me, then at the memorial. He moved forward to touch it and started saying something in Italian, but I had no idea what. He smiled at my confusion, fixed my gaze with his soft brown eyes, pointed at my notepad and started talking slowly. Then he made a diving gesture with his hand and a whistling sound as his hand swept down. He finished with a 'whooshing' sound and the use of both hands to then indicate an explosion.

Now the penny dropped, and the hairs stood up on the back of my neck. I looked towards the centre of the wheat field directly in front of us, beyond which, to the far west, the sun was now setting, its rays giving a warm golden hue to the feathered ears of wheat that swayed gently as eddies of warm breeze danced across them. I fumbled for words to ensure I had understood what he was indicating. I turned to face the memorial. One Italian word stood out etched in black upon the white marble-like stone of the memorial, *pilote*, and the surname alongside it, 'Ibbotson'. I repeated his gestures back to him and pointed to the centre of the field. The elderly gentleman smiled and, looking in my eyes, said simply, '*Sì.*' The hairs on my neck refused to lie flat. In the stillness of a warm summer evening with the sun about to fade, I stood somewhere in the middle of the Umbrian countryside next to an unknown gentleman who seemed to be trying to tell me he knew something about Desmond's crash. I spoke no Italian, he spoke no English, and there was no one to translate.

The sceptic in me began to question my initial thoughts. I tried to work out his background. He looked the right age, mid-seventies to eighties. His face was naturally lined and though not pale, neither was it red and weather beaten like that of a typical farmer. Who was he? Where had he come from? And where was an Italian speaker when I needed one?

I tried again to understand what he was saying. He ventured a few words in French. I replied in my very limited French to say simply that I was writing about Desmond and offered a few basic details about him. Then another idea came to me. I took out a pencil and flipped the paper on the pad over to a new page. I sketched a couple of tall trees and the field in front of us. I added a couple of artillery guns and a Spitfire diving down towards the ground with flames behind it. Using the sketch, a few hand gestures and words in French, I tried to communicate my thoughts more effectively. The elderly gentleman watched what I was doing intently. We sensed each other's frustration at not being able to completely understand each other, but I felt we were on the verge of a breakthrough. I showed him the sketch and asked him in French, 'Did you see the accident of the pilot Ibbotson in 1944?'

He turned and held my gaze with his now misty eyes. 'Yes,' he said, 'I saw everything.'

CHAPTER 1

The Unknown Eyewitness

A field near Castelnuovo
8 June 2007

I looked out across the field in front of us and tried to picture the scene sixty-two and a half years ago. Where had this man been standing, and what might he have seen? I knew only that the Spitfire had been on an air test, Assisi was in Allied hands and the front-line troops were 300km further north by that stage of the war. Bruno had described an explosion. This stranger next to me indicated that he had seen the same explosion.

Above my sketch of a Spitfire, I drew the mushroom shape of an open parachute with lines focusing to a body underneath. From the tail section I drew sharp zigzags as though a fire had taken hold and caused a pilot's worst nightmare – trapped in a burning aeroplane as it fell to earth.

Surely, if he had been shot down and the aircraft was on fire, Desmond would have tried to escape. I pointed to the parachute and asked the gentleman beside me if he had seen one. He looked, pointed to the stick man on the end of my pencil parachute then turned to face me and said simply, '*Non.*' I looked again at the memorial in front of me. The face was white marble with faint veins running across it. On the left side of the stone, just next to Desmond's picture, was a large semicircular grey gouge. What could simply have been the result of a machining process, where the cutter had struck a hidden fault line beneath the surface causing it to shatter and break off, had revealed a subtle, graduated depth. It looked as though the stone had been shot. The rough-edged white stone with its bullet-like wound reminded me of the many times Desmond had himself been shot at.

We talked a little more in French as I added some other potential hazards Desmond could have faced, but each one was met with an emphatic '*Non.*' The sun was casting soft golden hues across the wheat tops, and the shadows were lengthening. As we drifted slowly back to the roadside, I asked the gentleman if he was going to the memorial service tomorrow. There was his favourite word again: '*Non.*'

'Would you like to come to the service tomorrow?' I asked.

He smiled and nodded.

I showed him the timetable of events the RAF and Italian authorities had lined up. He agreed to go to the cemetery but did not look keen about going back to the Hotel Giotto afterwards, so I didn't press the matter.

Before we parted, I introduced myself and asked him his name. 'Pannacchi,' he said, 'Eugenio Pannacchi.' With a final farewell, he got in his car, a beaten-up Fiat with creaky doors and no power steering, and drove down the lane heading south towards the tiny village of Castelnuovo.

PART 2

What Happened to Desmond

The Man, the Ace and the Woman He Taught to Fly

CHAPTER 2

From Yorkshire to New Zealand and Back

1921–1940

In the first twelve-month period of Desmond's logbooks, there is no indication that he was an exceptional pilot. Indeed, he had hinted at having doubts himself. Yet the photos of his early childhood do not suggest he lacked confidence. Desmond was Horace and Sarah's first child and only son, born on 25 October 1921. Of all the pictures the family have of him, there was only one in which he was not grinning. It was taken on a visit to Albert Park in Auckland, New Zealand and, within the family group, only Sarah is managing to smile. Fifteen-year-old Desmond is on the far right of the picture, Horace the far left. Desmond bears a strong resemblance to his dad.

Desmond, loved by both parents, was adored by his mother. His dark hair, cheeky smile, happy disposition and blue eyes meant he could easily turn on the charm and get away with things that both his younger sisters, Muriel and Molly, would not, such as stealing sweets from the jars behind the till in his maternal grandma Ada's village post office when he thought no one was looking.

His family was tight knit and well known in the West Yorkshire village of Harewood. The house they lived in was tied accommodation: built and owned by the Earl of Harewood, whose family seat is the stately home Harewood House. Many of its residents, including Sarah, were employed by the estate. As a young man, Horace had joined the Royal Army Medical Corps and served in the First World War. After the war, he left the Army and took a job as the village postman. Ada ran the post office in Harewood.

Desmond preferred not to be called Desmond and was always known as 'Des' to his family. His school friends nicknamed him 'Dibby'. His RAF mates called him 'Ibby'. During his time at school and beyond, Desmond took after his father in enjoying sport – playing football and cricket for the school and village teams – but by playing to win and tackling others willingly, he developed a reputation for being a 'hard' footballer. Yet these were traits that would prove useful in the long run.

Desmond left Harrogate Grammar School in 1935. That same year, Sarah's father, Wilson McKie, came to stay with them at Harewood while on a trip around the world.[1] This wealthy, opinionated stranger from a distant land was also a communist. In talking about his life in New Zealand and the prospects for new immigrants, Wilson perhaps sensed his daughter was struggling and wanted to provide for her. His visit forced Horace and Sarah to think about their own lives and what sort of future they wanted for their children.

With a population of only just over 1.6 million people in 1935[2] that was overwhelmingly anglicised in both language and culture, Wilson assured the Ibbotsons they would be able to settle, afford a larger house and secure employment with a higher income.

At the time of his visit, a few of the milestones that would lead to war had passed. Hitler had become Chancellor in 1933, then Führer in 1934. In 1935, the existence of the Luftwaffe was revealed, and the Italians invaded Abyssinia (Ethiopia). Within six months, having already returned the Saarland to Germany, troops of the Wehrmacht occupied the Rhineland. Then, in 1936, the Nazis declared their support for General Franco's fascist forces in the Spanish Civil War.

After Wilson returned to New Zealand, the Ibbotsons considered the move. Perhaps fears of war persuaded them, or perhaps they saw the opportunity for a fresh start. Yet it was almost a year after Wilson's visit that Horace and Sarah and their three children finally left Harewood for New Zealand. They boarded the ocean liner MV *Rangitata* at the Port of London on 13 October 1936[3] and sailed westwards via the Panama

Canal and Pitcairn Island to start a completely new life. They arrived in Auckland a month later, during the early Antipodean summer.

Wilson not only paid for the family's passage to New Zealand but, in line with government entry requirements, agreed to sponsor the family from their arrival into the country, which meant he was committed to finding them employment as assisted immigrants. He gave Horace and Sarah some money to buy a property in one of the city's leafy suburbs, which they converted to a bed-and-breakfast guest house.

Desmond had turned 15 while at sea, at just about the time they were passing through Panama, and soon after arriving in Auckland, he enrolled at Seddon Memorial Technical College to learn a trade; working in a B&B clearly did not appeal to him. Although the country lacked a significant industrial base, there was a demand for skilled tradesmen, and the college offered courses in engineering and the building trades, including plumbing, carpentry and joinery.[4]

As the country's second city, Auckland offered the best opportunity for the family to establish themselves. Yet, as Desmond was finding his feet, Horace found it a struggle to settle down. Whether it was down to homesickness, a lack of prospects for him personally or that he resented the family being bankrolled by his father-in-law is unclear. Ultimately, it was Horace's decision to return to the UK, and if the family were to stay together, they would have to go with him. So, just six months later, on 6 May 1937, the Ibbotsons boarded the MV *Rangitane* and set sail for London.[5] After almost five weeks of travelling, the family arrived back in Harewood. Horace returned to work as a postman. Sarah took a job as a housekeeper at Harewood House. Muriel enrolled at Harrogate Grammar School to resume her education and Desmond, having taken carpentry and joinery classes in New Zealand, resumed his courses at night school. After completing his exams, Desmond managed to secure a job as an apprentice draughtsman at Cyril Stubbs & Co. Ltd near Leeds. The firm also had a sideline in coffin making. One evening, while having tea with the family, Desmond commented how much money he believed there was to be made in undertaking. Then, in front of his churchgoing parents, added, 'Though, if I had my way, I'd nail 'em all in face down!' Muriel thought this comment typical of Desmond's 'wicked, devilish sense of humour'.

As Desmond improved his skills in joinery and carpentry, in his spare time he made a beautiful sideboard for his parents. The craft also developed his judgement and patience, imbuing him with another sense that only comes with time and practice: 'a feel'. That sensory link between hand and eye improves the judgement of how much pressure to apply where and when.

These skills may not seem relevant at first, but an aeroplane is the tool with which the fighter pilot practises his craft and which requires that same intuitive feel. A pilot develops a balance between movement, muscle pressure and hand-eye coordination: left hand on the throttle, right hand on the control column while looking outside of the cockpit to judge the aeroplane's position relative to the ground or another aeroplane. With practice, as with a joiner's ability to cut and shape wood, a pilot's movements on the controls become instinctive, precise and smooth. A Spitfire especially required a delicate touch when handling it. The skills Desmond acquired in the classrooms and workshops of New Zealand and Yorkshire provided a unique grounding in ways that enabled him to fly a fighter plane instinctively when the time came.

In 1939, Desmond turned 18 and the stories in the press about the RAF's early exploits caught his attention. The night after war broke out, a Bomber Command squadron based at Leconfield in East Yorkshire became the first unit to conduct a raid on Germany, albeit to drop leaflets. After the Nazis invaded Norway and the Benelux countries in spring 1940, the newspapers and newsreels covered the desperate scraps the RAF fighter squadrons found themselves in as they tried to stop the Blitzkrieg rolling on through France. Then came the retreat from Dunkirk and, from mid-July as the RAF began to experience the first large-scale air raids on its airfields and radar stations, the imminent threat of invasion during the Battle of Britain.

During the First World War, pilots in the Royal Flying Corps (RFC) and Royal Naval Air Service (RNAS) were exclusively officers. Non-commissioned officers (NCOs) were allowed to fly only as gunners and observers. The services reflected both the societal structure from which the men were drawn and the attitudes of the senior officers. The RFC recruited volunteer pilots from the Army, many of whom were drawn from the cavalry regiments; the adage being that if they could ride a horse, they could fly an aeroplane. The RFC merged with the RNAS to form the RAF on 1 April 1918, and the preference to draw officers from public schools with the right background and money prevailed into the Second World War. Yet the RAF was arguably more forward looking in some areas than its forebears; it also encouraged recruits from non-public school backgrounds with technical skills.

It was at this point that Desmond decided to apply to join the RAF and took the bus into Leeds to sign up. He was successful at the interview and was sent to attend No. 9 Recruit Centre, Blackpool on 2 May 1940. Muriel said Desmond was inspired to join up after hearing about the exploits of RAF fighter pilots in the Battle of Britain, although this took place after he had signed up. One likely role model was Ginger Lacey. He was certainly the 'local hero' type, having seen action in France. Lacey was a fellow Yorkshireman, born in Wetherby, educated at Knaresborough Grammar School, who spent his early career as a sergeant pilot. Men such as Lacey showed Desmond that if he had the aptitude, social class might not be the barrier it had once been. And if recent history was anything to go by, compulsory conscription for every man of fighting age beckoned eventually.

Desmond was enlisted into the RAF Volunteer Reserve on 22 July 1940 at No. 3 Recruit Centre at RAF Padgate near Warrington where he attended No. 10 Aviation Candidates Selection Board for further aptitude tests, medical assessment and interviews. He passed these and was selected for training as a pilot/observer – a continuation of the First World War classification of aircrew. Desmond was then sent to RAF North Weald, a front-line airfield, on 17 August just at the height of the Battle of Britain. Glimpsing what may lie ahead for him, Desmond could see and hear the Hurricanes of 56 Squadron taking off to join other fighter formations as they tried to prevent the Luftwaffe attacking targets both in and surrounding London. After North Weald, he was ordered to attend No. 1 Receiving Wing at Babbacombe, near Torquay, in Devon, on 6 September for two weeks. During this time, he swapped his civilian clothes for an RAF uniform, learnt the basics of RAF discipline (how to march and salute) and was issued with his 'dog tags', or identity tokens, to be worn around the neck: one fireproof, one waterproof. These were hand-stamped with the wearer's initials, surname, service number, religion and the service (i.e. RAF) and would be used to identify him in the event of his death.[6]

Desmond was next posted to No. 2 Initial Training Wing (ITW) near Cambridge on 20 September 1940, to undergo six to ten weeks of training, including more drill and physical training (PT). The ITW trained aircrew of all trades (not just pilots but observers, flight engineers, bomb aimers and others too). Pilots were issued with their 'Sidcot' flying suits and studied navigation, meteorology, Morse code, RAF law and theory of flight.[7] Desmond did not record his experiences of basic training. Instead, it is only when he began flying training that his personal record starts, as he made notes in his logbook alongside the official record of each flight, despite uniformed personnel being forbidden from keeping journals or diaries while in service.

After finishing his basic service training, Desmond was sent back to Yorkshire to begin flying Tiger Moths at No. 4 Elementary Flying Training School (EFTS) based at Brough in East Yorkshire, on the north side of the river Humber, a few miles west of the city of Hull.

CHAPTER 3

No. 4 Elementary Flying Training School

Brough, Yorkshire
7 December 1940–26 February 1941

Here the student pilots had their first real contact with the RAF's aeroplanes as the focus switched to learning to fly, and they continued their ground school studies. Desmond took his first flight in a de Havilland Tiger Moth DH-82A biplane on 10 December 1940. Exposed as he was to the draught from the propellor on a winter's day, his first flight was very chilly despite the thick overalls, fleece-lined boots and gauntlets and leather helmet he wore.

The Tiger Moth had a single engine, two-bladed wooden propellor, tandem open cockpit and was constructed of doped fabric stretched over a wooden airframe. Slow, stable and manoeuvrable, it was an ideal airframe on which to learn the basics; it would forgive most ham-fisted pilots their errors. The instructors were not just assessing their students' ability to coordinate their hands and feet on the controls and fly the aeroplane in the right attitude at precise speeds and altitudes; they were also looking for their student's ability to follow instructions and understand what was happening around them. Desmond had been both a Boy Scout and an altar boy in his pre-teenage years and was good at sports, so he had the latent qualities needed: the capacity to obey instruction, confidence and coordination. War now brought a purpose and aroused many young men's sense of adventure and duty. Importantly too, he now wanted to fly the most advanced fighter of its day, an aeroplane that would become a British icon. He wanted to fly a Spitfire.

Desmond's home life had been turbulent of late, following the family's short-lived emigration to New Zealand and the emerging distance between his parents, whose marriage was vacillating between loving success and argumentative failure. As he began his first training course, he could be forgiven if he felt relief at being away from Harewood for the next ten weeks.

As a trainee, Desmond would watch the demonstration of a manoeuvre, listen to the instructions, then repeat the exercise exactly as the instructor had shown him – watch, listen, repeat. Did it wrong? Do it again. Not precise enough? Do it again. And so it went on until either Desmond failed the exercise (and therefore possibly the entire course) or the instructor declared it a 'pass' and moved straight on to the next exercise. After ten days of training, Desmond noted his first rising doubts in his logbook: 'I don't know if I'll make a pilot yet.' Student pilots were expected to go from their first flight with an instructor to taking the aircraft up solo in around 10 hours, and the twenty or so flights in the run-up to that goal were demanding given the variety of things to monitor and skills to master. The feeling of public failure and humiliation in front of your colleagues was ever present, as was the feeling of letting down your instructor.

Three days after his note of self-doubt, with 10 hours and 50 minutes of training under his belt and a successful 'check ride' with his instructor, Sgt Hewlett, Desmond went solo on Christmas Eve. 'Hooray!' he wrote. His skill as a pilot thus far was rated 'average' and he remained on course.

As part of their ground training, Desmond and his course mates also completed several sessions in the Link Trainer, the RAF's first real simulator.[1] Here too, Desmond was rated 'average', and his instructor stated he was 'inclined to overcontrol'– in pilot slang, known as 'chasing the instruments' – as he tried to achieve, then maintain the required readings on the dials.

Following three more weeks of training and having accumulated a total of 45 hours and 50 minutes flying time (dual and solo), Desmond, now a leading aircraftman (LAC), had completed his first flying course. To top it off, his superior officer rated his character as 'Very Good' in his end of year assessment.

Desmond felt more optimistic this time as he wrote, 'Posted onto single engined aircraft. I might make a fighter pilot yet.'

CHAPTER 4

No. 8 Service Flying Training School

Montrose, Scotland
8 March–20 May 1941

Desmond spent three months learning to fly the Miles Master, a single-engined, low-wing monoplane that was closer in appearance and performance to the front-line fighters it served as a bridge to. For the first two years of the war, pilot training was still mainly carried out in the UK. Eventually, the Empire Air Training Scheme and its companion, the British Flying Training Scheme, enabled the RAF to send trainee pilots overseas to certain members of the empire or the USA respectively, to carry out their training in safety. In the meantime, the safest places in the UK were the north of England, Wales and Scotland.

Although it too had a wooden airframe, the Master had a top speed of 300mph, which meant it was only between 30 and 70mph (depending on the engine type fitted) slower than the Hurricane fighter, which the successful trainees would progress to next. 'Jerry' Jarrold, who was also learning on the Master in early 1941, recalled:

The Master II was an excellent training aircraft and after the Tiger Moth it seemed to us to be like a fighter and had the same exhilaration when you flew it solo – which of course was the whole point. It seemed a massive aircraft and far more solid after the Tiger and very fast. We always made 3-point landings and you had to settle it in, which was good training for a Spitfire as the technique was the same; by the end of my Spitfire period I could drop the aircraft down on a spot. There were a few Hurricanes at the School and in the latter stages of the Course some chaps got to fly these, which, as we all thought we were heading for fighters, would have been a nice end to the Course.[1]

Montrose was not just a training base. Located on the Scottish east coast between Dundee and Aberdeen, the airfield faced the North Sea across which lay Nazi-occupied Norway. It was, therefore, within flying range of the Luftwaffe's fighter and bomber squadrons. As one of several airfields that guarded the approaches to Edinburgh, the Hurricane and Spitfire squadrons based there were responsible for defending the city and the naval bases at Rosyth and Cromarty from enemy raiders, conducting patrols and providing air cover for convoys passing through the North Sea.

The destinations of the trainees on the course that preceded Desmond's were varied. Of the forty-two successfully posted out, seventeen were officers, twenty-five were sergeants and all of them went off to join their respective operational training units (OTUs). There were thirteen 'wastage cases': five were killed, five transferred to twin-engine types, one was re-coursed to No. 28 course, one was rejected as unsuitable and the last individual, LAC P. Mitchell, was sentenced to 112 days' detention by the district court martial for committing a low-flying offence on 24 February 1941.[2]

The trainees on these courses were expected to follow exactly the same syllabus as they had on their Elementary Flying Training course, just more quickly because, while consolidating their flying skills on a new type, they also had to learn advanced skills, such as night flying. The Master was, therefore, an appropriately named aircraft. Pilots had to sharpen their instincts, refine their judgement and become more confident and precise in their decision making. A failure to do so may not just mean failing the course but could cost them their life.

Desmond went solo three days after his first flight in a Master and with just 4 hours' training 'on type'. His next flight was an introduction to low flying, which came with strict rules about what was and was not allowed. As they progressed, the temptation for trainees to 'buzz' or 'beat up' a building or ground feature by flying very low over it at speed could prove too much. If caught, it meant a court martial and potential dismissal, but if they misjudged their pass, the consequences could be fatal.

Despite the steady rate and tally of accidents on other courses around the same time, up to that point, in nearly six weeks of training, no one had been injured or killed on Desmond's own course, but unfortunately this did not last. On 25 April, LAC Nelson entered a spin just after completing a turn. The aircraft crashed and caught fire, killing the pilot. This accident was found to be due to pilot error rather than a technical malfunction.[3]

Desmond progressed without incident and completed exercises in navigation, slow flying, instrument flying and aerobatics, before finishing his course at the end of April. He made no further notes on his progress through this course, in part because of the intensity of the training. On the days they were not flying, the student pilots were either in the classroom learning the theories and principles of the various aspects of flying or were in the Link Trainer undergoing simulator training. On 1 May, Desmond wrote of his success, 'At last I am allowed to fly a fighter plane,' and kept his eye on one of the Hurricanes attached to the training school.

In mid-1941, all trainee fighter pilots had to practise the manoeuvres in the Master, then learn to fly the Hurricane before they could fly a Spitfire because the RAF had no two-seat trainer versions of either the Spitfire or Hurricane. The Hurricane was almost as fast as a Spitfire, partly because it used the same Rolls-Royce Merlin V12 engine but was more forgiving thanks to its wider undercarriage. Its (mainly) wood and canvas airframe meant it could absorb damage and be returned to airworthiness more quickly, efficiently and cheaply than the more delicate and expensive Spitfire with its aluminium airframe and stressed metal panelling.

Desmond made his first solo flight in a Hurricane on 6 May 1941, then flew exercises in the Master, followed by the Hurricane, including night landings. After a further 15 hours and 10 minutes of flying over ten days, Desmond took his 'wings test', an intense flight with his instructor, Fg Off Nichols, that lasted 1 hour and 20 minutes. The flight, a practical airborne examination, included various scenarios, manoeuvres and emergencies to test the students' decision-making skills as well as their flying ability. Desmond's only note about this flight on 16 May was a single word: 'Pass'. On 18 May, he flew again with the chief flying instructor (CFI), who agreed with Nichols' assessment and also granted Desmond a 'Pass'.

The instructors at Montrose had also judged Desmond's character and suitability to squadron life. The RAF Volunteer Reserve, in which Desmond had enlisted, looked for leadership qualities among its pilots. Overwhelmingly, most of those who were commissioned as officers across the RAF Regular, Volunteer Reserve and Auxiliary branches had been to public school and/or were university educated, which Desmond was not.

There was a notorious snobbery that pervaded the senior officer ranks. They judged a candidate's suitability for a commission, and their attitude towards 'grammar school boys', who were seen as cocky young men who did not know their place, meant those who were not recommended (the majority) became NCO pilots instead. As it strove to forge its own identity and prove its worth as an independent fighting arm, the RAF would become more meritocratic in time. Some of this progression was forced upon its squadrons as a result of the losses suffered during operations, but some of it was also rooted in the RAF's experience overseas, where front-line conditions were very different from those in the UK. In the years ahead, Desmond would see those enlightened leaders promote men under them who had not just proven themselves in battle but could also lead others into battle. Given the choice between flying Spitfires or being an officer though, Desmond would have preferred to fly Spitfires.

The next few days left Desmond on a high. Aged 19, he graduated from advanced training and, although his proficiency as a pilot after a total of 118 hours basic and advanced training was still only marked as 'average', he was selected to fly Spitfires. He scribbled a simple hurried note in his logbook: 'SPITs!' His income almost doubled from 5s 6d as an LAC to 9s 6d as he was promoted through two ranks – senior aircraftman (SAC) and corporal – up to sergeant (service no. 1107760).

The fact aircrew started their operational flying careers with the rank of sergeant, irrespective of their length of service, caused some degree of consternation and friction with the other time-served sergeants in ground trades. The rationale stemmed from the belief that aircrew of sergeant rank or above would receive better treatment from the enemy if they were to end up as prisoners of war (PoWs).

Desmond left Montrose on 22 May 1941 and returned to Harewood on leave, this time in uniform with the coveted pilot's wings stitched just above the left breast pocket of his No.1 dress jacket and the triple chevrons of a sergeant on his upper arms. Around this time, Desmond had a formal portrait taken at a local studio. Though he had, and would continue to be, photographed many times in his short life, there were only two formal studio portrait photographs taken of him in his life, and this was one. He was promoted again to the rank of flight sergeant on 1 June 1941 but would have to wait until his next course before he could obtain the new rank badges.

CHAPTER 5

53 Operational Training Unit

Heston, Middlesex
9 June–20 July 1941

Desmond reported to No. 5 Course along with six officers and thirty-eight other sergeant pilots, including Canadian Ray Sherk, with whom he quickly became friends. Heston airfield was located in Middlesex, just north-east of what is now London's Heathrow Airport.

Among the team of instructors were several Battle of Britain veterans on rest from operations. The CFI, who had been there since February 1941, was Flt Lt Billy Drake. He had seen action in France flying Hurricanes with 1 Squadron and managed to escape before the country fell to the Germans. On his return to the UK, he had flown ops as a flight commander with 91 Squadron based at Manston in Kent – the closest RAF airfield to occupied France. As CFI, Billy oversaw Desmond's conversion to Spitfires.

Alongside Billy were Flt Lt Roy Mottram DFC (Distinguished Flying Cross) and Flt Lt Arthur Victor 'Darky' Clowes DFM (Distinguished Flying Medal), who had arrived at Heston just one month earlier. Having also seen action in France, Clowes was already an ace. Drake, Mottram and Clowes were all in their early twenties; through a mix of luck and losses, skill and experience, they had been promoted to positions of leadership. They were each destined to lead squadrons of their own, which Desmond would eventually join.

Desmond began the six-week course with a familiarisation flight in a Miles Master on 12 June. The day after, he took to the air again for his very first flight in a Spitfire, a Mk II (no. 4165) that was reassigned to the OTU after service in the Battle of Britain. Even though it was a battle-worn version, it was still the fighter Desmond most wanted to fly, and its speed and lightness of handling did not disappoint him. 'Gee! They are marvellous,' he wrote afterwards. A fraction over twelve months since he had walked into the RAF recruiting office in Leeds, he was flying a Spitfire. The aeroplane that had first captured his imagination had now captured his heart. His first love affair had begun.

On 14 June, Desmond took his third flight in a Spitfire. As he prepared for landing, he pumped the lever on the cockpit wall by his right knee to lower the undercarriage – there being no button to press to do the job in those early aircraft. All indications were normal, and the indicator on the instrument panel showed the wheels locked down. He continued his final approach, crossing the end of the runway threshold as expected, lined up nicely on the centreline.

As the wheels touched the runway surface and the weight of the Spitfire bore down, the undercarriage collapsed. The fighter smacked down hard onto the runway, severely damaging the propellor, and slid noisily to a halt as the station fire engines raced to the scene. Shocked and cursing his luck, Desmond slid the canopy back, quickly undid his straps and stepped out onto the back of the wing. One the RAF's most valuable fighter planes lay slumped in front of him with its propellor twisted and bent.

The aircraft was later hoisted onto the back of an articulated low loader and taken back to the hangars for assessment and, if possible, repair. Desmond slunk over to the CO's office to explain what had happened. Usually, a belly landing would render damage significant enough that the plane would have to be sent away to the maintenance unit for more extensive work. If he had been found to be negligent, Desmond could have faced a severe reprimand. A few hours later, the engineering officer reported that the Spitfire had no oil in the hydraulic system, thus no means of the undercarriage taking the weight of the plane as it landed. If the airman responsible for checking the oil in the undercarriage system was found to have been negligent, it would be *him* who faced disciplinary action instead. Desmond had done nothing wrong. Cleared to fly again the day after, Desmond took a Spitfire up to 30,000ft, the highest he had yet been, in order to familiarise himself with the changes in performance a fighter encounters at such extreme heights.

That same day, on his second sortie, he spent nearly 2 hours navigating to Winchester, Swindon and Cambridge, practising his map-reading skills and forced-landing procedures. Pilots needed to practise one of the most important emergency procedures by simulating the occurrence of a total or partial engine failure. The pilot does not need to put the aircraft down on the ground but will run through the routines and approaches as though they were to make a landing.

Even with the engine switched off completely, Spitfires would stay sufficiently stable in the air to allow the pilot to glide back to earth and carry out a 'dead stick' landing. However, they had to commit to landing in a suitable place quickly: without any power from the engine, the Spitfire became a nose-heavy, inefficient glider that brought itself back to earth whether the pilot liked it or not.

When Desmond returned to Heston to practise his emergency landings, he found he could not lower the undercarriage. The wheels were still locked up in the wing. He had no choice but to crash-land another Spitfire on the same airfield. This time, with no wheels to support the aeroplane, Desmond had to switch the engine off completely on final approach to reduce the chance of a fire immediately on impact and gently bellyflop or 'pancake' the Spitfire on to its underside as best he could.

Once more, he heard the scream of metal being scratched along the runway, the 'whack' as the propellor blades spun into the ground and, as he felt the straps hold him back from a bodily impact with the instrument panel, thanked God no fire had broken out. He clambered out of what had seemed to be a perfectly serviceable fighter when he got into it, but which was now another collapsed and creaking wreck at the side of the runway.

One can imagine the fire crew arriving again and one of them saying to Desmond: 'Oh, it's you again. You need to be careful, Flight. If you keep this up, we'll soon have no Spitfires left, and the boss will have to start taking the cost of repairs out of your wages!' Desmond probably wondered if he was going to be allowed to continue flying at all. Once again, he was going to have to visit the CO's office to explain what had happened and how it was that he had managed to return, within two days, two Spitfires in a worse condition than when he had borrowed them. Although he did not know it at the time and as embarrassing as it had been to wreck two Spitfires in less than a week, the fact he was not to blame had shown Desmond that he could handle an emergency and walk away from a crash when several of his colleagues had not. Two days later, he was back in the air and carrying on learning.

A month earlier, at the end of May, Fighter Command Organisation Circular 81 'promulgated a decision that half of 53 OTU was to move to Llandow, there to be reinforced by drafting. The other half is to remain at Heston, to be summarily reinforced and to form 61 OTU.'[1] Half of the unit earmarked for the move now left in the third week of June for Llandow in South Wales, 20 miles west of Cardiff. Desmond was among them.

Shortly after arriving at Llandow, the pilots of No. 5 Course began practising formation flying. The standard fighter formation at the time was the 'Vic' of three: a leader and two wingmen flying in an arrowhead, or inverted 'v' pattern.

On the evening of Monday 7 July, three Spitfires took off from Llandow to practise low-level formation flying between the hills behind Aberfan in the Vale of Merthyr. Two Canadian pilots, Sgts Gerald 'Jerrie' Fenwick Manuel and Louis 'Curly' Goldberg, were part of the Vic formation; the other pilot is unknown. At around 6.30 p.m., as they passed over the village of Merthyr Vale, an eyewitness saw Manuel's Spitfire, at the back of the flight, accelerate slightly and overshoot the formation leader (Goldberg). As he did so, their wingtips touched, and the Spitfires collided mid-air at a height of around 500ft, causing both pilots to lose control. Seconds later, Goldberg crashed in a field and was killed instantly, while Manuel's Spitfire came down on an end-of-terrace house in Mount Pleasant and exploded in flames, killing three residents (a mother and two daughters) along with the pilot. Two days later, the pilots were buried at the cemetery in Merthyr Tydfil. Desmond and the other trainees attended the funeral. Sgt Ray Sherk was one of the pall bearers.[2]

The same day the funeral was taking place, tragedy struck again when two more aircraft collided while practising formation flying. This time Sgt Frederick George Thomas McGahey collided mid-air with Sgt W. Saunders. Saunders was lucky and managed to bail out, but sadly McGahey was killed when his fighter came down in a field near Tydraw Farm, Colwinston, only a few miles east of Llandow. His body was later dispatched to Belfast for burial by his family.

Then on 10 July, Sgt Marion Arthur Plomteaux (RCAF) was also killed in a flying accident when out practising air-to-air combat, or 'dog-fighting'. He misjudged a manoeuvre, stalled and spun into a field near Marcross, a few miles south-east of Llandow, before he could recover the Spitfire or bail out. Plomteaux was an American originally from Albuquerque, New Mexico, who had crossed the border to Canada to enlist in the Royal Canadian Air Force (RCAF) and been sent over to the UK to fight. He was buried at Boverton cemetery near Llantrisant on 14 July.[3] He was also the fourth pilot killed in four days.

While Desmond was out practising aerobatics over Devon on 11 July, his engine developed low oil pressure, which could have led to his engine seizing up. If he had turned north and headed for Llandow (the furthest airfield away), it could have meant him ditching in the Bristol Channel or, if he had remained over land, he may have had to bail out. Instead, he decided to make his first forced landing at an airfield close to Barnstaple (probably RAF Chivenor), flying back to Llandow when the mechanics had inspected his engine and given him the all clear.

Desmond flew the remaining ten days of his course without major incident, although he failed to practise live firing his machine guns in flight on two occasions due to stoppages. He took his last flight with the OTU on 20 July, by which time he had acquired 50 hours 25 minutes on Spitfires alone. That was five times the number of hours some new pilots had acquired before they had been drafted to front-line units during the Battle of Britain just twelve months earlier.

There are two signatures certifying Desmond's completion of this course and subsequent suitability to continue to a fighter squadron. One of which is from Wg Cdr Edgar Ryder. The other is on the 'ticket' fixed in Desmond's logbook. It is dated Saturday 26 July 1941. The instructor rated Desmond again as being of 'average' ability, and it is signed by

Billy Drake. Desmond left South Wales and, with Ray Sherk, headed for Leconfield in North Yorkshire to start his first tour with 129 Squadron.

Billy, who had chafed at being rested as an instructor, continued to push, prod and plead with anyone who would listen to get him back on operations, but he would be stuck at Llandow until early September. It would be another year until Desmond and Billy crossed paths again.

CHAPTER 6

129 Squadron

Leconfield, Yorkshire
27 July–27 August 1941

Just eight months had elapsed between Desmond's first tentative flight in a Tiger Moth biplane to graduation as a fighter pilot on Spitfires and his first operational posting with the newly resurrected 129 Squadron. It had been twenty-three years since 129 Squadron had last been operational, and even then it had only enjoyed a brief existence. First formed on 1 March 1918 as a day bomber squadron, it was then disbanded barely four months later, on 4 July 1918, without achieving operational status.

The squadron was re-formed at RAF Leconfield near Hull on 16 June 1941. The cost was financed by the Indian government purchasing British war bonds, so the squadron was christened 'Mysore' after the province in south-western India. The squadron crest showed Gandaberunda – the double-headed eagle of Hindu myths, which possessed immense strength and was capable of fighting the forces of destruction – holding an elephant in each set of talons. Initially equipped with ageing and comparatively sluggish Mk I Spitfires, 129 Squadron would go on to serve until the end of the war.

The process of being raised to operational status fell under the leadership of the 29-year-old commanding officer (CO). Sqn Ldr Dennis Lockhart Armitage. Armitage was from Little Hulton, near Bolton in Lancashire. Just three months earlier, he had been a junior officer on

266 Squadron. Within that time, he had been promoted twice, awarded a DFC and given his own squadron to raise from scratch.

Armitage had to ensure his pilots could handle their fighters in combat, which involved them getting as much practice in formation flying, attack procedures, air-to-air fighting and live firing of their guns as possible. He had to weld together a motley assortment of pilots into a cohesive and effective fighting unit. The pilots had come from all manner of backgrounds and squadrons. They included Rhodesians, Americans, Canadians, Australians and one pilot from Jamaica. A couple of combat-experienced pilots had followed Armitage over from 266 Squadron. Others, like Desmond, were fresh from an OTU or were drafted in from other operational squadrons as replacements. Among these new pilots were two American 'Eagles' from 121 Squadron, also based at Leconfield: Plt Offs Fred Scudday and J. Warner.

Ironically, given the USA was still not officially in the war, Scudday and Warner were probably the most experienced flyers in the squadron apart from their leaders. The three Eagle squadrons in the RAF (121, 71 and 133) had been formed in September 1940 in response to the British government's call for foreign flyers from North America who were sufficiently experienced and willing to fly with the RAF.[1] The successful volunteers underwent the normal RAF preliminary training, including passing through the OTUs, before being posted to the Eagle squadrons, which remained subordinate to the RAF Fighter Command structure and were led by RAF COs and flight commanders. Once America entered the war, these Eagle pilots had the option of continuing with the RAF or joining the US Army Air Force (USAAF).

One of the genuine Canadians who, along with Ray Sherk had joined the RAF and now 129 Squadron, was James 'Jimmy' Whalen from Vancouver in British Columbia. Jimmy had only received his RAF wings in January 1941 at the age of 20 and had been one of the very first to join the squadron, arriving in mid-June as a sergeant pilot. He had wanted to be a fighter pilot for several years. Shortly after the war started, and as some way of helping Britain to recruit more pilots, the RCAF dropped its graduate standard for pilots, which prompted Jimmy to drop out of his first year at the University of British Columbia and join up in 1940.

On completion of his service training, Jimmy was granted a commission as a pilot officer. So pleased was he to be flying at last that, during his advanced flying training in north-eastern Canada, he let his confidence get the better of him. While out flying solo in a Harvard training aircraft, he decided to fly low underneath the Ottawa–Hull Bridge. Having flown safely through the gap, he immediately pulled up into a loop over the top of the bridge, completing the manoeuvre by flying underneath it again and out the other side. Unfortunately for him, a concerned witness had noted the number of the aircraft and reported him to the authorities. When the CO found out, he stripped Jimmy of his commission and reduced him to the rank of sergeant. There he stayed until 26 August 1941 when, now flying with 129 Squadron, the RAF decided to promote him back up to pilot officer. Unauthorised low flying was forbidden, but his experience and above-average talents counted more. Besides, the RAF perhaps considered he had served his punishment.

At Leconfield, the officers and NCOs were segregated, meaning they ate, slept and socialised in different messes. As sergeant pilots, Desmond, Ray and Jimmy lived and worked closely together and became good friends.

The work-up to operational status was intense and, once achieved, the pilots would then conduct local air defence patrols around Hull, convoy patrols over the North Sea and, using a rota of pilots, maintain a readiness state in order to scramble at a few minutes' notice to intercept any incoming raiders. To that end, the pilots would practise taking off and landing in formation, 'snapper' attacks – one or two Spitfires pretending to be enemy raiders that had to be intercepted – and general air combat.

Desmond practised air combat with both Jimmy and Ray through those summer days using camera guns fitted in the leading edges of the Spitfires' wings to record their results. Ray's performance was not mentioned in his daily notes, but Desmond noted that Jimmy 'takes some holding. Often I can't,' meaning Jimmy could often outturn or break away from Desmond's faint attacks and out-fox him.

Jimmy and Desmond had both enjoyed an outdoorsy childhood – Jimmy on the Vancouver beaches and parks near his home, occasionally in the mountains beyond, Desmond in the fields, streams and woods around Harewood. As they chased each other around in the blue skies of late summer out over the sea, or over the North Yorkshire Moors, Jimmy's six months' additional flying and aerobatic experience told on

Desmond, and it is easy to picture Jimmy watch Desmond's Spitfire slide closer in, conning him into thinking that he was going to get a shot in, then break away and out-manoeuvre, laughing at Desmond's frustration over the radio as he did so.

Time off base for the pilots was limited. When their chance did come, Desmond was much closer to Harewood than he had been in South Wales, and during late August he took a couple of days' leave to visit his family. Muriel recalled that Desmond had turned up at home at least twice in a two-seater sports car. Desmond never owned a car himself – they were expensive, and petrol was rationed anyway – and appeared to have borrowed this particular sports car and driven it to Harewood.

One weekend, he pulled up to the front of his parents' house in full uniform, playing up to the popular image of a dashing Spitfire pilot. His parents, grandma and sisters made a fuss of him as he unloaded his bags from the shelf behind the driver's seat. Then Muriel noticed something odd about the soft-top roof. It was missing altogether.

'Where's the roof, Des?' Muriel asked, pointing to the space over the car's interior.

'Er, it's back at Leconfield,' Desmond replied.

'Why, lad? It's not that sunny today. You had the roof up last time,' his dad chimed in.

Desmond paused momentarily, then decided to confess.

'I accidentally backed it into the wing of a Spitfire ... with the hood up,' he said, grinning sheepishly.

Horace and Muriel laughed, and Sarah tutted, shook her head and went back indoors. So much for the glamorous Spitfire pilot.

There were other occasions when Desmond returned to Harewood and visited his family, but they were unofficial and fleeting because, with RAF Leconfield only 45 miles due east of Harewood and around 10 minutes' flying time away, Desmond visited them in a Spitfire.

The training schedules allowed for a certain type of sortie that appear in the records as 'General Handling' or 'Local Flying'; these were a chance for pilots to practise flying exercises by themselves away from the local airfield, in clear airspace. The intention was that the pilot would responsibly look to perfect those turns, drills, aerobatics or other manoeuvres that may need a bit more polish, or use the time to familiarise himself with the local area.

Where a pilot was confident and competent in all these manoeuvres, and the weather was good, he essentially had a chance to use one of the RAF's aeroplanes for his own purposes. As Jimmy Whalen had found out, there were strict orders banning low flying, which meant a disciplinary offence if caught. It is a strange dichotomy in the make-up of a fighter pilot. The RAF wanted young men who were keen, capable and able to cope with the rigours of the job. They should be intelligent, independent-minded, resourceful and self-disciplined. In trying to recruit men who they could mould to their requirements, they needed them to follow the rules but also to be able to think for themselves and carry on with a mission should their leaders be put out of action. Therefore, pilots were both risk-takers and rule followers. The challenge for the pilots was knowing when to follow the rules and when to take the risks. If they broke the rules and misjudged the situation, it could, of course, be fatal.

Desmond was no exception: there were at least three occasions during August 1941, which he recorded in his logbook, where this could have happened. Of course, he never noted that he did any unauthorised low flying because his flight commander and CO would see the logbooks at the end of each month to verify and sign off each pilot's recorded hours, but he was seen by people on the ground.

Muriel recalled that from time to time during that summer, Desmond would often 'beat up' his family's house in Harewood village. On hearing the deep, familiar growl of the Spitfire's Merlin engine in the near distance, rising in pitch and getting louder and louder as it dived toward them, Sarah would call out to the two girls, 'It's our Des. He's 'ere again,' and dash outside just in time to see the Spitfire as it zoomed low and fast right over the house, before it pulled up into the sky and shot away again, waggling its wings. When I asked Muriel how low she thought he might have been, she just laughed and said, 'Certainly lower than he should have been.' The last opportunity Desmond would have had to buzz his house was on 17 August 1941. Just four days later the squadron was declared operational and prepared to move south to Westhampnett near Chichester – the former RAF base that is now home to Goodwood racetrack. Desmond thought he would be going with them but instead he was posted out by himself to Hornchurch in Essex on 27 August. His new squadron was No. 54, a famous and well-renowned squadron of elite pilots based at a distinguished airfield. The posting would still have meant a great deal to Desmond, given what he had read about the pilots whose reputations had been made during the Battle of Britain. It must have felt to him as though he was about to meet his heroes. The squadron would certainly test all his abilities as a fighter pilot and forge his combat skills. It was a shame his mates were not going with him. Desmond would not see Jimmy again, but he would be posted to the same place as Ray in the months ahead. Just not where he expected.

CHAPTER 7

54 Squadron

Hornchurch, Essex
28 August 1941–1 October 1942

After a long journey down from Yorkshire, across central London and beyond the outskirts to Essex, Desmond reported to his new squadron that cold wet morning of Thursday 28 August 1941. Once he had been introduced to the other pilots, Desmond went over to the operations room to sign for his new Spitfire, a Mk Vb no. R7343 – 'K'. As was the usual practice for a new arrival, he had been told to take this one up and have a look around, to familiarise himself with the airfield and its surrounding area on a 'sector recce'. Of course, his new colleagues would be watching him. As he walked out of the crew room to a nearby aeroplane, a dozen pairs of eyes followed his every step, judging his manner and ability from the outset. Starting it up in one go would give a good impression, start it in two and they would be ribbing him in the mess after standdown.

Desmond took off at 10.35 a.m. and spent an hour in the air. This Mk V Spitfire was impressively different to the battle weary 1As he had been flying up to the week before. He noted, 'Spit 5's amazingly light to handle after Spit I's especially at high speed (over 300mph).' By the standards of the day, this was remarkably fast. The last world land speed record to be set before the war was 369mph, achieved by John Cobb in August 1939.[1] In the spring of the same year, Germany had twice claimed a world air speed record – first achieving a speed of 463mph in a single-engined propellor-driven Heinkel in April, before breaking that record with a speed of 469mph in a specially designed Messerschmitt ME109R in May.[2]

The Mk V version of the Spitfire was produced in response to the changing requirements of the RAF and, in particular, to counter the latest version of the Messerschmitt (Bf) 109 then in service with the Luftwaffe, the 109E (christened 'Emil' by the Germans) and the new 109F.[3]

The ME109 fighter had been developed originally under the guise of being a fast aeroplane for delivering mail across Germany in the mid-1930s and, having seen some action at the tail end of the Spanish Civil War as part of the German Condor Legion, had blooded some of the Luftwaffe fighter pilots for the forthcoming war in Europe. The aeroplane had also received some refinements including an armour-plated seat, strengthened canopy and two wing-mounted 20mm cannons.

The British had a lucky break when a German pilot happened to land a 109E on the wrong side of the Franco-German border in November 1939. It was hurriedly shipped back to the UK and flight tested against the Spitfire Mk I and Hurricane.

Comparisons in design, engine performance and handling capabilities were made and the results reported to the British manufacturers and chiefs of staff. The decision to temporarily halt the planned development of the Spitfire Mk II and Griffon-powered Mk IV led to the stop-gap version, the Mk V, being introduced instead. The Mk V represented a significant jump in overall performance for relatively little effort. From a starting point of 1000bhp in 1936, the new Merlin 45 and 46 engines now developed 1230bhp. Fitting them to the new Mk V airframes now gave the Spitfire a top speed of 369mph and the ability to climb to 35,000ft in 15 minutes.[4]

The increase in power and speed were not the only changes. On the basic airframe, retaining the slender appearance of the Mk I, the only significant change was to the ailerons – the movable sections of each wing's outboard trailing edge, which enable an aircraft to bank (roll) and turn left or right. The Mk I ailerons were fabric covered, while the Mk V had metal-skinned ailerons. The stressed metal skin over these control surfaces enabled the Spitfire to roll much faster (almost double the normal rate at high speeds) and greatly reduced the heavy pressures felt on the control column when in a high-speed dive or attempting roll manoeuvres at speed, but it had taken several years to make the improvement. Supermarine's renowned test pilot Jeffrey Quill had been aware of the problem early in the Spitfire's development and, after a brief period on operations with 65 Squadron, during which he shot down two ME109s, Quill had test flown one of the prototypes fitted with metal-skinned ailerons, on 7 November 1940. Unable to find fault, he took it to Boscombe Down, where it was flown further by other test pilots, who all reported the same result. On their collective word, the recommendations reached the Air Ministry, the manufacturers and the squadrons such that, with immediate effect, the new Spitfires were ordered to be fitted with metal ailerons and a programme of retrofitting the old ones was begun.[5] It was these new ailerons that gave Desmond and his fellow pilots a much lighter feel on the controls, especially over 300mph, and enabled the Spitfire pilots to respond more quickly in an engagement.

The Mk Vs were also now being fitted with 20mm cannons like the ME109s but, due to the Spitfire's thinner wings, they had to be mounted differently. The firing mechanisms were recessed in the section facing closest to the cockpit, with the barrels extending forward of the leading edge of each wing by about 2ft, giving the Spitfire a new and very distinctive silhouette.

The size of the cannon shells made the fighter more lethal because, as the RAF pilots had learnt to their cost in the Battle of Britain when they fell under the guns of the ME109s, it took fewer hits from fewer 20mm rounds to bring down an aircraft. The damage was done not by the size of the bullet going *into* the aeroplane's exterior surfaces, but by the size and momentum of it coming *out* of the other side. Depending on what it hit on its journey through the target, the cannon shell (the shaped projectile head) changed its shape, direction and exit point.

The cannons did give the pilots some trouble as they were prone to sudden stoppages. If one of them stopped firing, it would throw the Spitfire off balance, causing it to skid in the direction of the malfunctioning cannon. However, they gave pilots the advantage over the standard machine guns as the higher muzzle velocity coupled with a bigger, heavier round meant any hits were much more effective, so a capable pilot with a good eye was more likely to down his opponent's aeroplane rather than just damage it. Lighter on the stick, quicker acceleration, faster and nimbler all round, the Mk V was a favourite straight away with the pilots who flew it, Desmond included.

Desmond arrived at Hornchurch to a new squadron, new leadership and a new aircraft. Unlike 129 Squadron, 54 was an established squadron with a fighting history dating back to the middle of the First World War and had covered the retreat from Dunkirk and fought in the Battle of Britain.

The pilots had a reputation for hard fighting and hard socialising. These men lived and flew as they fought: with verve, skill, bravery and not a little dash. Desmond may have felt a tinge of sadness at having left his friends behind; however, Hornchurch was no bad place to be. The posting was the closest he would ever get to walking in the footsteps of those he had most admired.

Hornchurch was not far from the coast but was (in 1941) just beyond the outskirts of London, a few miles north of the River Thames. As a sector station, Hornchurch would receive orders from Fighter Command Headquarters via the Group HQ and pass them on to the satellite airfields located within the same geographical area of responsibility (the sector). The northern boundary of the Hornchurch sector ran from the suburbs of London due east through Essex and out beyond Rochford into the North Sea. The southern boundary headed south-east out between Biggin Hill and Gravesend, past Folkestone and the Straits of Dover into the English Channel. Hornchurch, therefore, guarded the shortest route the Germans could fly from their bases in France to hit southern England and London – the seat of government and royalty, but also home to the world's busiest port and docks.

The Dover Straits are the narrowest point of the shipping lanes between the Channel and the North Sea, so the Hornchurch Wing also had to protect the passage of vital convoys, the coastal ports and towns of Folkestone, Dover, Ramsgate, Rochester and Gravesend, oil terminals and power stations, not to mention the radar stations, airfields and army barracks. Although the Luftwaffe's presence in the skies of southern England was not as formidable as it had been the year before, the Luftwaffe was still giving the Hornchurch boys a hard time.

Their station commander, Gp Capt Harry 'Broady' Broadhurst's excellent leadership was marked by an aggressive fighting spirit that permeated through the three squadrons under his command. Broadhurst had started his military career as a soldier in the Royal Artillery before switching to the RAF in 1926 and had proven to be an excellent marksman in the air. Broadhurst had been badly shot up when flying a Hurricane over France in the winter of 1939–40 and only just made it back to England. Although this little escapade saw him feature in the pages of the *Sunday Despatch*, individual press attention was something he wanted his pilots to avoid.[6]

Under Broady was the wing leader, Wg Cdr Eric Stapleton. Under him were the three squadron commanders: Sqn Ldrs Newell 'Fanny' Orton of 54, E.H. Thomas of 611 and Hiram Smith of 603. These three squadrons formed the 'Hornchurch Wing'.

Fanny's two flight commanders were Flt Lt Roy Mottram, in charge of A Flight (an ex-92 Squadron Battle of Britain veteran), who had recently been notified that he was to receive the DFC for displaying 'exceptional zeal and immense enthusiasm during the many offensive sweeps carried out' by the squadron,[7] and Flt Lt Edward Francis John 'Jack' Charles (who had been born in Coventry but raised in Canada) in charge of B Flight. Desmond joined B Flight and spent the last few days of August flying practice dogfights with other sergeant pilots and an experienced officer before flying with Jack Charles himself. Although Desmond had now accumulated 29 hours on Spitfires, he and the other new arrivals were still being assessed on how well they fitted in with the squadron professionally and socially, and the flight commanders were alert to who was any good or not.

On 30 August, Jack Charles took Desmond and Sgt Pook up for an evening sortie covering formation aerobatics to see how good they were at sticking close to their leader. Jack reputedly had 'the best eyes on the Wing' and was 'one of its outstanding pilots who always saw the enemy first and who always seemed to fire his guns'.[8] He was already an ace, having acquired six confirmed kills and five and a half 'probables' – the half coming from a shared attack. There could hardly be a better pilot for Desmond to learn his fighting skills from, and a few days later Desmond was deemed fit for operations.

The squadron had its own way of encouraging pilots to pay attention when engaged in combat exercises. If a pilot lost a 'life' by being jumped by an opponent, he could be fined from his wages. But pilots also lost money by placing personal bets with each other as to who would get one over on the other and 'shoot' him down; just as in the local pub or at a dance, they would bet each other who could successfully chat up the best-looking women.

The first significant loss in months for the squadron came when Roy Mottram was killed on 31 August over northern France. The squadron had been escorting a formation of bombers over Lille, and Roy was brought down when he engaged a formation of enemy aircraft sent up to intercept them. The RAF escort formation had been shadowed at the time by ME109s. Roy was seen to turn away from his own formation and became involved in a dogfight at between 20,000 and 23,000ft. Escorting pilots from 603 Squadron saw Roy being pursued by six enemy fighters between Poperinge and the coast. He was last heard to say that he would spin out of the engagement, but he never returned and was later found to have been shot down at Neuf-Berquin. After only just over a year's operational flying, with three confirmed destroyed, three probables and several 'assists', Roy had just missed out on becoming an ace, but he was highly respected, and the squadron noted it had 'lost one of the best Flight Commanders that any squadron could wish to have'.[9]

Desmond's first operational sortie took place on 2 September when the squadron was unexpectedly called to readiness shortly after dawn. They took off at 8.30 a.m. and were told to join up with a few Hurricanes from 242 Squadron to escort a 'Roadstead'[10] formation of three Blenheims tasked with bombing ships anchored in the English Channel, 2 miles off Dunkirk. The target was a merchant vessel of about 3,000 tonnes and its escort of two flak ships sat at anchor just to the north of the merchantman. Somehow, the Blenheims failed to see the merchant ship and turned back.

But the escorting Spitfires and Hurricanes did find the target vessels. The section leaders called their wingmen into formation behind them, dropped to very low level over the water and twenty-four fighters took turns to (as they put it) 'tickle the decks' of the two smaller ships with their machine guns, before pulling up and away to avoid the ships' masts and guns.

Desmond and the squadron 'flew back at 0 ft' over the Channel, landing at Hornchurch with 20 gallons of fuel left – less than the reserve they normally allowed themselves to make it home safely.[11] The brevity with which Desmond commented on this particular flight belies the reality of what often happened on such missions. The Spitfires flew at very low level to get a better shot at the target, but on the way back they did so to avoid the enemy guns dotted around the French coast as well.

Flying at 'nought feet' meant just a few feet above the waves, and it took great concentration, skill and considerable nerve to be able to hold a fighter racing at full pelt so close to the sea. The Spitfire's altimeter used barometric (air) pressure fed directly into the instrument via a thin metal tube.

There was a margin for error in pressure readings, particularly when flying at some distance away from the home airfield and below 30ft, because a barometric altimeter will not work effectively below around 30ft above the surface – be it land or water.

Pilots could fly their aircraft at very low level yet in relative safety above flat land or water, even though their altimeters may have legitimately registered a height of 0ft, as long as they had reasonable visibility. During bad weather, or with limited visibility, very low flying could only be done safely when the altimeter could give a reading.

All aircraft returned safely from the operation, which had been a good lesson for Desmond. Over the coming weeks and months, he would become accustomed to flying at wave-top or tree-top height as the squadron took part in low-level raids against targets in France.

From now on, the clock was counting down towards the 250 hours (or approximately 170 operational sorties) Desmond required to complete a tour of operations. Back at base that evening, the pilots relaxed by going along to the first station dance of the season.

Come midday on 4 September, the early morning mist and fog had cleared, leaving perfect flying conditions, and the squadron was duly rostered to fly in Circus 93,[12] which took off at 3.30 p.m. led by Wg Cdr Eric Stapleton, with Plt Off 'Streak' Harris (from 54 Squadron's A Flight) as his number two. The wing was to escort a formation of eighteen Blenheims on another daylight raid to the Pas-de-Calais area where they were to bomb the Mazingarbe chemical works. This would be the first of a series of raids on Mazingarbe, a small industrial town lying between Bethune and Lens and 12 miles to the north of Arras.

The good weather that day meant a full strength 'show' by the wing, and all three Hornchurch squadrons took twelve Spitfires each up in support of the bombers in the mid-afternoon. As was usual with a 'Circus' formation, the fighters outnumbered the bombers. The Spitfires from 54 Squadron were led by the Station Commander, Harry Broadhurst.

This was Desmond's first time flying in such a large formation, and he was flying as number two (wingman) to Plt Off Evans. The Spitfires rendezvoused with the Blenheims over Manston, crossed the enemy coast just north-east of Calais and were shortly over the target area at Mazingarbe. The bombers successfully dropped their bombs, which was not always the case on these raids, and the Spitfires were warned of an imminent attack by around fifteen to twenty ME109s.

All the pilots in the formation normally kept radio, or radio/telephone (R/T), silence until the last minute but could still hear the instructions and dialogue between the formation leader and the ground controller back in England. Only on sight of the enemy would one of the formation call the leader's attention and transmit a warning.

Listening carefully to what was going on, Desmond's heart rate began to rise as the Spitfires were guided into position, ready to engage the Germans. He recalled the simple order Evans had given him: 'Stick to me like glue.' Desmond looked around, wondering where the Germans might appear from. Gradually, the two formations closed on each other and awaited the order to attack.

The controllers on the ground were experienced in getting formations of RAF fighters into position to meet formations of enemy aircraft sent up to intercept them. But Neville Duke recalled that, when flying similar raids over enemy territory, on at least one occasion in August 1941 the controller at Biggin Hill, whose job it was to guide a circus of fighters into battle, had simply given up. The Luftwaffe had at one point put up so many fighters in opposition to the RAF bombers and fighters that the controller announced dryly over the radio, 'Many 109s covering northern France at all heights' and just left the pilots to get on with it.

Wg Cdr Stapleton saw the formation of Messerschmitts, 1,000ft below and ahead of them at 24,000ft, beginning to make a determined attack on the Blenheim bombers. Now he called some of the Spitfires in to attack this group of Messerschmitts. Just as they did so, another formation of ME109s was seen to dive in from 28,000ft onto 54 Squadron. The leader of 611 Squadron called eight of his aircraft in to counterattack them, to cover 54 Squadron. It was these ME109s that gave Desmond his first taste of action as he and Evans were told to 'break' into them as they swooped down at speed. In the melee that followed, Desmond managed to briefly latch on to a 109 and turn his Spitfire left and right as he tried to keep up with it. He came within range, took a shot, but missed.

As this was going on, the remaining four Spitfires of 611 then climbed to attack a third formation of ME109s that had appeared higher still, and a section of 603 Squadron dropped in to help 611 engage them. The remnants of the escort, a small number of 603, stayed 'up top' to act as cover in case any more enemy fighters showed up.

Now all hell broke loose, and Spitfires and Messerschmitts dived, weaved, looped and turned, alternately firing at each other whenever they had chance, even if it was only for a second or two. The Germans had managed to completely separate the Spitfire formations, who fought hard for several minutes in singles or pairs. But as they ran low on fuel and ammunition, the Spitfires had to break off and make for home as fast as they could, streaming out of France at 0ft again.

Although now separated from their original formations, Harris was still seen accompanying Wg Cdr Stapleton as they crossed the coast, with Harris weaving hard. As the Spitfires descended and raced across the French coast, they weaved and dropped to wave-top height to try to dodge the gunfire from the enemy machine guns, anti-aircraft guns and large-calibre flak batteries dotted along the coast.

Those who could landed back at Hornchurch in ones and twos. For a while it looked as if at least five pilots from 54 Squadron were missing, but slowly news came in. The Czech, Flt Sgt Pavlu, landed late at Hornchurch. Sgt Aitken was forced to land at Hawkinge near Folkestone close to the coast. Sgt Bax diverted to Coltishall near the Norfolk coast. The last two unaccounted for were Evans and Harris. Desmond had been with his leader, Evans, on the first attack, diving into a formation of 109s but had lost him just as he fired at an ME109. Soon he realised his fuel was running low and made his own way across the Channel to Hornchurch. They waited for some time for news to come in, either from returning pilots or a phone call from another airfield to say he was safe, but none arrived. Evans, along with Harris, did not come back.

Despite the two losses, reports of the day's actions reached the ears of High Command, and the following day the AOC himself, Trafford

Leigh-Mallory, signalled the wing with the message: 'Very well done Hornchurch Wing. Congratulations on yesterday's battle.'

Inclement weather then effectively closed down operations over France until the middle of September, so the new pilots trained in the local area with the more experienced pilots instead. They agreed that 'all was good and the reputation of the fighting 54th would undoubtedly be upheld'.[13]

Wondering if his flight commanders had been right in their assessment, Fanny Orton took Desmond and a few others from B Flight up to practise their dogfighting skills. Going up against highly experienced leaders, aces who had been awarded gallantry medals for their actions over Dunkirk and during the Battle of Britain, was a real test of mettle and competence for Desmond and his colleagues, even though experience was no guarantee of survival.

As the weather cleared, operations resumed, and on 17 September 54 Squadron was assigned two Circus operations: one escorting Blenheims to hit Mazingarbe power station and chemical works again and another escorting twin-engined Hampdens to hit a shell factory at Marquise. Of the twenty-four Blenheims sent over, only ten saw the targets and dropped their bombs, while the handful of Hampdens could not identify their target so did not bomb.

Yet, on both raids, several thousand feet above the frustrated bombers, the escorting Spitfires were dealing with an enemy that, while not seen as 'terribly good' since the RAF pilots managed to take fairly easy evasive action, was actually very determined and swarmed around the Spitfires. This time, 54 Squadron lost three more pilots on the first raid, two who had just joined the squadron (Sgts Overton and Draper) and the boss himself, Fanny Orton. During the fighting, Sqn Ldr Orton was seen by his wingman to be on the tail of a 109, pursuing it and shooting chunks off it. Orton was therefore credited with a probable kill but, sadly, was not seen again. He was immediately replaced by Sqn Ldr Scott-Malden.

Sqn Ldr David 'Scotty' Scott-Malden DFM was already based at Hornchurch serving with 603 (City of Edinburgh) Squadron, so was promoted and just walked across the tarmac to join his new squadron. He would go on to earn the DFC and achieve eventual promotion to the rank of air vice-marshal. Scotty had flown exceptionally well during his time with 603 Squadron and was a good choice. He was also thought to be one of the first Volunteer Reserve officers to take command of a fighter squadron.

On the second raid, just after crossing the French coast, the Luftwaffe engaged the Spitfires again. Sgt Preece was shot down and crashed in the Channel but was later picked up by one of the RAF's Air Sea Rescue motor launches and returned to Hornchurch. The motor launch crew faced an extremely difficult task of spotting a head bobbing about in a vast seascape, even when the pilot's head may have been kept above the waterline by an inflated 'Mae West' life jacket. Two more probables were claimed by the 54 Squadron pilots that day, but not by Desmond. The pilots who returned reported they had been in 'a terrific battle – you could fire at 109s all the time,' and they, equally, fired back.[14] Desmond agreed, having been pursued by the Germans and shot at too, but he managed to evade them well enough to avoid being hit.

It had been a disastrous day for the squadron given the losses, but there had been plenty of lessons for Desmond, who had been with the squadron for less than a month. He had seen first-hand what air-to-air fighting really meant and what happened when you either took your eye off the ball or were just plain unlucky. The rule of thumb was that pilots who survived their first five operations had a higher-than-average chance of surviving the rest of their tour. That day, Desmond had completed his fifth operation.

While the rest of the squadron were on ops, for the next four days it is possible Desmond took a few days' leave and returned home to Harewood – not by Spitfire as he had done a few weeks earlier but by train instead. The family photos of him in his uniform with pilot's wings and sergeant chevrons date from the summer of 1941. Perhaps the loss of several of his contemporaries may have prompted him to record such moments and achievements for posterity as soon as he could.

The images show him smartly dressed and groomed for the camera, reflecting the standards he was expected to maintain when on duty. This would contrast with the more informal approach seen in months to come, as his time in combat intensified.

When Desmond did return to flying nine days later, he was part of an escort sortie to a squadron of Hurricanes sent out to attack five suspected enemy minesweepers in the Channel just off Gravelines. As the fighters swooped onto their target, the escorting Spitfires were intercepted, and Desmond got into a fight with an ME109E. This time he got in close enough to see his bullets strike home, but the 109 survived the encounter when its pilot realised he was going to come off worse so broke away from the fight and turned for home. Desmond decided not to follow him. He could only claim the 109 as a 'damaged', but it was the first time he had successfully engaged and hit an enemy aircraft. His confidence and skill were growing as he came closer to getting his first confirmed victory.

On 27 September, the squadron was tasked to take part in Circus 103B, an offensive sweep back to Mazingarbe. Desmond was flying as Blue 2 (wingman to the Blue Section leader). They were 15 miles inland, north-east from Le Touquet on the French coast and flying at 14,000ft when a formation of ME109Es intercepted the RAF fighters and bombers, while a section of them made straight for the Blenheims. Blue Section were ordered to engage them. Immediately, Desmond pushed the throttle forward to get a boost of power. He wrote: 'Three 109s dived in front of me from my starboard (right) side as though to attack the bombers which were about a mile in front of me.' Blue Section each picked one of the German aeroplanes that were focused on making a swift attack on the bombers. Desmond got behind his ME109 and gave it a quick burst. The pilot reacted by rolling inverted and accelerated away using the ME109's superior speed in a dive to its best advantage.

In the early days, a Spitfire's guns were harmonised to 400yds so the bullets would all converge at a specific point ahead but, after the RAF's experience in the Battle of Britain, that distance was commonly reduced to 250yds. In this fight, Desmond closed to 200yds, racing straight down at over 300mph, almost vertical behind his opponent. He continued:

> I fired a short burst from astern as the leading 109 turned in front of me and he went down in a vertical dive with several pieces falling away from the rudder and tail unit. I followed him down for 2,000ft and when I last saw the enemy aircraft, it was in a very steep dive with more small pieces coming off. I had to pull away and returned to the English coast behind the bombers.[15]

It was a frustrating outcome for this operation because, yet again, the Blenheims had failed to identify and drop their bombs on the Mazingarbe power station and, despite his best efforts, Desmond could only claim his ME109 as a damaged.

As he regained level flight, Desmond spotted and paired up with Sgt Fenton. As they proceeded back across the Channel together, they spotted a lone Blenheim heading back to England at sea level. Over a brief radio discussion, Desmond and Fenton decided to escort it home. They positioned themselves in a loose 'V' just off each wing and throttled back to keep level with the lumbering Blenheim. The lower altitude and cruising speed also helped them all conserve their remaining fuel.

As they approached the south coast, Desmond saw one of the other escorting Spitfires crash-land on the shore at Dungeness.[16] Once safely inland, Desmond and Fenton left the Blenheim and landed at Lympne to refuel before flying back to Hornchurch. The rest of the 54 Squadron pilots also had to make their own way back in loose groups, pairs or solo, but they were fortunate to have suffered no losses this time.

The next day, while escorting a formation of three more Blenheims and twelve 'Hurri-bombers' (Hurricane fighters carrying bombs and fitted with 20mm cannon) to Ostend on the Belgian coast, Desmond got into another dogfight. But on this, his eighth operational sortie, he got enough hits on a 109F to cause it such significant damage that he could claim it as a probable.

A 'probable' claim meant the stricken aeroplane was severely damaged to an extent that indicated it was unlikely to make it back to base, but the action had not been reliably witnessed by any other pilots. To be able to claim a confirmed 'kill', in the absence of the plane's destruction being filmed by a gun camera, it had to be witnessed by another pilot. Sometimes eyewitnesses on the ground would report an aircraft crash. The police would then notify the Air Ministry, who would notify the squadron. If the two accounts matched, the pilot would be credited with a confirmed kill or destroyed. As September gave way to October, the number of days between operations began to increase as the autumn weather worsened and limited the opportunities for daytime bombing raids.

Operations over enemy-held territory continued where possible, but Bomber Command conducted mainly nighttime raids over Germany.

As the threat of imminent invasion receded, the RAF chief, Sir Hugh 'Stuffy' Dowding, decided the Spitfires and Hurricanes should now conduct offensive fighter sweeps on a deceptively simple premise – fly over to France and see who wanted a fight. However, this rather vague policy of 'leaning forward into France' contrasted sharply with two essential facets of the RAF's victory in the Battle of Britain.

First, the RAF had home advantage. The Allied pilots were highly motivated because they were fighting for the countryside, villages and homes they were flying over, which was where they and their loved ones lived. And, if they were shot down and bailed out, they could be back with their squadron in a matter of hours.

Second, by flying over home turf, the Spitfire and Hurricanes had more operational time in the air and could, therefore, spend longer fighting the enemy, for whom time was tight and fuel precious. The German ME109s, similar in size and range to the RAF fighters, normally had no more than 10 minutes combat time before having to head home. If they were shot down and bailed out over England, the Luftwaffe pilots would become PoWs.

Now that situation was reversed at the stroke of Dowding's pen. Not only were the RAF fighters limited to a similar air combat time of around 10 minutes, if their pilots were shot down beyond the Channel, they were now over enemy-held territory where few civilians spoke English, and few pilots spoke either French or German. The pilots would not know who to trust. If they were captured still in uniform and not shot out of hand, they would be interrogated and shipped off to a PoW camp for months. If later they were captured dressed in civilian clothing trying to escape, they were liable to be viewed as spies and shot. The home advantage enjoyed by the RAF's fighter aircraft was completely lost under this new policy, designed to show that Britain, and specifically the RAF, was still capable of taking the fight to the enemy.

CHAPTER 8

54 Squadron – French Rhubarbs and Scottish Hail

2 October 1941–7 June 1942

The first time 54 Squadron was rostered for an offensive fighter sweep was on 2 October. It was also the first time Desmond was chosen to lead a section. This would be his ninth op, but already he was flexing his leadership muscles. The twelve Spitfires took off as normal, formed three sections in line astern and began the climb to height. Frustratingly, Desmond had to return home due to a fault with the oxygen system. One of his colleagues took his place as leader and, although Luftwaffe fighters were in the area, the raid went ahead without incident.

Desmond's next opportunity came on the afternoon of 11 October when two pairs of Spitfires were sent out over the coast of occupied Belgium on a 'Rhubarb'.[1] One pair was led by the CO, Sqn Ldr Scott-Malden, his number two being Sgt Guthrie. The second pair was B Flight commander Jack Charles, with Desmond as his number two. Two 'old hands' leading two newcomers. The flight was uneventful, there was no contact with enemy fighters and the formation returned safely.

Rhubarbs were at best controversial and at worst an often-loathed type of operational sortie that involved deliberate penetration of enemy territory to hit designated targets and/or scout for targets of opportunity. These occasional forays across the Channel into the French and Belgian plains were carried out aggressively at high speed and frequently at very low level. In part, this was as much due to the prevailing weather conditions as the tactics because, when the weather prevented larger raids taking place, the only sorties that could be flown were Rhubarbs.

Many pilots grew to resent these types of raids because they were deliberately being put at increased risk for very little tangible gain. The price was likely to be the loss of a well-trained and valuable pilot. Flying as an escort to bombers and engaging in dogfights was seen as a fairer kind of sport. Ferreting around alone in the enemy countryside for what may or may not turn out to be a German vehicle, train or group of soldiers seemed a grubbier side to a pilot's job. Though some pilots did feel more at ease with the random nature of the task they were given and arguably looked on it as a chance to wreak havoc or personal revenge.

Later in the evening of 11 October, a handful of pilots took off to practise air-to-air fighting in pairs. Desmond led Sgt McDonald off to the south, out over the Kent Weald. McDonald was a Canadian, fresh out of the OTU at Heston, and had been with the squadron less than a fortnight. Now Desmond was showing him how to handle a Spitfire as a weapon. What followed for Desmond though was a reminder of how leaders are tested when things go wrong.

Near the end of the sortie, after chasing each other round the sky, practising dogfight manoeuvres, Desmond's radio packed up. Something else occurred to him too. While flying at between 10,000 and 15,000ft the daylight had remained reasonably bright up above the clouds, even as the sun slunk slowly towards the horizon. Realising that both fuel and light were fading, Desmond decided to end the exercise and turn for home. He looked around, below and underneath the wings to try to find a feature he recognised, but the ground was in complete shadow. He started looking round the cramped cockpit for his maps but realised they too had disappeared. They were probably trapped somewhere inaccessible on the cockpit floor as a result of him not stowing them correctly before starting the violent aerobatics.

He turned north, looking for the south coast and began a straight and level descent, all the time hoping his wingman had kept him in sight and, not being able to raise him on the radio, would come looking for him. He was now responsible for getting both himself and the 'new boy' home, but he was unable to see McDonald let alone communicate with him, or anyone else for that matter, and was unable to fix his position with a map. This could pose a serious problem.

Just then, McDonald's Spitfire slid into close formation just behind his left wing. Desmond began pointing, trying to tell him he had a problem. The pilot looked blankly at him. Desmond reached up and pulled the canopy back. Cold air rushed in, and the engine roared louder. Desmond pointed to his earpiece, showing his radio had failed. He gestured to McDonald to keep close as they were about to descend. Desmond thrust his hand forward to show the direction. McDonald acknowledged, then disappeared into wispy cloud. Desmond looked ahead. He was also descending into cloud but could just make out a gap below. He pulled the canopy shut and focused on his instruments, so he didn't become disorientated. After a few seconds in gloom, the cloud thinned and cleared. He looked out to his left. McDonald was gone.

Dusk had by now given way to early nighttime. For all his hours in Spitfires to date, Desmond had very little night flying experience. The countryside below had lost its features as towns and villages followed blackout procedures in case of air raids. Desmond was truly alone. He decided to turn east and let down over the Channel to try to pick out the cliffs. As long as he was on the right side of the Channel, he stood a chance of making it back.

Passing through 5,000ft he could make out the line of cliffs and silvery sheen of the sea below. He nudged a little closer to the coastline and scanned the gloomy land behind, thinking about what options he might have. His fuel gauge showed less than a quarter tank full – nowhere near enough to reach Hornchurch. He thought about crash landing – but in the dark, with no lights? If he made it down to 20ft, he could still easily fly straight into a wood or the side of a blacked-out building. His only other alternative was to bail out: point the Spitfire out to sea, put it in a gentle dive and jump over the side. But he would have no reference point to know when he was approaching the ground and could easily break both his legs. Or, if he drifted out over the sea, he would surely drown. What a choice.

What decided it for him was a bright flash – not a light, but a reflection. A glint or two was enough to attract his eye. Soon, he could discern a distinct narrow line of water – the Royal Military Canal – and just beyond that, two thin silver lines that marked the railway running east to west to Folkestone. He knew Lympne airfield was between the two features and the surrounding ground was mostly flat marshland. He began to descend. He couldn't see the airfield yet, but if he dropped low enough and circled the area in a wide loop, perhaps they might see him.

Indeed, someone on the ground recognised the sound of the Spitfire's engine and saw the crackles of flame from the exhaust. A lamp flashed its beam up towards him. He turned towards it. Out of the gloom, he could make out the faint lights of the runway lamps that had been turned on and finally landed, bumpily but safely at Lympne. He had been airborne for two hours, lost his wingman and landed, with the needle on the petrol gauge just above zero, at the wrong airfield. Hornchurch was nearly 60 miles away to the north. But at least he hadn't crashed another Spitfire and lost that too.

With the help of a groundcrew, he put the Spitfire to bed in a hangar and walked over to the sergeants' mess to telephone Hornchurch, He explained to the duty operations officer what had happened and was relieved to be told McDonald had managed to find his own way to Hawkinge airfield (situated to the north of Folkestone) and landed safely. The pair spent the night at separate sergeants' messes before refuelling and returning to Hornchurch the following morning to a ribbing from the other pilots about staying out late, trying to become night-fighter aces and so on.

The remainder of the month was spent either practising formation flying or, when on ops, convoy patrols. The odd Circus and Rhubarb took place but, while still engaging enemy fighters, there were no additions to Desmond's tally.

In November, 54 Squadron was ordered to move far away from the action over Kent and the south coast. It was usual for squadrons to be rotated through sectors on the front line, and once they had either been depleted or faced an extended period of action in one particular sector, they were sent north for a rest and a chance to regroup. In reality though, it seems all the changes were intended to gradually dismantle the squadron, and the present composition of the Hornchurch Wing. The reorganisation saw 611 Squadron leave for a new base at Drem in the Turnhouse sector near Edinburgh.

Desmond was temporarily reassigned to A Flight. All the Spitfire Vs were left at Hornchurch to be collected by 124 Squadron and taken to their base at Biggin Hill instead. All that was moving to Scotland were the pilots, groundcrew, all their essential equipment and personal belongings. They boarded a specially laid-on train and began their 31-hour journey to Caithness on 17 November.[2]

The base at Castletown was far more isolated and spread out than at Hornchurch. The surroundings were bleak, the Spitfires were old Mk IIb types, and the tasks felt menial: all convoy patrols and training sorties with just an occasional alert when a twin-engined German JU-88 bomber flew in on a solo raid to drop a few bombs on or around the nearby bases. It wasn't all bad – taking off north-west on the main runway, pilots would fly directly over the shallow Dunnet Bay fringed by a wide sandy beach. To the north-east of the bay was the officers' mess, the Dunnet Hotel. The little town from which the airfield took its name lay a couple of miles to the west. In peacetime, it made for a beautiful location for a quiet holiday, far from the hustle and bustle of industrial towns and cities. But such remote locations could be notoriously bleak in the late autumn and winter months when the rain was driven horizontally by the fierce onshore winds.

From the beginning of December, Desmond was sent away from 54 Squadron on detachment to No. 4 Delivery Flight (DF) at Grangemouth (180 miles to the south of Castletown) on a rest from ops. Going north to a quieter sector was one thing, but he felt in no need of a rest and was keen to return to operations. The DF was formed on 13 April 1941 with a flight lieutenant as CO, half a dozen pilots, one twin-engined Dominie biplane and a Humber Snipe utility car.[3]

When Desmond joined the DF, there were only eight pilots, including himself, on strength (compared to the usual twenty to thirty on a fighter squadron). It is possible he was posted in following the death of Sgt Brady who, flying solo without any R/T, flew into the side of a hill near Aberdeen on 8 November 1941, resulting in the unit's first fatality.[4] It was a timely reminder for Desmond that he had been lucky not to have flown into one of the hills of the Weald a month earlier when he had lost his radio and his wingman.

A large proportion of the Spitfires at Castletown were required to be on readiness, which meant a maximum of four aircraft could be used for practice and training new pilots at any one time. Flying for both 54 Squadron at Castletown and 4 DF was restricted even further by the frequent low cloud, wind, rain, 'armour-piercing hail', shorter days and recurrent minor accidents.[5] The squadron were keen to keep their fighting strength current, and it was useful having one of their own pilots posted to the DF who could help maintain that, but they still had to wait several days for replacement parts, due to the weather.

On 9 December, Desmond was tasked to deliver a Mk IIB Spitfire to Castletown for 54 Squadron. They sent up a section of 'Spits' to carry out a practice intercept and escort him in but as they tried to do so, he spotted them and decided to have some fun. He watched them turn in to intercept him and said that he 'just opened the throttle and left them behind' to chase him.

Desmond was based at Castletown for only thirteen days, but in that time an official war photographer arrived at the base and took a picture of him posing in the cockpit of a Spitfire. Desmond was strapped in, lifejacket and flying helmet on. He turned to face the camera, looking over his left shoulder, his hand ready to shut the side panel, as though he was waiting for the shutter to click, then he could start the engine and fly off to tackle the enemy.

Sixty years later, I found that photograph in the Imperial War Museum Photographic Archives and had a copy made. When it arrived in the post, I took it round to show Muriel, who immediately recognised her brother despite having never seen the full photograph before. I wasn't completely certain because he looked a little different, but Muriel was adamant. 'That's my brother,' she said firmly, holding the photo in one hand and pointing at his face with the forefinger of the other, 'I'd recognise him anywhere.' That same photo, heavily cropped to show just his face, was published in a copy of *The War Illustrated* above a short announcement two years after it was taken, when Desmond was abroad. Muriel spotted it, cut it out and stuck it in the scrapbook she had devoted to her brother. It would not be the last time Desmond appeared in the papers.

Desmond continued to fly all over Scotland, the Isle of Man and Northern Ireland ferrying aircraft around. Often, he would be flown to another airfield for the job and, on such occasions, he would fly as second pilot in the DF's twin-engined Dominie to pick up the particular aircraft (usually a Spitfire) and fly it on to the destination unit. Once there, he would either be flown back to Grangemouth in another communications aircraft or travel back by rail. This little interlude carried on until 19 December 1941.

It was at this time the 54 Squadron adjutant resentfully noted that no sooner were pilots arriving on the squadron and being trained up to operational standard than they were posted out. The blunt truth was that Churchill had decided to draw land and air assets out of the Western Desert in mid-1941, where they had been successfully pushing the Italian and German forces back towards Libya and away from Egypt, in order to defend the Greek islands, specifically Crete.[6] The withdrawal of some Allied units from the desert had allowed the Axis armies time to re-arm and stem the Allied advance across the desert. Without Allied air superiority to hamper them, the Germans and Italians began pushing back, and the characteristic waxing and waning of armies across the north of Africa started to play out once more.

With the RAF drafting more squadrons to Greece, it needed to replenish its existing front-line units in Egypt and send out reinforcements from the UK, and volunteers were being sought from resting fighter units across the UK. No. 54 Squadron received its request for volunteers from 14 Group Headquarters based in Inverness.

Over the autumn of 1941, 54 Squadron had acquired a proportionally large contingent of pilots from overseas who, along with the ex-Hornchurch pilots, had gradually been sent abroad to be replaced with fresh RAF pilots from the OTUs. The whole composition and character of 54 Squadron, one of the RAF's elite squadrons, was changing completely and was no longer the unit Desmond had known. In fact, the squadron's declining status meant it was practically becoming an OTU. Bored with ferrying aircraft around, and with few friends left on 54 Squadron, Desmond may have succumbed to 14 Group's request and applied for a posting overseas. Most of Desmond's mates had already left, either for the Middle East, Malta or, in a couple of cases, back to the USA and Australia.

Although Desmond's service record formally states that he returned to 54 Squadron on 23 December following his secondment to the DF, he never flew with them again. It is most likely he visited his family that Christmas, but it would be the last Christmas they would all spend together. A few weeks later still, what was left of the 'fighting 54th' set sail for Australia and service in the Far East.

Once his overseas posting was confirmed on 26 February 1942, Desmond would have been granted leave to visit his family once more before departing. Desmond's tales of adventure were a welcome and fun distraction; however, there were undercurrents of tension between Desmond's parents because Horace was having an affair.

During that precious time, neither Desmond nor Muriel nor indeed any of his family considered the possibility that he might not come back. Such thoughts would be in the back of his mother's mind though, despite the bravado reassurances from Desmond that he was good at flying Spitfires, had fought the enemy at close range and not been harmed. He was full of stories about flying over France and the south of England, then up to Scotland for patrols over convoys and across the country delivering aeroplanes. Plus, the friends he'd made, the parties and dances he'd been to, the girls he'd met – what did they have to worry about? He would be away a few months, then no doubt be posted back to England and would see them again soon. This was, of course, in the days before the siege of Tobruk, Malta and the retreat across Egypt when it looked like Hitler's war machine would take the whole of Eastern Europe and the Middle East.

When he finally left, it took a journey of six weeks by land and sea before Desmond arrived at the training base near Alexandria towards the end of April. He was just in time to join the developing crisis in Egypt when the British and Allied forces were being pushed all the way back to Cairo.

It was a situation as desperate as when the Nazis advanced through France and the Low Countries in the spring of 1940, nearly two years earlier. For Desmond, although new experiences and achievements lay ahead, it was to be the last time he saw England or his family again.

Family at Harewood, c. 1927. L–R: Amy, Grandma Ada, Desmond, Muriel, Sally, Sarah. (Ibbotson family album)

L–R: Des, Muriel and Peter Nettleton on Horace's motorbike. (Ibbotson family album)

Captioned by Sarah: 'My three – Brownie and scout and very fat Mollie.' L–R: Muriel, Desmond holding Mollie. (Ibbotson family album)

At the River Wharfe, Harewood – Muriel, Des and two cousins, 1930s. (Ibbotson family album)

Desmond, Cub Scout cricketer, 1933. (Ibbotson family album)

The Ibbotsons (Des back right) in Albert Park, Auckland, New Zealand, 1937. (Ibbotson family album)

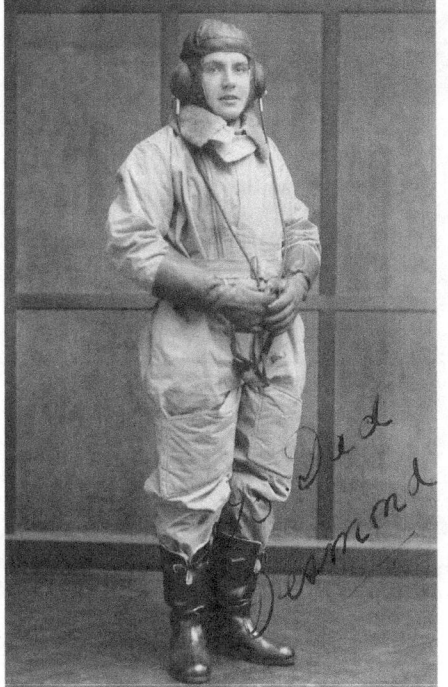

Above left: Desmond and Horace Ibbotson in their local team football kit, 1937. (Ibbotson family album)

Above right: Desmond on leave from training, with Grandma Ada, Harewood, 1941. (Ibbotson family album)

Left: Des in flying training, 1940. The handwriting reads, 'To Dad, Desmond'. (Ibbotson family album)

Des on gaining his RAF wings, 2 July 1941. (Ibbotson family album)

Desmond as a sergeant pilot – at home at the family-run post office in Harewood while on leave from 129 Squadron based at Leconfield, 1941. (Ibbotson family album)

No. 129 Squadron, Leconfield, Yorkshire, August 1941. Norm Peat (top), Des (seated), Jimmy Whalen (standing). (Photo taken by and courtesy of Ray Sherk)

28–30 November 1941. Sgt Desmond Ibbotson, aged 20, 54 Squadron, Castletown, Caithness, Scotland. A few days later Desmond transferred to No. 4 Delivery Flight. (Piemags/ww2archive/Alamy stock photo)

Desmond's photograph of 'Morrison with my kite' shows Sgt J.H. Morrison (RNZAF). He served with 112 Squadron from 18 August to 30 September 1942, during which his Kittyhawk (No. ET795) mysteriously caught fire in mid-air, and he crash-landed near El Haouaria – his second such accident in a fortnight. He suffered cuts to the head and wrist but was otherwise all right. He returned to the squadron fit for flying but was then posted to another unit. (Ibbotson family album)

Curtiss Kittyhawk Mark I, AK772 'GA-Y' 'London Pride', of 112 Squadron RAF, is prepared for a sortie at Gambut Main, Libya. The groundcrew can just be seen assisting the pilot to strap himself into the cockpit. The aircraft is carrying a 250lb general-purpose bomb, fitted with a surface-burst impact fuse under the fuselage. Note also the plugs placed in the exhaust stubs to keep the desert sand out. (Piemags/ww2archive/Alamy stock photo)

No. 112 Squadron pilots sharing a tin of corned beef and 'hard-tac' biscuits, June/July 1942 (L–R): Plt Off Brian A.F. 'Compo' Cudden (KIA, 11 December 1942); Flt Lt Walker DFC (KIA, Burma, 8 February 1944); Sgt D. Hogg (PoW, 21 October 1942); Sgt 'Nobby' A. Clarke (believed to be misidentified); Plt Off 'Johnny' Johnson (MIA, 24 July 1942); Sgt H.G.E. 'Tommy' Thomas (MIA, 5 September 1942 but possibly survived); Fg Off (later Sqn Ldr) William M. 'Babe' Whitamore (KIA, Burma, 17 March 1944, aged 21). (Ibbotson family album)

June 1942 (L–R): Plt Off Cuddon, Plt Off Johnson, Flt Lt Walker DFC, Sgt D.J.B. White, Des, Johnny S. Barrow. Kneeling: Flt Sgt J.B. 'Paddy' Agnew. (Ibbotson family album)

Sqn Ldr Billy Drake photographed while CO No. 112 Squadron RAF at Gambut, Libya. Billy had been CFI at 53 OTU, Llandow. He certified Desmond there and promoted him to pilot officer while CO of 112 Squadron. As CO, Billy enjoyed a period of considerable success in North Africa, shooting down fourteen enemy aircraft before he was taken off operations in December 1943 to serve on the staff at RAF Headquarters Middle East. (Piemags/ww2archive/Alamy stock photo)

June 1942, North Africa, the 'Desert Fox', Generalfeldmarschall Erwin J.E. Rommel with Generalleutnant Georg von Bismarck. (Bundesarchiv, Bild 101I-784-0232-37A/Otto/CC-BY-SA 3.0)

Mammut Moritz in the desert, 1942. This command vehicle is actually a captured British Associated Equipment Company Dorchester command vehicle and was the same type Desmond was taken to for interrogation by senior Afrika Korps officers when he was captured at Mersa Matruh on 7 November 1942. (Sueddeutsche Zeitung photo/Alamy stock photo)

Desmond (second left, wearing sunglasses) when Churchill visited the Western Desert, 3 August 1942. (Ibbotson family album)

Desmond after escaping Rommel's troops and arriving at LG13 near Mersa Matruh on the afternoon of 8 November 1942. He was awarded the 'Flying Boot'. (Ibbotson family album)

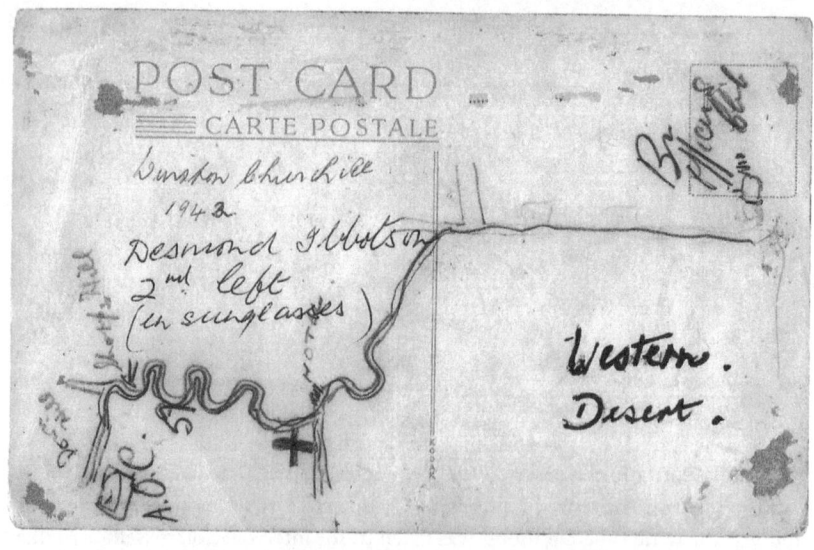

The map on the back of the photo of when Churchill visited the Western Desert, 3 August 1942. (Ibbotson family album)

Desmond's Late Arrivals Club certificate, 8 November 1942. (Ibbotson family album)

Around 23 February 1943. Des poses in his 601 Squadron Spitfire after the award of his first DFC. Note the seven swastikas on the cowling. (Ibbotson family album)

Bill Gwynne, Ibby, 'Red' Schofield and WO Reggie Breeze (equipment officer), Bou Grara, Tunisia, spring 1943.

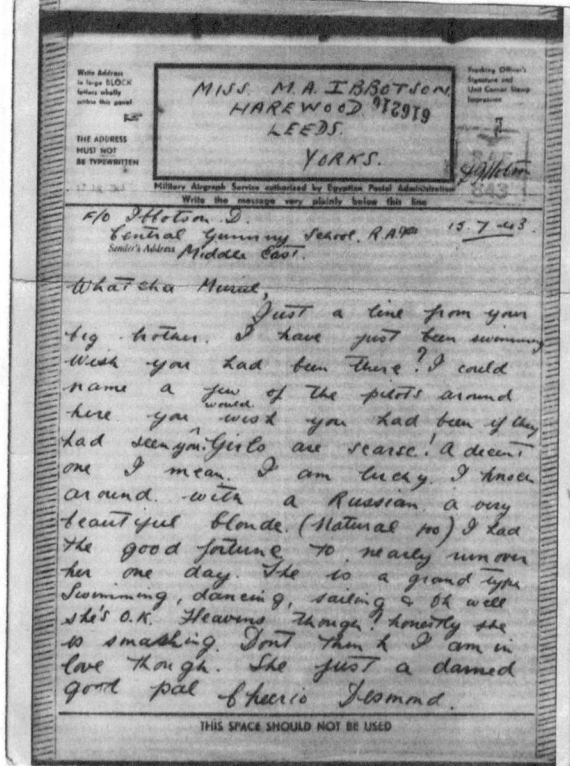

Desmond's airgraph letter to Muriel, 15 July 1943. (Ibbotson family album)

CHAPTER 9

112 Squadron – The Western Desert

North Africa
8–30 June 1942

Desmond reported to the operations tent of the Desert Air Force (DAF) Training Flight on 8 June 1942. He was 20 years old. It was a year since he had begun conversion training at 53 OTU to fly Spitfires. Now, he had to learn to fly the Curtiss P-40 Kittyhawk.

Affectionately known as 'Kitties', these aeroplanes had been designed and built in America and were, like the Spitfire, single-seat, single-engined fighters. Due to performance and reliability problems suffered by the original American Pratt & Whitney engines, the RAF had decided to refit the original fighter with the same Rolls-Royce Merlin engines used in the Spitfire and Hurricane. Standardising the engines also helped with the servicing and maintenance requirements.

The Luftwaffe had already used the purpose-built Junkers Ju-87 Stuka dive-bombers to support its armoured units and infantry in Poland, the Low Countries and France and had shipped them over to the desert to provide the same support. The RAF had to rely on modified fighters to do the same job, which is where the Kittyhawks came in and where the DAF had to teach its pilots how to drop bombs accurately.

The strategic situation was critical. If Egypt went the way of France, the Germans would capture the Suez Canal, and in doing so prevent the British from using a shortcut to their empire in the Far East, tighten their control of the Mediterranean and drive onto the Persian oilfields. Middle Eastern oil would fuel the expansion of Nazism for years to come, as well as providing the Germans with a southern route into Russia. Added to that, exactly two years earlier, the Italians declared war on Britain and its allies and expanded their existing forces in North Africa and occupied Ethiopia (then called Abyssinia).

All Desmond had wanted was another shot at action, somewhere warmer than Scotland, where he could continue to fly Spitfires and shoot down enemy aircraft. His experience in England had been all-too brief – two squadrons in a little over nine months. He had the skills, and the fighter units at home needed pilots, but it seemed the RAF was not willing to give him the opportunity he wanted to prove himself.

Was it snobbery? Was it because someone higher up had looked with displeasure at how many Spitfires he had crashed, rather than how many enemy aircraft he had damaged? Why had he just been shunted around the UK when it was quite obvious, in his mind, that keen, young and capable pilots like him should be out on the front-line squadrons doing what they had been trained to do? The result of his pushing to get to another squadron and more action was Egypt.

As he stood on the dusty rock-strewn ground outside the large Emperor tent that served as the operations room, shielding his eyes from the sun's glare as he tried to locate his new 'kite', he must have wondered what the hell he had got himself into now. Had he listened to the old maxim, 'If an officer says he wants volunteers, don't put your hand up'? Obviously not.

Desmond spotted the Kitty parked in a line of aircraft and walked over to it. His feet would become accustomed to the sharp, angular rocks that pushed at the soles of his boots. He stood by the left wing and paused to take in the sight of this new fighter he was about to fly for the first time. Everything about the shape of it said American: broad, thick wings rested on a wide undercarriage supported by rough-cut tyres. Despite it also being a single-seater and using the same engine, it was larger than a Hurricane and uglier than a Spitfire. There was nothing graceful or sleek about it, just oozing functionality. Seen from the front, its distinctive radiator shape gave the Kittyhawk a knowing grin, as though it was happy to be carrying bombs and bullets.

The squadron Desmond was now in training to join, 112 Squadron, made use of this aeroplane's unique jawline. In 1941, Fg Off Brunton had the idea of painting a set of shark's teeth around each side of the radiator and menacing eyes just behind the exhausts. Gerry Westenra, a New Zealand pilot and one of the flight commanders, recommended the markings be adopted. The CO at the time agreed, and the scheme was quickly adopted by all the squadron's Kittyhawks, which led to the nickname, 'Shark Squadron', and was retained for the rest of the war. Away in the Pacific Far East, an American fighter squadron (The Flying Tigers) adopted a similar design on its Tomahawks and Warhawks, but the RAF unit was the first in this war.[1] The rest of the paint scheme was a blend of light and dark-brown desert camouflage on the upper surfaces with light-blue underneath.

Over the next seven days, Desmond flew a total of 9 hours solo in the Kittyhawk, except for his first flight in a two-seat Harvard trainer – in which his instructor trained him to land on the aeroplane's main wheels as opposed to the three-point landings he was used to. The Kittyhawk had toe-operated brakes, as opposed to the hand-operated brake lever located on the control column of the Spitfire, and it also had a tailwheel that could unlock if the Kittyhawk started to swing on landing and the pilot over-corrected the resulting tail movement.

The training flight syllabus was rudimentary and progress rapid. Each sortie covered a different skill that had to be learnt in an hour or less. On only his second flight, Desmond was sent solo to practise handling and landings. Then came formation flying and attacks, dogfighting, shadow shooting, aerobatics and, arguably the most important skill he would need in this theatre, low flying – all covered and completed in around 5 hours, actually half the time it had taken him to first go solo in a Tiger Moth having never flown an aeroplane before. It showed that not only were Desmond's basic skills now instinctive, but he could adapt and learn quickly.

Desmond joined 112 Squadron on 15 June 1942 as soon as he was declared qualified to fly the Kittyhawk. The squadron was the longest serving one in North Africa. It was part of 239 Wing, which comprised four squadrons (two Australian squadrons – Nos 3 RAAF and 450 RAAF

– and two British squadrons – 112 RAF and 250 RAF) all based on the same airstrip at Gambut Main and all flying the Kittyhawk. Their leader was 24-year-old Billy Drake, Desmond's CFI from 53 OTU, Llandow, who had been promoted to squadron leader in December 1941 and briefly commanded 128 Squadron in Sierra Leone before taking over command of Shark Squadron. It was Billy who insisted that replacement pilots should first accumulate 5–10 hours' air experience on Kittyhawks, practising dive-bombing and strafing.[2]

While Desmond had been grappling with the controls of a new fighter, Billy had been trying to work out how he was going to control a bunch of tough, battle-hardened fighter pilots who eyed him with both curiosity and borderline contempt. They were a mix of British, American, Canadian, Australian, South African, Polish and Czech nationalities, with an equally wide range of backgrounds. Their previous CO had been a highly respected and renowned pilot with a tally of enemy fighters destroyed, which had earned him the nickname 'Killer' Caldwell. The temporary CO in place when Billy arrived to take charge was a flight commander who had fully expected to have been appointed as the new squadron leader. Billy walked into a tense situation with an irregular bunch of tired and edgy pilots. Furthermore, the normally strict separation between sergeants and officers had blurred to the point of virtual irrelevance. There were only a couple of large communal Emperor tents that served as the ops room/CO's office and mess. The pilots shared two-man tents.

Billy (his christened name, not the usual contraction of William), like Desmond, had spent part of his secondary education abroad, having emigrated at the wish of his father. On his return to England, his parents had discussed with him what a suitable career might be – perhaps a diplomat or doctor like his father. After a sequence of events that included taking a pleasure flight with Alan Cobham's Flying Circus, Billy responded to an RAF recruiting advertisement in *Aeroplane* magazine and joined the RAF as a regular on a short service commission in 1935. His parents did not want him to join up but agreed to an interview, believing he would be turned down.

When he joined No. 1 (Fighter) Squadron as part of the Advanced Air Striking Force in France, he had some success too, destroying four enemy aircraft and claiming several others as probables and damaged.

As the Germans rolled through France, Billy came off worst from a dogfight, bailed out and escaped west with the help of an American ambulance driver, Helen Ahrenfeldt, whom he had met some weeks earlier when on leave in Paris. It had been love at first sight for both of them. So, when he was shot down and wounded during what was to be his last sortie in France, Helen arranged for him to be treated in the American hospital in Paris. Then, when he had to flee the advancing Germans, who were expected in the city within 24 hours, she lent him her car with a full tank of fuel. He drove to Le Mans, found his squadron at a nearby airfield and got a flight back to Tangmere near Chichester, via Jersey, with a ferry pilot.

While a flight commander during the Battle of France, Billy had nearly become an ace. He was then sent to 53 OTU for a rest and to work as a CFI, where he first crossed paths with Desmond. By the time Billy joined 112 Squadron, he was an ace with a total of six destroyed, four probables and three damaged. His first DFC was announced on his 23rd birthday, 20 December 1940.[3] Billy had failed his own CFI's test at the first attempt when he flew his aircraft too close to the stalling point and had the controls quickly taken off him by the instructor. After a short time on remedial training with his original instructor, Billy retook his test and passed. Desmond passed first time, with Billy as his CFI.

Sixty-two years later, I met Billy at Duxford Air Show. He remembered Desmond immediately: his eyes flickered with new attention as that name connected him to the desert war all those years ago. I had to tell him Desmond had been killed in 1944, and the momentary hope of possibly catching up with someone from that time was extinguished.

Desmond would have recognised Billy when he arrived in Libya. Whether Billy recognised him is unclear, but they certainly became well acquainted. For Desmond, swapping Scottish sleet for Libyan sunshine had its benefit. But there were no other creature comforts: no single rooms, sprung beds, catered mess hall or off-base facilities in a local town. The nearest city where they could spend their leave was Alexandria, 300 miles away on the coast. When Desmond stepped down from the cockpit, debriefed and made his way 'home', he walked a few yards to a two-man tent that he shared with George 'Felix' Knoll, a fellow sergeant pilot who had fled his native Czechoslovakia to England to train with the RAF and fight back against the Nazis.

The beds were a rolled-out mat and a couple of thin blankets to keep off the nighttime cold.

Food was usually ration boxes of tinned beef and hardtack biscuits. There was little or no fruit. Flies were an ever-present menace, flitting haphazardly between the pilots' food and the latrines. Water was tightly rationed and split between drinking and washing. Rather than full uniform, pilots wore a combination of regulation issue short-sleeved shirts, shorts or trousers, socks and either shoes or desert boots, occasionally jumpers and waist-length battledress jackets. Rips and tears were repaired, stains ignored. Even when wearing desert clothing, it was uncomfortable in the cockpits with the canopy closed and rarely any cloud cover around to intercept the sun's rays. If the temperature was manageable, the glare from the sun was intense.

Dust, of course, was a serious problem. Hot winds off the Sahara to the south would travel north, bringing huge clouds of fine sand with them. The fine particles drifted in through any opening like beige, gritty fog and settled on any stationary surface and in any liquid. If they penetrated the engines of tanks, trucks or aeroplanes, they would render them utterly immobile until the dust had been removed.

The first few ops Desmond flew were to escort bombers, but these gradually reduced as the Kittyhawks changed from fighter interception to ground attack. The reason was partly that the aircraft was much better suited to low-level work, being somewhat inferior to the Messerschmitts above 10,000ft. Hence the escorts were flown at heights below that, if at all possible. Another factor was that the DAF was just beginning to take delivery of a small number of Spitfires, which could take over the fighter escort role and engage the 109s at higher altitudes.

The Allies were fighting a combination of German and Italian forces. The Italians had been in North and Eastern Africa since the mid-1930s but had very nearly been beaten out by the British in 1940 and 1941. When defeat looked imminent, Hitler agreed to send in the Afrika Korps. Leading the Korps was General Erwin Rommel. Following his victory in France in 1940, when he had commanded a division of over 60,000 soldiers and tanks to drive the British and French into ignominious surrender, Rommel's star was in the ascendancy. He was personally chosen by Hitler to lead the Afrika Korps. Because of the compassion he showed the British captives, he was respected as a fair commander.

Rommel achieved early success in North Africa too and drove the Allies back across the Libyan border and deep into Egypt, but he failed to capture Tobruk, a strategically important port town and vital supply hub. The Allies regrouped, pushed back, relieved Tobruk and looked set to advance right through Libya. Rommel was determined to take Tobruk, counter-attacked and finally surrounded it on 19 June 1942, having battered the British tanks of the 4th Armoured Brigade at Sidi Rezegh. At this stage, Rommel's panzer divisions had also pushed the Allied forces back to such an extent the DAF was unable to provide proper air support to the garrison.

On 21 June, the Tobruk garrison, having held out for an eight-month siege, finally fell into German hands after two days of renewed attacks by the Afrika Korps. Not only did the Germans capture over 30,000 soldiers, but also their weapons, ammunition, food and fuel supplies, including 10,000 cubic litres of petrol – enough to keep the Korps going for many weeks.

Churchill was most disappointed, especially as many of the troops in Tobruk had hardly been engaged in the fight to stop Rommel's advance. But General Klopper, the South African commander of the garrison, had been offered support to surrender, as the senior commanders realised that to hold out much longer would result in the loss of more lives when the garrison could not be properly sustained.

On receiving the news of Rommel's victory, Hitler promoted him to the rank of general field marshal. Rommel continued the march forward and led his troops across the border into Egypt on 23 June, forcing the Allies further and further back.

During this period, Desmond and his mates were regularly flying two sorties a day, escorting bombers and learning to attack targets on the ground. The Kittyhawk's low-level performance was further enhanced because it was a very good gun platform. The three 0.50in guns (nicknamed '50 cals') in each wing, carried a powerful punch in a strafing run. The 250lb bombs had a long nose fuse, or striker. When the striker hit first, it caused the bomb to explode while it was still about 2ft in the air. The blast effect and resulting shrapnel had a devastating effect on 'soft' targets such as trucks and particularly soldiers.

The AOC, Arthur 'Mary' Coningham, had realised the value of fitting a tactical bomb load (2 x 250lb or 1 x 500lb) under a Kittyhawk to attack ground targets. On 25 June, he ordered that the Afrika Korps supply columns (easily visible from above when moving around due to their dust trails), camps, airfields and ports be bombed round the clock. This was done by twin-engined, medium-range bombers in conjunction with the single-engined fighter-bombers such as the Kittyhawk.

The technique Desmond and the other pilots practised began with a medium-steep dive on the target at a 30–45° angle from a few thousand feet above, aiming through the gunsight. The pilot began to pull out at between 3,000 and 2,000ft, counted out a 5-second delay and released the bomb. Once the bomb had been dispatched, rather than pull up and climb away, pilots were taught to turn away instead, drop down to very low level and stay low all the way home, machine gunning anything they came across that they thought might be the enemy.

On one of two raids Desmond flew on 25 June, as directed, he dropped a single 250lb and had a go at shooting up an enemy truck, hitting it in the back. He returned on his second sortie to strafe another section of motorised transport (MT) and the German troops he saw within the spread of his guns. Similarly, the next day he dropped his first 500lb bomb and shot up two trucks, which made 'the Jerries duck'.

From 26 June onwards, Desmond and many of the squadron pilots began to average four sorties a day, mainly escort work and fighter cover. Indeed, the squadron claimed a record for the largest number of sorties flown in a single day – sixty-nine – which is commendable given the average length of each sortie was about an hour long. On returning to the airfield, each aircraft had to be refuelled and re-armed ready for the next mission. The groundcrews managed to keep an average of five aircraft serviceable at approximately hourly periods. To maintain a high level of serviceability during the day, the groundcrews often worked through the night and at a rate that exceeded what most front-line groundcrews achieved during the height of the Battle of Britain.

The reality of the desert war then was that the British and Allied forces were being beaten. The RAF and Eighth Army were falling back in what became known as the 'Great Retreat', leapfrogging and zig-zagging eastwards towards Cairo as the Axis forces continued to press home their attacks and push the Allies further back. During the last week of June, the Allies were retreating so fast the DAF pilots could take off from one airfield on an operation and land at another an hour later.

The Sharks had sent up their first batch of aircraft at 6.25 a.m. on 26 June. The last went up at 7.20 p.m., just as the pilots thought their day had ended because there was a 'flap on', meaning several pilots had to forego their meals. All the pilots were 'thoroughly tired', but the activity was not quite over because that evening the squadron had to move bases yet again, leapfrogging its way from its current base, LG102 at Sidi Haneish, via LG105 on 27 June to LG 106 at El Daba.[4]

For the next few days, the intensity of operations dwindled a little. The Luftwaffe curtailed its ops too as it suffered from serviceability problems, aircrew fatigue and fuel shortages, meaning that at any one time it could not put more than 50 per cent of its aircraft into the air.[5] Neither was it ever quite as efficient as the DAF at moving from base to base at short notice.

On 29 June, Desmond flew as co-pilot to his flight commander, Flt Lt Geoff Garton, in a Wellington twin-engined bomber. The Sharks temporarily shared El Daba with at least one squadron of Wellingtons. Most of them were clapped-out Mk I Wellingtons scavenged from squadrons back in Britain that were converting to long-range, four-engined bombers such as the Halifax, Stirling and Lancaster. Ordered to move airfields again and short of a crew to rescue this bomber, Garton decided he would fly it out and asked if any of the pilots had any multi-engined experience. Desmond had. Quickly, the pair of them climbed through the rear door of the bomber, hunched their way up through the narrow fuselage and settled into the cockpit, Garton in the left seat, Desmond on the right next to him. They started the engines and flew off to the relative safety of another LG further east. Subsequent to this action, Geoff Garton 'was awarded the DFC having flown a bomber out of one of the airfields in the retreat, never having flown a "heavy" before'.[6]

If ever something sounds like the boss getting all the glory for his subordinate's effort, that must be it! Strictly speaking, Flt Sgt Ibbotson had never flown a 'heavy' either but was the more experienced of the two despite his lower rank, so if medals were being handed out, a DFM might have been appropriate, given that they were chased off the airfield by the approaching Germans and both were equally exposed to the imminent danger.[7]

Under the then DAF commander, Tommy Elmhirst's efficient and organised system, every man knew that absolutely nothing could be left behind that would be of material advantage to the enemy. The maintenance crews worked with the bare essentials – anything more would hamper their readiness to move quickly. Where aircraft were flyable but not fit for ops, they would be flown regardless – one was flown out with an instrument panel missing – or were simply towed behind trucks. Any left behind were doused in petrol and set ablaze. Where trucks were temporarily unserviceable but ultimately seen as repairable, they were towed out too.[8] At the end of June, the DAF and the Allied armies had reached the end of the line. Just 60 miles further east behind them was Alexandria and behind that to the south was Cairo.

CHAPTER 10

112 Squadron – The Great Retreat

North Africa
1 July–10 October 1942

On 1 July, Cecil Beaton went to his office at GHQ in Cairo to be told everyone was on 12 hours' notice to leave. The news of the retreat of the British and advance of the German armies caused havoc and widespread panic in the city. The personnel in British headquarters offices were busily destroying and burning secret papers in what became known as Ash Wednesday. In Beaton's office, Sqn Ldr Houghton showed Beaton a map with a line on it indicating the 30-mile-wide strip of land between El Alamein and the Qattara depression. 'The last line of defence,' he said, pointing to it. 'If that goes, there's nothing left.'[1] Already, Allied supply columns were heading for the city and Alexandria in readiness for final evacuation. Benito Mussolini had arrived in Derna, Libya, expecting to lead a victory parade through the streets of Cairo.[2] A few days earlier, Rommel had confidently stated his expectation that a breakthrough on the Alamein front would see him in Cairo and Alexandria by the end of June. Rommel realised his supply lines were now so long, his reserves of men and materiel so low that he had to make a break for it while the Allies were still on their knees and reeling from the chaotic retreat of the last few weeks. Otherwise, time was on the Allies' side. They still controlled the Gulf of Suez and could now begin to re-arm. Their supply lines were much shorter, and they still had superiority in tanks and aircraft. Hitler kept good faith in his favourite general. Following a series of defeats and the fall of Tobruk, Churchill was about to sack his.

July saw an intensification of effort on both sides: Rommel determined to carry the momentum of his advance to press home the final blows on the Allies, capture Cairo and the Suez Canal beyond before his supplies ran out, and Auchinleck determined to regroup, dig in and stop Rommel's advance before his supplies too ran out.

The DAF's emphasis on attacking ground troops and positions meant there was less opportunity for pilots to engage with enemy aircraft. In a month of solid flying, Desmond noted that he only saw enemy aircraft once. On 4 July, he flew three sorties, the second of which was through 'the heaviest flak I have seen in the Middle East'. On the third sortie, the Sharks came across a Stuka party and set about them with some vigour. 'Babe' Whitamore claimed both a Stuka and an ME109F as damaged. In the same fight, Desmond singled out one of the Stukas, carefully positioned it in his gunsight and, ignoring the flak from the Germans below and the return fire from the Stuka's rear gunner, gave it a full burst. The Stuka, slowed by the bomb still attached underneath it, could not escape and crashed into the desert below. Nine months after his last encounter with an enemy aeroplane when he claimed a probable, Desmond was itching to report this as a confirmed kill, but the intelligence officer could only credit him with a probable because there were no other witnesses. That was until some soldiers from the 7th Armoured Division (later known as the famous 'Desert Rats') contacted the squadron to report a Stuka had crashed in flames near their position. With that confirmation, Desmond had now officially destroyed his first enemy aircraft.

Desmond had the 7th Armoured Division to thank the day after too. Sent out in the mid-morning to bomb LG21, the flight ran into heavy flak. With Desmond were Joe Crichton, Fg Off Bruce, Flt Lt 'Jimmy' Walker (leading) and Sgt Greaves. Desmond managed to drop both bombs in the dispersal area, clearly intending to hit one of the parked aircraft. He turned and strafed two lorries and a petrol tanker, which promptly burst into flames, before he was hit by groundfire. The damage was instantaneous and caused the engine to splutter and falter. Still the flashes of tracer bullets from below zipped past, above and below the wings. Desmond turned east, away from the target area, trying to put as much distance between him and the German gunners as he could and, within seconds of being hit, prepared to immediately force land. The flashes of tracer rounds gradually faded away like hounds that had lost the scent of the fox.

With no time to be certain if the ground would take the weight of a stricken Kittyhawk, Desmond put it down in among a squadron of tanks spaced several yards apart and slid to a halt. As the dust cleared, he flung the straps off his shoulders, scrambled out of the cockpit, jumped onto the wing and stepped onto the desert below. Checking himself over, he found he was uninjured and that, to his relief, he had come down near some British tanks. He walked over to one of them. The tank commander leant over the top of the turret, pulled his radio headset to one side and directed Desmond towards their command vehicles not far away.

His aircraft was the only one lost on that sortie, and his mates reported him as missing, 'last seen over the Qattara Depression', well south of El Alamein.[3] One of the armoured vehicles travelling behind the tanks picked him up and gave him a lift back to the squadron base. Joe Crichton, who had been with Desmond on that raid, recalled:

> We lost many men while dive-bombing and strafing, flak and small arms fire were our big bug bear and we all received plenty of shrapnel. I got hit five times in seven trips at one spell. But we usually dove down and bombed, then kept on through the MTs and stayed right on the deck, many times having to pull up to go over trucks and tanks. At one stage we had orders not to bomb below 500 feet as a few had come back with shrapnel from their own bombs.[4]

Desmond noted that he spent the rest of this day and the next one with the 7th Armoured Division and he 'met General Gut', which is a misspelling of General Gott's surname. General William Henry Ewart 'Strafer' Gott was commander of XIII Corps, which included 7th Armoured Division, whose forces were in the area. His nickname came during his First World War service as a junior officer when his fellow officers came across a popular German slogan, '*Gott strafe* England'

(God punish England). The name stuck and he was known as Strafer for the rest of his life.[5] When he met Desmond, Gott was about to assume command of the Eighth Army in the prelude to the forthcoming Allied counter-offensive, but it would not fall to him to lead the British and Commonwealth armies to victory.

Flying ground attack missions was dangerous and frustrating on all sides. The Allied armies complained about the RAF continually hitting their own troops. The RAF complained the Allied soldiers fired on them too.[6] It was very different to being in England and flying across the Channel to tempt the Luftwaffe into a fight.

Desmond flew as wingman to Billy Drake for the first time on 10 July during an evening raid on an enemy landing ground the Sharks had used themselves only a fortnight before. Billy led a formation of Kittyhawks escorting bombers. The enemy fighters engaged them and, in the ensuing dogfight, Desmond 'was attacked twice by 109s and once by MC202s'. This was also the first time Desmond had encountered any Italian fighters – specifically the Macchi-Castoldi MC202, a single-engine, single-seat fighter roughly comparable in performance to the ME109E and Hurricane. The Allies were fighting hard to keep Rommel's forces at bay, as an excerpt from Desmond's logbook indicates:

> July 11 (52) Tac recce strafe and bomb. Bombing and straffed "eyeties".
> Hit two lorries and LMG (Light Machine Gun).
> July 12 (53) Bombing raid. Dropped 500lb bomb on MT etc.
> July 13 (54) Bomber support for AIF (Australian Infantry Force).
>   Dropped 500lb bomb on MT etc.
> July 13 (55) Bombing raid. Top cover. Dropped 500lb bomb
>   on MT etc.
> July 14 (56) Bombing raid. Top cover. Dropped 500lb bomb
>   on MT etc.
> July 15 (57) Tac Recce & bombing. Top cover Bags of ack-ack.
>   Bombed MT.
> July 16 (58) Bombing raid. Top cover. Bombs on target. Plenty of
>   ack-ack. No e/a (enemy aircraft).
> July 16 (59) Bombing raid. Top cover. Bombs on target. no ack-ack.
>   No e/a.

On the evening of Wednesday 22 July, Desmond and seven others flew an evening bombing raid. It was during this operation that he claimed another victory when the squadron encountered a German raiding force of twenty dive-bombers and fighter escort. Desmond 'put a beautiful burst into a 109F' but, without seeing it either blow up mid-air or crash, could only claim it as a probable.

On the last day of July, the squadron was tasked to strike at Rommel's panzer headquarters. Geoff Garton led ten Kittyhawks out to attack, with top cover provided by 250 Squadron. The records state there were 'no visible results'[7] but Desmond noted that he 'got a hit on a 109F and then was shot at by another 109. (Hit in engine, cockpit and tail)'. This was the closest he had come to being shot and wounded.

After two ops on 2 August, when the squadron was stood down from ops for the day, Billy returned to his office to catch up on some paperwork, among which were a few signals confirming enemy positions, dispositions and RAF personnel movements. One of them was the following message from 239 Wing HQ:

> A signal was received from Advanced Air Headquarters (Western Desert) releasing the wing and squadrons from operations for a rest and training period, the intention being to grant all personnel seven days leave, followed by ten days intensive training to build up the squadrons for further intensive operations.[8]

The frequency of raids on both sides dropped. Rommel's forces were at the point of exhaustion and had paused temporarily to regroup. Rommel, who kept up a daily correspondence with his beloved wife, Lucie, on all but the most intensely active days, wrote a letter to her on 2 August. As always, he headed it '*Liebste* [darling] Lu':

> 2/8/42. Except for intense air activity against my supply lines, it's all quiet. I'm glad of every day's respite we get. A lot of sickness. Many of our older officers, unfortunately are going down at present. I myself am feeling very tired and limp, though I have got a chance to look after myself a bit just at the moment. Unfortunately, the British railway from Tobruk up to the front is not in operation. We're waiting for locomotives. The struggle to hold on to the Alamein line once it

was taken gave us the severest fighting we've seen in Africa. We've all got heat diarrhoea now but it's bearable. A year ago I had jaundice. That was worse.[9]

Rommel knew he had precious little time left if he was to break the Allied lines at El Alamein and make the dash for Cairo. The British knew it too, and both sides used the time to rest front-line soldiers and airmen where possible and regroup. Billy's squadron was granted seven days off, so all the pilots went to Beirut in Lebanon for a few days of welcome respite from operations and the chance of a hot bath and decent food for a change, all except Desmond. When he had last been sent away from ops, he had questioned the logic of it quite indignantly. He had barely begun doing what he had spent months being trained, itching to do, when suddenly he had been sent away from Hornchurch in Essex up to Scotland 'for a rest?' Now he was sitting outside, chatting with a couple of mates, beginning to relax after the day's flying was over when the adjutant called his attention and beckoned him over into Billy Drake's 'office'. The office was, as with virtually everything in the desert, a makeshift affair. The CO was quartered in the back end of a truck with the canvas awning draped from one side, camouflage netting stretched over it and two small wooden steps leading up to the doorway.

Billy told Desmond that, while the squadron was being stood down for a week, he would not be joining them. Billy unfolded two sheets of typed paper and passed them to Desmond. Underneath the notice that he was to receive a commission was another message with orders that Desmond fly to 239 Wing Base Training Flight (BTF) that evening, where he would spend the week undergoing section leader training before returning to the squadron.

Billy opened the desk drawer to his left, took out some pilot officer rank slides and handed them to Desmond, confirming his 'promotion-in-the-field'. It reflected Billy's judgement and trust in a young pilot whom he believed could lead from the front with an instinct nurtured and honed through the weeks of fighting.

Billy later paid a personal tribute to Desmond when he said he 'was one of my best pilots … a delightful man, sound as a rock. He could always be relied upon to do what he was told and do it well – he was completely and utterly reliable.'[10]

Billy also highlighted some of the characteristics required in both a pilot and a leader:

> [The various factors included] ... target identification, decisions regarding tactics to be employed and actual execution. A leader also had to assess the overall situation and allocate targets or tasks to the various subunits and pilots. Speed of thought, quick reactions and the ability to assess situations rapidly were the essential requirements of successful leadership in controlling and leading fighting units [of anywhere from four to 24 aircraft]. A natural gift for leadership together with combat experience were the qualities looked for ... from flight commanders to squadron and wing leaders.[11]

Billy had seen Desmond perform very effectively at first-hand during forty-two of the operations the squadron had carried out during a six-week period in June and July in some of the most intense fighting of the desert war so far. Although the Army and the RAF were retreating, morale among the Shark Squadron pilots remained high, despite the strain of combat and almost-daily losses.

Billy also remarked on the lack of gunnery training the pilots received prior to joining their front-line squadrons. Getting into a dogfight was one thing, but air combat and gunnery skills were quite another. Desmond had shown he was not afraid of a fight. Indeed, he approached it with the same enthusiasm he had shown playing a football match for his local team back in Harewood. Chasing an enemy fighter was almost like chasing an opposing striker with the ball at his feet, just another sport.

So, Desmond left for 239 Wing BTF at LG222 and, from 3 August, spent the next eight days learning how to lead different-sized formations of aircraft that a flight commander would typically be expected to lead. Three days later, returning to the landing ground after leading a section of six Kittyhawks, Desmond's engine suddenly cut out at low level, forcing him to crash-land for a fourth time – this time within the airfield boundaries.

That evening, in the officers' mess, there was talk that something important must be going on because generals of various ranks were being flown in. Speculation grew as to what it might be: either pulling everyone back to Cairo for evacuation or assembling what remained of soldiers, guns, tanks and aircraft for a 'big push'.

Churchill met with Auchinleck on 3 August and pressured him to take an early offensive. 'The Auk' refused and told Churchill the truth – that the Eighth Army was down to its last resources. Rommel, he explained, would be equally weakened after the recent skirmishes, but with their superior quality in guns and armour, it would take more numbers on the Allied side to overcome them. For such an offensive, huge reserves of fuel and munitions were needed, and to launch one now would be wasteful and foolhardy. The earliest time for the attack would be mid-September.[12] Earlier in July, during a visit to Washington DC, Churchill had secured from President Roosevelt the delivery of 300 of the latest Sherman tanks, 100 105mm self-propelled guns and a complement of sixty-five four-engined Liberator heavy bombers, thirty of which were diverted from their destination in India.[13]

Churchill did not like what he was told during his meeting with Auchinleck, nor did he like what he was hearing from soldiers within the upper echelons of Army Command, who were disloyal to or critical of Auchinleck despite having made mistakes themselves. The British Army did not appear to have faith in, or support for, its leader. Auchinleck was right in his assessment of what was the right thing to do, and he was also right in his memo to Churchill, offering him the sword with which to finish him off when he wrote, 'I fear that the position is now much what it was a year ago when I took over command, except that the enemy now has Tobruk which may be of considerable advantage to him.'[14] Auchinleck was now in line to be sacked; neither Churchill nor Auchinleck's immediate superior, Brooke, had confidence in him.

Churchill opted against Brooke's suggestion of Lt Gen Montgomery as successor and, after speaking to him personally, chose Strafer Gott instead, but would ultimately only ever meet with him once.[15] Churchill decided to split the Middle East Command and left El Alamein for Cairo to finalise the appointments and new command structure. Then, within 48 hours, tragedy struck.

Lt Gen Gott was requested to fly to Cairo on 7 August. He never made it. A section of six ME109s from II/JG 27, acting on intelligence gleaned from the interception of uncoded and insecure British radio traffic, were sent up to find the general's aircraft. They located it heading west at low level, barely 50ft, hugging the ground to mask the movement of its shadow underneath. The fighters dived down and, as pairs, took it in turns to shoot out the unescorted Whitley bomber's engines. Jimmy James, the pilot, managed to force land the plane but it caught fire on impact when the fuel tanks in the wing ruptured. The 109s turned and attacked it again. The pilot and co-pilot got out through the front escape hatch but the force of the impact on landing had collapsed the undercarriage and buckled and jammed the fuselage door, trapping the VIPs and General Gott inside. The fire consumed the whole wreckage.[16]

At around the same time, at 239 Wing BTF, Desmond and his colleagues were treated to a brief visit from Churchill himself who, before leaving for a conference in Cairo, toured the airfields and forward areas. A photo of Desmond, seen grinning in the background among a group of cheering pilots as Churchill walked past them, made it into Sarah's album back home in Harewood.

When Churchill heard the tragic news about General Gott, he appointed Lt Gen Bernard Law Montgomery in his replacement as the leader of the Eighth Army. The expectation of a swift and long-awaited victory now fell on Montgomery's shoulders.

On his return to 112 Squadron a few days later, while out leading Yellow Section covering a bombing raid, Desmond had engine trouble again. By his own account, he only just made the aerodrome. The engine temperatures were 'off the clock', but he landed the aircraft in one piece in a sandstorm.

On the intervening days, while ops were suspended, Desmond practised leading formation flying as he put what he had learnt during his week away to good use. At the end of August, he took part in a morning fighter sweep. Billy Drake led Red Section; Desmond led Yellow Section. They flew together as top cover for 3 Squadron (RAAF) and 450 Squadron (known as the 'Desert Harassers').

About halfway through the sweep, while flying at a height of 15,000ft over the forward area near Deir El Abyad, a mixed formation of fifteen ME109s and Italian MC202s were seen, and 'four Italian machines daringly attacked but without doing any harm'.[17] The squadron diary blandly records that 'enemy fighters were seen and attacked without result',[18] but it was a tougher fight than it seemed. Desmond called his section into the fight, which quickly descended into a free-for-all but was, said Desmond:

The best combat I have yet been in. We were dived on [from] (7 o'clock) by 4 MC202s. Took avoiding action and then fought with about 15. MC202s were doing upward rolls and beautiful aerobatics. I had two good bursts. 1 head-on, the MC202 gave way. They had too much height and speed for us. Every time you got on one's tail 2 attacked you. I was attacked no less than 7 times. Was very sorry when I did not get one.

The MC202 'Folgore' (Thunderbolt) was superior in speed and general performance to the Kittyhawk, but Desmond held his own against it and when outnumbered. He demonstrated a brave, almost reckless, manoeuvre by flying straight at an enemy fighter with a closing speed of around 500mph. Desmond held his nerve; the Italian did not and broke off first. August turned to September, and Desmond's next fight would see him very nearly killed.

On 3 September, the New Zealand Division started a counter-offensive to push the Germans back. They got bogged down in the soft sand within a few miles but did succeed in forcing the Afrika Korps and 15th Panzer Division to begin to retreat. During the second sortie of that morning, Danny Saville led eight Kittyhawks in two sections of four aircraft out to cover a formation of Baltimore bombers. Danny also led the lower section while Desmond led the top four. Half an hour after take-off, they saw eleven 109s of II/JG 27. The 109s spotted them too. On seeing the 109s, Danny immediately called his section in to the attack, surprising the Germans below them. As they peeled away, Desmond waited for the right time, then called his section in behind. He rolled the Kittyhawk hard over onto its back and pulled the stick firmly back into his stomach to begin the dive. Below him, he could see the ME109s 'breaking', turning up towards them to face the attack. They were going to stay and fight. As the distance between them closed, each picked their target and positioned themselves ready. Desmond wrote that, in the ensuing dogfight, he:

Was attacked by 10 ME109Fs. Got a 2 second burst at 1 109F & saw a big piece come from his port aileron and then a lot of smoke. Was attacked time and time again. Hit through cockpit, shattered instruments. The first time I (myself) have had a cut or scratch from Jerry.

From the details he later gave to the intelligence officer, Desmond was singled out and attacked by four or five 109s while he was in a turn, which may have been immediately after he had put a burst into the 109 he was pursuing. Eager not to let this one get away, as his Italian opponent had the other day, Desmond's mind was fully focused on the fighter in front of him as he squeezed the 'fire' button to give it a 2-second burst. He soon found that hanging on that second or two longer 'just to make sure' was extremely risky. The cannon shells from the 109 that attacked him only just missed Desmond's head. The German was close in behind him and had judged his aim almost to perfection. With the engine at full power, it was only when the instrument panel suddenly exploded, sending splinters of glass and metal everywhere, that he realised the danger and broke away before his pursuer could get any more rounds into the cockpit.

Desmond managed to return safely to base and handed the Kittyhawk over to the mechanics to repair the instrument panel and other superficial damage.[19] But he was concerned that, because he had been on his own in the fight, it could only be claimed as a probable. As the others in the section landed and gave their reports to the intelligence officer, Desmond was relieved to finally be credited with his second confirmed victory, almost two months after his first.

On 13 September, the wing was scrambled to intercept a large raid conducted by Stukas bombing the El Alamein area, which were escorted by twelve ME109s from I Gruppe, eleven from III/JG 27 and fourteen from III/JG 53. Billy Drake shot down a 109.[20] Desmond was again involved, and Sgt Morrison was flying as his wingman. Desmond said he:

> Jumped 12 109s. Shot at one, missed then put a long burst from astern into another which went down trailing black smoke. Was attacked by two & then emptied my guns into a 109F from 150yds which was badly hit but kept tearing along west. 650 rounds fired.

Although he had hit two separate German fighters, Desmond could only claim the first one as a probable, because no one else could verify its destruction and, despite him having 'badly hit' the second one, it continued flying so he could only claim it as a damaged. Desmond continued to get in really close to his target (150yds or less) before firing to give himself the best chance of a successful hit, even though it was not always enough to down an opponent. As for his wingman, Sgt J.H. Morrison, he was attacked by an ME109, which set his Kittyhawk on fire. Morrison crash-landed with the wheels up, escaped his burning aeroplane and walked back to base.

The next few weeks were, according to Billy Drake, a quiet period. Rommel had lost the Battle of Gazala at the end of August, and with it the last real chance of breaking the Allied lines and driving through to Cairo, the Suez Canal and beyond, but he remained stubbornly difficult to push back. The Luftwaffe continued, with albeit fewer attacks around El Alamein, while the DAF flew a reduced number of medium- and low-level raids against the Luftwaffe airfields.

On days when they were stood down from ops, the Sharks flew training sorties. Desmond continued to lead sections of four and six, both in practice and on ground attack raids into mid-October, bringing his total up to ninety-eight operations, but he would not see his hundredth with the Sharks.

Billy called Desmond into his office once again and told him he was being posted to 601 County of London Squadron of the Auxiliary Air Force, nicknamed 'the Millionaires' after the pre-war aristocratic young men who formed their core of pilots. The squadron had seen action in the Battle of Britain before sailing for Malta in the spring but had only been in the desert for just over three months.

Desmond stepped out of Billy's caravan, went over to his tent to pack his kit bag and hitched a lift to Emergency Landing Ground 92, the airfield currently being used by 92, 601 and 145 Squadrons, which together comprised 244 Wing.

It was a new airfield, but just another dusty desert airstrip, set on a wide, flat expanse of sand, lined by rows of tents, runway boundaries marked by upturned 50-gallon oil drums and fringed with sandbagged gun emplacements, barrels pointed skywards. The bland food and weather were the same – warm days, cold nights. On the other hand, this posting marked Desmond's return to flying his favourite aircraft: the Spitfire.

CHAPTER 11

601 Squadron – El Alamein and Escape

North Africa
11 October–8 November 1942

Desmond reported to his new unit on 11 October. The squadron was led by Sqn Ldr Arthur Victor 'Darky' Clowes, who had quite a record as a pilot, with at least ten victories to his name. He had been a sergeant pilot before and during the Battle of France flying Hurricanes for No. 1 Squadron alongside Billy Drake and Fanny Orton. Clowes had been awarded the DFM (in August 1940) and DFC (in May 1941) before 'resting' as an instructor at 53 OTU. He returned to operations in command of 79 Squadron before arriving in the desert to continue his second tour, where he had been in charge of 601 Squadron since August 1942.[1]

Desmond found he already knew one of the pilots there. His friend Babe Whitamore had arrived on the squadron a few weeks earlier. He also learnt his mate from 53 OTU and 129 Squadron, Ray Sherk, had been on the squadron too. Ray had been posted out to join 601 Squadron at around the same time as Desmond had joined 112 Squadron. Although both squadrons were then in different wings and based at different airfields, Ray had often been flying Spitfires as top cover while Desmond had been flying a Kittyhawk a several hundred feet below on the same raid. In fact, Desmond was disappointed to find they had missed each other by only two weeks. Ray had been out on patrol one day with two other pilots when they intercepted and shot down a German JU-52 transport aircraft. Turning for home, Ray's engine failed, and he force landed in the Qattara Depression. He was captured by the Italians and flown to a PoW camp in Italy.[2] It is possible that when Ray went missing, Desmond was posted in as his replacement, having a similar background to Ray, including front-line experience in Spitfires.

Desmond took up one of the Spitfire Mk VC fighters to re-familiarise himself with the Spitfire – having been ten months since he had last flown one – and, in particular, how to handle the narrow undercarriage of the slender Spitfire when landing on rough desert terrain. The Mk Vc Spitfire was the same as the Vb Desmond had flown from Hornchurch, except that it had a large Vokes air filter fitted underneath the engine to reduce the intake of dust into the engine, which gave it a distinctive 'chin'.

Desmond spent a week on the squadron before participating in his first op with 601, when he managed to latch on to a 109, chase it briefly and shoot at it. The bullets hit the glycol coolant system in the engine, and it started to trail white smoke. Desmond followed, but the 109 escaped by slipping into a layer of cloud at 2,000ft and continued heading out to sea. Desmond claimed this as another damaged. The next op was his 100th. This time, he chased an Italian MC202 Thunderbolt. He latched on to its tail and fired at it but missed. Then, as he closed to around 100yds, he was thrown off by its slipstream.

The pilots on the squadron were among those thousands of soldiers and aircrew anxiously awaiting their orders for the forthcoming offensive. They knew it was imminent, but no one knew the date, or the hour, apart from a few senior officers.

Rommel had been ordered home in September for six weeks' compulsory sick leave. His physical health was at risk after two years of constant strain, and he was close to collapse. Prior to leaving, he had dispersed his forces as he thought best and left new commanders in charge. Rommel had sought and received assurances from Marshal Cavallero, Field Marshal Kesselring and Hitler himself that the supplies he required would be sent to him, but he still feared he would be let down. The Italians seemed to keep as much as possible for themselves, while Hitler and his inner circle of senior commanders were more interested in keeping the Russian front going.

Rommel's defences comprised thin cover at the front (within minefields), backed up by infantry strongholds, followed by minefields several kilometres deep with artillery and Panzers in the rear. The intention was that the initial defences should hold up the British advance until the commanders could work out where the main attack was coming from, then deploy Panzers and infantry to counter it.

Meanwhile, Montgomery was very pleased with the way the recent battle of Alam Halfa had gone. Rommel's forces had been stopped, then forced to retreat, proving at last that they were beatable, though in reality it was a victory significantly aided by lack of supplies on the German/Axis side rather than outstanding tactical manoeuvring. Many of the defence plans had been put in place by Auchinleck, and Montgomery had not sought to change them because he, in fact, agreed with them. Montgomery's earlier briefing report down to divisional commander level stated:

> This battle for which we are preparing will be a real rough house and will involve a very great deal of hard fighting. If we are successful it will mean the end of the war in North Africa, apart from general "clearing up" operations; it will be the turning point of the whole war. Therefore we can take no chances. There will be no tip and run tactics in this battle; it will be a killing match; the German is a good soldier and the only way to beat him is to kill him in battle.[3]

During the night of 22 October, the British and Commonwealth infantry across the front began to move forward into their slit trenches ahead of the main defence line. They were ordered not to move and to keep quiet until the attack began.

The next afternoon, Desmond flew again with B Flight on an offensive sweep ahead of Kittyhawks from 260 Squadron and Tomahawks of 5 Squadron SAAF (South African Air Force). Eighteen ME109s plus some MC202s engaged them at 17,000ft, with Babe Whitamore claiming one of the 202s as shot down into the sea. Desmond got behind one of the Messerschmitts and was in a prime position to shoot it down, but his cannons failed at the critical moment. The lucky enemy pilot got away unharmed, with just the memory of seeing a Spitfire swooping in menacingly behind him.

At 9.40 p.m. the massive barrage Montgomery had planned began, and all along the El Alamein front, artillery shells of all sizes flew towards the enemy positions beyond. Rommel, who had now returned from sick leave, had situated German units among the Italian divisions to stiffen their resolve and ensure they remained in the fight. The barrage, the heaviest seen since the First World War, was to last all night and reminded all those young soldiers huddled waiting in their slit trenches, just what their fathers and uncles before them had faced twenty-five years earlier. On the airfields and landing grounds near the front, the pilots stood outside their tents, watching the flashes that scattered in rippling bursts across the far horizon. The sound of the guns booming could be heard as a faint rumble. The Battle of El Alamein had begun.

Desmond was involved in another scrap on 25 October (his 21st birthday) when, on a sweep over Daba, he and three colleagues in the section saw two formations of ME109s. One was a group of six, the other was a section of four above them. The 601 Squadron section leader, Bruce Ingram, led them in to attack the top four ME109s.

Desmond and his wingman, Sgt Toller, quickly climbed to 28,000ft, where he spotted three more 109s below him at 25,000ft just south-east of Daba. Desmond radioed Toller to follow him and dive down to attack them. Two of the Germans saw them coming and broke away, but the other stayed put, flying on, perhaps oblivious to the imminent danger. With his speed increasing rapidly in the dive and only a few seconds left in which to make his attack, Desmond manoeuvred carefully into position above this lone fighter. He wrote: 'I jumped three [109s] at 25,000ft. The leader stayed and fought. I had no cannons but I hit him three times. He jettisoned the hood and dived away towards our lines.'[4]

Desmond claimed this one as damaged and said he had no cannons because, not for the first time, they had failed to fire. Two days earlier, he had chased a 109F to the point where he had a 'lovely sight' on it, but just as he pressed the 'fire' button, the cannons failed and the 109 got away.

Despite the intense barrage and massive numbers of troops and tanks thrown forward at the start of the offensive, Montgomery had not yet succeeded in breaking through the northern sector of the front. It had taken more than 24 hours to penetrate the thick belt of mines more than a mile deep in the first stage of the advance, almost sarcastically named Operation Lightfoot.

On hearing the battle commence, Rommel's panzers were ordered forward to bolster their own defences, which had so far halted the progress of the British along the coast. Operation Supercharge, the second phase of Montgomery's offensive, was launched on 2 November and successfully forced the Afrika Korps and Panzer Army in to retreat. Stukas were sent up, with fighter escorts, to try to stop the Allied advance.

On 601 Squadron's second sortie, at 9.10 a.m. on 2 November, eight ME109Fs saw the nine Spitfires first and attacked them. In the dogfight that followed, Desmond claimed another victory. This time he got in close, very close (to around 20yds directly behind his opponent), before shooting him down. His enemy's aeroplane immediately caught fire and went down in flames.

In the days that followed, whenever he took to the air, Desmond could catch a glimpse of the intense fighting taking place on the ground beneath him. Sometimes, if he was low enough, he would see the burnt-out vehicles, wheels separated from axles, turrets upside down but yards away from the tank they had been on top of, their hulls now heaps of twisted metal slumped in the dirt.

On 4 November, Desmond saw a big battle going on below him. He didn't know this was a desperate attempt by Rommel to hold the Allied advance and that he had previously requested permission from Hitler to withdraw. But the Führer was having none of it. Ignorant of the reality on the ground and perceiving a weakness in leadership, Hitler replied with his infamous 'death or glory' telegram in a short rebuke to Rommel's tactical assessment. The message read:

> In the difficult position in which you are placed there can be no thought but to hold out, to take not one step back ... To your troops you can show no other road than the road that leads to victory or to death.[5]

'Difficult' was an understatement, and it put Rommel in an impossible position. He could sacrifice an entire army just to keep favour with Hitler but lose the battle for Egypt, or he could save his army with a fighting retreat and risk incurring Hitler's wrath and a bullet in Berlin. Rommel decided to ignore the telegram. He organised his troops quickly so they could carry out a tactical withdrawal if the British pressed home the next phase of the attack. But the weather began to turn against them.

Heavy downpours of rain from the night of 6 November hampered British efforts to pursue Rommel's forces by bogging down the tanks and planes. The conditions under wheel and foot were no better for Montgomery than for Rommel, but whereas Montgomery practically stopped short, Rommel kept his forces moving, albeit very slowly.

The divisions of the Afrika Korps gathered in the area were severely depleted.[6] A lot of this destruction had been wrought by the fighters and bombers of the DAF, which had not just destroyed the weaponry and soldiers but disrupted reinforcements and prevented supplies from reaching the front.

By 9.30 a.m. on 6 November, Korps HQ was travelling on its own and had reached a point 22km south-south-east of Mersa Matruh where it stopped. In the area south-west of Mersa Matruh, the ground was very soft after the heavy rains. The panzers were desperately short of fuel, and orders were given that the airfields around the town were to be searched for any fuel left.

The high volume of traffic caused jams on the main road and in the town itself, which could not be cleared due to the rain and mines at the roadside. Convoys trying to reach the front line to resupply the troops could not make it through either. Officers of all ranks had lost their heads and were making hasty and ill-considered decisions and, in places, panic had broken out. Some vehicles were set on fire, whether on or beside the road, and artillery guns were abandoned or destroyed because there were no tractors for them. A large number of vehicles had left their units and were streaming back without orders. Some got stuck in thick mud, leaving the soldiers no choice but to get out and blow them up along with their heavy field artillery and anti-aircraft guns.

Due to the bad weather, the first week of November had been reasonably quiet for the squadron as the Germans now retreated. For the first time since the Allied Great Retreat in the summer, 601 Squadron moved forwards on 6 November from LG92 to ELG21 at Daba.

One of the keys to the successful advance of both the Allied and Axis armies had been their ability to intercept each other's radio traffic and figure out where the opposing forces were going from and to and in what numbers. To the British, it had always seemed that Rommel instinctively knew where to position his units to either attack or defend against their moves. In fact, Rommel had for months been receiving intercepted messages from a secret unit – *Horch Kompanie* 621 – which had, in part, been listening in to sloppy Allied operators on the battlefield who had not been obeying basic R/T security. He had combined these with stolen copies of detailed reports, written by an American military attaché based in Egypt, whom the British had given free access to their battle plans so as to keep President Roosevelt informed, to build up a detailed picture of Allied manoeuvres. *Horch Kompanie* 621 continued to function until captured by the Allies in July 1942. Shortly after, the British eventually uncovered the leak of reports from the embassy concerned and plugged it before the Battle of El Alamein.[7] From then on, Rommel was (in intelligence terms) almost blind.

As for the British, thanks to the efforts of three Polish mathematicians some years earlier, they had acquired a few early Enigma machines and set up a code-breaking facility at Bletchley Park – code-named 'Ultra'. Messages between the Nazi leadership in Berlin and the Afrika Korps commanders were intercepted, decrypted and sent to Allied commanders sparingly, using language plausible enough not to alert the Germans that their messages were being read. One of the messages intercepted by Ultra was sent at what would become a key point in Desmond's story, just as Rommel was working out what he wanted his Luftwaffe and Italian commanders to do to counter the Allied offensive.

Now, three months to the day after Lt Gen Strafer Gott's flight was intercepted by German fighters and he was killed, British intelligence intercepted a message sent during the afternoon of 6 November 1942. Marked 'Top-Secret', it revealed Rommel was travelling to a conference of the Axis High Command in North Africa the following morning, on 7 November, in Sidi Barani, around 85 miles west of Mersa Matruh. Those called to attend were *Generalfeldmarschall* Albert Kesselring, His Excellency Barbasetti and General Gandin.[8]

Whenever he could, Rommel flew a single-engined Fieseler Storch, as the roads were strafed regularly by the RAF. Whether on this occasion Rommel flew to Sidi Barrani or risked taking a staff car along the main coastal highway instead is not known.

That Saturday morning, six pilots of B Flight 601 Squadron were briefed shortly after breakfast and given specific given orders to 'Patrol Road Matruh–Sidi Barrani'[9] They were Flt Lt Bruce Ingram (flight commander and formation leader), Plt Off Donald E. Llewellyn, Lt Bennetts, Lt A. Bartleman, Fg Off Babe Whitamore and Desmond. In his own daily briefing to the pilots, the squadron intelligence officer, Kenneth Carew-Gibbs, told them about the disposition of friendly and enemy forces and which airfields would be safe to land on in an emergency.

They took off at 8.45 a.m. and headed westwards climbing to their patrol height of 7,000ft. Within minutes they spotted a formation of enemy planes heading in the opposite direction comprising nine ME109s escorting nine JU-87 Stukas and three JU-88 twin-engined bombers that were after the British soldiers and tanks whose formations could be seen off to the east.

Bruce Ingram had no choice. With the enemy in sight, he had to attack the bombers despite the fact that doing so could draw the Messerschmitts in behind them, and the Spitfires were outnumbered three to one. The section began to form into line astern behind their leader.

Ingram picked his moment. He called over the radio, 'Tally Ho!', rolled his Spitfire onto its back and began his dive. He kept focused on the Stukas below, as their rear gunners swung their machine guns round to meet them. Each of the Spitfires banked over to the left at 1-second intervals and followed their leader racing headlong towards the enemy formation, all guns armed, ready to fire. As they did so, the Messerschmitts, lurking a few hundred feet above, now fell in behind them. Before the Spitfires could properly get in among the Stukas, a dogfight ensued with the 109s. The Stukas tried to sneak off towards the east along with the JU-88s.

Turning away from the bombers, the Spitfires engaged the Messerschmitts. Ingram got a 109 and Llewellyn another before he was shot down. A third 109 went down as a result of the efforts of Babe Whitamore and Lt Bennetts, who each claimed a share of it.

The Spitfires now turned their attention back to the JU-88s and the Stukas, picking them up just west of Charing Cross. Ingram called his section into attack again, and this time they went straight into the formation of Stukas, followed again by the Messerschmitts. Desmond managed to shoot down two Stukas, the first of which went down in flames. The second claim was recorded initially as a probable after Desmond was overheard on the radio shooting it down, but it was later confirmed. It was this fight that made him an ace and, moreover, a Spitfire ace at that.

Unfortunately though, another fighter got in unseen behind him and opened fire. The first Desmond knew about it was when the bullets started slamming into his Spitfire, causing it to buck. He heard the 'thunk' of 20mm rounds puncturing the airframe seemingly all around him as they progressed up the wing root. Then one entered the petrol tank located directly behind the Merlin engine. As the fuel bled from the ruptured tank, the loss of power from the engine was sudden and dramatic. Desmond had to land quickly before it either seized up or blew up.

Below him he made out Landing Ground No. 8 (LG08) near Mersa Matruh, just inland from the coast, and prepared to make a crash landing. Only a fortnight before, this airstrip had been classed as unserviceable. Recent repairs had been undertaken but full work had not been completed, and pilots were advised to take care on landing.

Unable to lower the undercarriage, Desmond belly landed his Spitfire (No. BR135, UF-V) on the rough desert earth, slid noisily to a halt and popped the hood. Frustrated by his bad turn of luck, he proceeded to undo his seat harness, then his parachute and clamber out of the aircraft.

Llewellyn and Desmond had both been shot down. Both followed standard procedure and decided not to take to their parachutes but instead picked a landing ground to land on. Within 5 minutes of each other and only a few miles apart, both pilots believed they had landed close to their own side. But only one of them was right.

Llewellyn landed on ELG101, leaving his aircraft badly damaged, but he could walk away from this wreck. He made his way north to the coast road and headed eastwards until he reached safety.

Desmond who, like Llewellyn, had now been shot down for the second time, started to walk away from his wrecked Spitfire. Having seen off the remaining enemy fighters, his four remaining colleagues witnessed his landing and circled nearby at a safe enough distance from the German guns.

Desmond could make out some vehicles in the distance coming towards him. He believed them to be British, thinking he was simply going to be picked up as he had been a month before and dropped back at the airfield. At the pre-flight briefing, the pilots had been told that LG08 was still in British hands. Unfortunately, this was not true.

As the vehicles and troops drew nearer, Desmond could see the 'funny coloured cars' and make out the peaked caps of Afrika Korps soldiers. How his heart must have sunk as he realised it was the enemy coming for him. As a front-line pilot he carried a standard issue service revolver, but it only held six rounds and would be no match for the machine pistols the dozen or so soldiers each carried, let alone the large-calibre machine guns on the accompanying half-track and armoured car that were all now pointing ominously at him. Desmond had no choice but to give himself up.

One of the German soldiers walked up to him. Unexpectedly, he introduced himself in English and directed Desmond to get into the back of the half-track, at which point he was, to use a contemporary expression, 'in the bag' – a PoW – just like his old mate Ray Sherk.

As the half-track drove back to join a group of vehicles at the perimeter of the airfield, Desmond wondered if he would finally catch up with Ray again. He looked at the Germans facing him, their automatic weapons laid across their laps pointing in his direction. They looked back at him but said nothing.

The rest of the Spitfires returned to base and reported Desmond as 'missing believed safe'. So far, the Germans hadn't made a move against him, hadn't roughed him up or even yelled at him. In fact, they had been disarmingly polite. It was all rather strange.

When the vehicles stopped, he dismounted under watchful eyes and was taken immediately to what he could clearly see to be a truck whose rear had been converted to be an office. On the side was a large black swastika. He was, once again, in a senior officer's caravan – only, this time, it was known as a *Mammut* (mammoth), and it was Rommel's. In fact, the truck was called a 'Dorchester' originally because it had belonged to the British and was one of three purpose-built armoured command vehicles built by the Associated Equipment Company (AEC) in England. The living quarters contained an iron-framed bed, en-suite toilet and wash basin – hence the British name, Dorchester, after the renowned London hotel. The British generals who used them had been captured in 1941 when they had left their vehicles to attend a meeting elsewhere but were apprehended on their way back by the Afrika Korps, who then commandeered the trucks for their own use. Rommel had assigned one to Lt Gen Streich of the 5th Light Division but kept the other two for himself and named them 'Max' and 'Moritz'. The Germans subsequently found the caravans were completely intact with some personal belongings still inside. Among them, Rommel took possession of a pair of field glasses which, when seen in later newsreel films and portrait photographs of him, became a steadfast part of his image from then on.[10]

The story of what happened to Desmond over the next 24 hours blurs between myth and reality. Desmond had been taken immediately to see the most senior officer available and was shown into Rommel's *Mammut* – 'a well-appointed caravan at the edge of the airfield'. There, he was reportedly introduced to 'a man he unhesitatingly recognised as Rommel himself',[11] the man he had quite possibly been sent to kill.

It is true that Rommel did make every effort to meet captured PoWs when the opportunity arose, and there are five well-documented cases of when this happened between 1940 and 1944.[12] He saw it as an opportunity to gauge the enemy's state of mind, their morale and what their perception of the war's progress was, rather than extracting any tactical information from them – although a pilot could provide a useful amount if interrogated properly.

It was said the two exchanged pleasantries, and Desmond was assured he would be well treated. After a brief conversation, he was then taken outside and escorted by armed guards onto another vehicle to be driven further west, deeper behind enemy lines, towards either a troopship or an aeroplane across the Mediterranean to Italy.

As the truck bumped and swayed across the desert and onto the cratered coastal highway, Desmond contemplated what he should do next. Should he try to escape now, or wait until he got to Italy? If he waited until he was about to cross the Med, the greater the risk that whatever ship or transport aircraft he was put on would be attacked by the British not knowing he was in it. If he waited until he was in Italy, the weather in November and December would be a potentially greater threat than the Germans. Desmond spoke neither Italian nor German and, while he did not speak any Arabic either, he was still relatively close to Allied lines, and some Arabs were loyal to the British. The muzzle of another machine pistol pointing towards him meant attempting to escape was futile for now.

There were several stops that afternoon, sometimes for an hour or more, occasionally to swap to another vehicle. Each time Desmond got out of the truck, he considered whether he could or should make a run for it. But there were too many Germans around. All he could do was be patient and bide his time. An hour later, the truck slowed and pulled off the road again, heading a short distance into the desert. Eventually, it came to a stop. The cab doors opened, and the soldiers walked round to let the truck's tailgate down so Desmond could get out. After a break, the guards walked Desmond towards another truck.

It was after sunset during the transfer to the fourth truck, and possibly the last one before he would be transported to Italy, that Desmond made his move while the guards weren't paying attention, and he slipped away into the darkness. He crept a few yards, checked he hadn't been seen then broke into a gentle run heading away from the vehicles. After about 200yds, he came across a tank rut about a foot deep. Sensing it was the only cover around, he dropped into it, lay face down and hid. For several minutes he stayed still, hardly daring to breathe, his ears straining to hear whether the noise of the guards searching for him was coming closer.[13] Eventually the search died down, and Desmond set off again, towards the coastal highway. When he found it, he followed the route eastwards back to Mersa Matruh and, beyond that, the Allied lines.

Walking at a steady pace, parallel to but a safe distance from the highway, he picked his way past the clustered wreckage of dozens of tanks and trucks that littered the roadside and nearby desert. He knew he had to put as much distance between him and his captors as possible while also avoiding any German positions, because the darkness would not hide him much longer. He explained afterwards:

> I crept and walked through two Jerry camps. After walking for six hours I heard sheep in the distance and found some Arabs. They hid me until all the Jerries had retreated towards Sidi Barrani. Our tanks came later and picked me up. Eventually I returned to the squadron [and] learnt that the squadron had shot down seven enemy aircraft on that show.

By the afternoon of Sunday 8 November, Desmond was back with the squadron, now based at ELG13.[14] There happened to be an official war photographer on the base, looking for a story about the successes and escapades a front-line squadron had to tell about its part in the Battle of El Alamein. Desmond's escape fitted the bill nicely and the photographer captured a close-up image of Desmond, laughing as he celebrated his lucky escape. Neither of them knew that picture would become a lasting tribute to him.

CHAPTER 12

601 Squadron – The Advance to Tunis

9 November 1942–31 May 1943

Sometime after his escape, Desmond received a certificate of the 'Flying Boot', which brought with it membership to the Late Arrivals Club, whose motto was: 'It is never too late to come back.' He pinned the certificate in his logbook, where it remains to this day. The Late Arrivals Club is unique. It was founded during the Western Desert campaign in 1941 as a result of a brief newspaper article written by Sqn Ldr George Houghton, a public relations officer then based in Cairo. He had written about a pilot who had been shot down and spent a few days walking back to rejoin his unit, and described him as a 'late arrival'. Other aircrew who had shared similar experiences wrote to him with the idea of setting up an informal club. Houghton designed the certificate and emblem of a winged flying boot, which was made into a badge and worn by some aircrew on their sleeves. Almost 500 certificates and badges were awarded before the end of the desert campaign.[1]

While Rommel had been contending with Allied advances in the east, over 1,500 miles away to the west, Anglo-American divisions had landed on the shores of French Algeria and Morocco in Operation Torch and begun to flood ashore to take up positions on the Axis rear flanks. Now the Italians and Rommel's Afrika Korps had to fight on two fronts. The

Royal Navy's domination of the Mediterranean made resupply to the Axis forces extremely challenging, and the increasing number of land battles meant this was slowly becoming a battle of attrition. Desmond returned to flying three days later and, aside from routine patrols over Allied columns creeping steadily westwards with the occasional strafing attack on enemy trucks, there was not much to report. From Mishiefa to Gambut to Gazala, they leapfrogged through mid- and late November, watching the Allies retake Tobruk on 12 November, then crossing the Egyptian–Libyan border on the morning of 13 November.

The supply trucks of the British Royal Army Service Corps (RASC) were now driving long distances, sometimes as many as 100 miles a day for a single trip, shuttling petrol and ammunition back and forth to the forward tanks and troops pursuing Rommel's army back across the desert. Montgomery decided to pause just west of Tobruk and concentrate on regrouping his supplies for the next stage.

The soldiers and pilots often found themselves passing through sites of recently fought battles. Occasionally, as the squadrons moved up by road, they might stop to salvage items from the back of abandoned German trucks whose contents had not been badly damaged by shot or shell. Sometimes, they would also find the mangled remains of occupants still in the vehicles the pilots themselves had recently hit during a strafing run. One pilot reflected in his diary: 'Thought a lot about the blackened corpses we passed coming up. I guess it is necessary if this damned war is to be won.'[2]

Some squadrons also managed to acquire aircraft left behind by the retreating Germans, which they converted for their own use. These included a Fieseler Storch light aircraft (repainted white and used by the AOC as his own personal aeroplane), a twin-engined Heinkel He 111 bomber, a Messerschmitt 109 and a JU-87 Stuka, acquired by 601 Squadron on 12 November when they captured LG20. Once they were deemed airworthy, the Allied pilots took turns at flying them just for fun and ferrying people and materiel around.

The Millionaires repainted their Stuka in RAF camouflage colours, complete with roundels, the squadron code letters 'UF- ?', generous yellow bands round the rear fuselage just forward of the tail section and red flying sword emblems.[3] It would accompany the squadron right across Libya towards Tunisia.

The squadron stayed off operational flying for the last days of November and instead continued to dash forward, from Marturba to Gambut, Gazala, El Adem and Zawiyat Msus, ending up at El Hasseiate landing ground on 3 December, 550 miles away from their start point in Egypt.

Two days later, eleven Spitfires took off in the mid-afternoon on a fighter sweep of the Marble Arch area ahead of Kittybombers. They saw between sixty and eighty single-engined fighters dotted about the enemy aerodrome at Marble Arch. As they were about to return home, they sighted six ME109s ahead of them, with two more below.

It was these two 109s that Desmond and his section went down to attack. Desmond carefully manoeuvred his aircraft into position behind one of them, closed to 250yds and opened fire. Glycol coolant begin to stream out of the 109's engine, which then caught fire. Desmond pursued the plane until concentrated enemy flak from the airfield below and two 109s on his port side, which made to attack him in return, forced him to break away. His last sight of that bullet-riddled ME109 had been at 5,000ft. It later crashed and was, therefore, confirmed as destroyed. This was Desmond's sixth confirmed kill.

On 7 December, following another fruitless scramble by two Spitfires, the squadron was sent up in the early afternoon on another fighter sweep of the Marble Arch and Aghiela area near the Libyan coast. 'The Arch' (or Arco Philaenorum to use its official title, named after two Carthaginian brothers who were buried there – the Philaenae) was a huge fascist-style memorial, erected on the orders of Benito Mussolini before the war to straddle the section of coast road between Tripoli and Benghazi.[4] It was a distinctive if highly incongruous feature in an otherwise bland and barren landscape.

Climbing up to 15,000ft, the Spitfires headed for their patrol area. They soon caught sight of a *Schwarme* formation of four ME109s just west of Aghiela. Immediately, the Spitfires banked hard over and dived down to attack them. Fg Off Samuel shot one down almost straight away. Sgt Steele damaged a second. Desmond picked his target, slid in behind one of the 109s and, after a brief engagement, shot it down into the sea 5 or 6 miles north-east of Aghiela. The enemy pilot did not bail out.[5]

In response, the victim's wingman turned in behind Desmond and fired. His bullets blew the wingtip off Desmond's Spitfire. Desmond flicked the Spitfire onto its back and simultaneously slammed the throttle forward to try to shake off his opponent. The German followed, kept pace with him and fired again, sending bright-orange balls of tracer rounds streaking past. Small black clouds of smoke appeared in front of Desmond as anti-aircraft guns in the desert down below opened fire too. Shrapnel hit Desmond's engine, bucking the aircraft and knocking it about violently. The Spitfire began to cough and lose power rapidly. Realising he would not make it home, Desmond looked around. The good thing was that the ground fire had also sent the remaining 109 packing. Watching the altimeter unwind and the desert floor grow steadily closer, Desmond tried to identify a place where he could put down. He managed to force land on an advanced landing ground that was identified only by a grid reference (XB9797).[6] Luckily, this time it was not on an enemy airstrip.

This was the third time Desmond had been shot down. In countless similar situations, other pilots had taken to their parachutes, but Desmond never felt the need to. Instead, each time he had been forced down – either by gunfire or engine failure – Desmond stayed strapped in his seat, at the controls and fought to bring the damaged aeroplane safely back down to the ground.

A few days after this, on 11 December, Desmond was sent out to Nagrah to fetch a new Spitfire from HQ 239 Wing to replace the one he had been shot down in. While he was away, his squadron sent up twelve Spitfires to conduct a sweep over the Marble Arch area ahead of several Shark Squadron Kittyhawks. The formation was intercepted by several German and Italian fighters. Three Kittyhawk pilots were brought down, two of which Desmond knew well: Billy Drake, who was leading the Kittyhawks, was attacked by no less than seven ME109s. He fought back and managed to shoot down two of them but in doing so used up all the petrol in his tanks. As he descended, Billy saw some British forward reconnaissance troops (the 11th Hussars nicknamed the 'Cherrypickers'), force landed nearby and, with their assistance, returned to the squadron soon after.[7] The other pilot shot down was Plt Off 'Compo' Cuddon, who was listed as missing, but his body was never found.

By mid-December, the Eighth Army was preparing to take El Agheila and march on the Libyan capital, Tripoli. Rommel's troops had burnt or otherwise destroyed anything in Benghazi they could not take with them in the retreat westwards. From that point on, there were no significant flying operations to speak of.

Christmas Day 1942 was more relaxed. The AOC released everyone except essential staff from duty. The cooks had worked all night and laid on a wonderful spread, with the help of last-minute arrivals of NAAFI[8] supplies, including turkey, pork, Christmas pudding, wine and various trimmings.[9]

Back on flying duty a few days later, on 28 December, Desmond took a Spitfire up for another cannon test. Unexpectedly though, his engine cut out as he returned. Desmond was too low to bail out, and the Spitfire was dropping like a stone. All he could do was prepare for impact and hope he could get the undercarriage down in time, his hand furiously working the hydraulic pump by his right knee. He missed the roughly marked runway and 'pranged outside the 'drome 30yds from an army gunpit'.

Desmond took some time off ops. Unable to return home during this time, he took his leave far behind the lines in the usual rest haunts of Alexandria and Cairo. Years later, his sister Muriel recalled that Desmond managed to meet up with his Uncle Billy. Tucked away in one of the family albums was an old, unsent postcard. On the reverse were a few handwritten notes near the edges. In the middle was a sketch-map of Egypt showing the route from an airfield in the south to an officers' rest hotel near Suez. This could have been their meeting place.

Uncle Billy was Sarah's half-brother, William John Kirkwood. He lived in the mill town of Accrington. Accrington's military past was, and remains, synonymous with the First World War; the town's pals battalion had then been almost entirely wiped out during the morning of the first day of the Battle of the Somme in 1916.

Billy had joined the East Lancashire Regiment as a private in the mid-1920s, worked his way up through the ranks and, according to Muriel, was a PT instructor at the Royal Military Academy Sandhurst. By the time he met up with Desmond again in North Africa, he too was a junior officer (a lieutenant) and attached to the Military Police.[10]

Over a few bottles of beer in the officers' hotel bar, they shared tales of their time in the desert. Eventually, the discussion turned to news from home. Billy told Desmond his dad had been caught having an affair with Sarah's sister, and Sarah was seeking a divorce. Desmond mulled things over. He wondered how his sisters were. Muriel was not yet 18, and Molly was only 10. If Desmond did go home, would he be able to look his dad in the eye again? The conversation with Billy turned back to the war and how long it would take to kick the Germans out of Africa, but the atmosphere had changed, despite the hopeful exchanges about how things would turn out in the desert and in Yorkshire. They left the bar and agreed they should meet up again soon. But a few weeks later, in early April, Billy was travelling in a vehicle that ran over a landmine. He was injured in the explosion and taken to the nearest military hospital, where he later died of his wounds.[11]

By the time Desmond was back flying on ops again, on 10 January 1943, the squadron had crossed Libya's western border and moved into southern Tunisia, supporting the Allies' push for Tripoli on the coast. Desmond was mainly engaged in either bringing new aircraft up from 59 Repair and Servicing Unit at Hamraiet (including a new clipped-wing ('clippy') Spit-bomber[12] designed for low-level ground attack raids), or 'breaking in' new pilots by taking them up to practise shadow shooting and aerobatics. The squadron had the honour of being the first unit in Egypt to take delivery of the new Spit-bomber. But from the end of January into early February, there were several days of dust storms, which prevented any operational flying. The first test flight of the new Spit-bomber on squadron service (and the first by any front-line unit in the Egyptian theatre) took place on 4 February, and there was competition between the pilots to be the first to fly it.

The honour of that first flight went to Desmond, who had more experience of Spitfires than anyone else on the squadron, and he found the clippy to be much faster than the regular Mk Vs. These Spit-bombers had been first converted in Malta when standard Mk V airframes were fitted with a couple of improvised bomb racks so that a 250lb bomb could be carried underneath each wing.[13] They were brought into service to act as dive-bombers and to work alongside the Kittyhawks and Hurricanes already in service. The technique was to release the bombs in a steep, 60–70° dive from around 7,000ft. Of course, once this bomb load was gone, the Spitfire could immediately revert to its primary role as a fighter and engage any enemy aircraft.

On the day the Eighth Army entered Tripoli, Desmond had his first flight as pilot in the Stuka, flying it to Hamraiet.[14] After it had been refitted with a new wingtip and aileron, Desmond took it up again for a 20-minute formal test flight to ensure the airframe repairs were up to scratch. This 'tame' Stuka was used as an aerial taxi for shopping trips to collect supplies for the mess (crates of beer, wine, cigarettes, papers, letters), equipment for the mechanics (including, on one occasion, spare tyres) and to ferry personnel to and from various landing grounds as the squadron continued to advance. The groundcrew looked after this flying war trophy as well as any of their own Spitfires, using any spare parts they could lay their hands on to keep it going.

The Millionaires were not the only squadron to use irregular aircraft to go shopping. One squadron used a captured Heinkel HE-111 twin-engined bomber. Other squadrons used His Majesty's fighters and bombers to collect supplies. For example, an old Hurricane of 87 Squadron had its guns and ammunition removed, and the long-range tanks were cleaned to make way for bottles of spirits, wine and packets of cigarettes in the wing recesses. One pilot from 92 Squadron emptied a 4-gallon jerrycan of petrol, stowed it in the cockpit of his Spitfire, flew to Castel Benito, refilled the jerrycan with Chianti and flew home with both feet on one rudder pedal. According to Neville Duke, the wine was good and did the job, although it did have an aftertaste of petrol about it.

A VIP visit to Castel Benito took place on 3 February when Winston Churchill, having finished the conference in Casablanca with Roosevelt and American, British and French Combined Chiefs of Staff, landed at the airfield in his B-24 Liberator. Desmond, who had just been promoted to flying officer, was away at the time collecting another Spit-bomber, so he missed the chance to see Churchill again. All the squadrons were paraded for the prime minister, who passed slowly along the front of them in an open-top chauffeur driven car to resounding cheers from all.[15]

For the remainder of February, Desmond only flew a Spitfire once and spent the rest of the time flying the Stuka, accumulating a total of 12 hours flying time in it. His experience is rather unique – not just because the opportunity to fly these aircraft was so rare, but very few of the other pilots acquired as much first-hand experience on the Stuka as Desmond did.

The airfield at Castel Benito was near the coast and was the first grass airstrip that 601 had seen since they had left Britain. It had only very recently been captured from the Germans as they continued to retreat. The squadron's A and B Flights were finally reunited there on 16 February. During this time of relative calm, Desmond received the news he was to be awarded the DFC. The squadron record book states, rather blandly, that it was for 'courage, determination and devotion to duty'. Yet, the citation for the award of this, Desmond's first medal, as it appeared in the *London Gazette* at the time states:

> In the campaign in the Western Desert, Pilot Officer Ibbotson has flown with great distinction and has destroyed at least 7 enemy aircraft. Throughout his keenness and determination have been inspiring. On one occasion he crash landed near Mersa Matruh but aided by friendly Arabs, he was enabled to rejoin his unit.[16]

Desmond received his medal on 23 February and took a 7-hour trip from the airfield at Castel Benito as a passenger in a twin-engined Hudson, stopping to refuel at El Adem before going on to Cairo for the event and a few days' leave afterwards.

While he was away, the squadron lost its tame Stuka, Desmond's 'pet' aeroplane. According to a post-war source it was the detection of corrosion to the wing spar that put an end to the pilots' joyriding.[17] This was not the case according to Desmond though. The Hazbub main airfield had been subjected to frequent barrages from German artillery on the nearby hills. Despite vague assurances that patrols of Gurkhas would be sent out to deal with the problem and silence the guns, nothing was ever done about it.[18] When Desmond returned, he found the same guns had launched a barrage at Castel Benito on 1 March. Almost all the Spitfires managed to evacuate to nearby airfields except for one, which was badly damaged on take-off when a shell exploded underneath it, causing the pilot to crash 3 miles from the airfield. The attempt to rescue the Stuka was fruitless though. 'Lost Stuka,' wrote Desmond, 'we were shelled off the aerodrome. It let us down it would not start.' What became of it is unknown. The squadron temporarily dispersed its Spitfires and Spit-bombers around four separate landing grounds: Hazbub, El Assa, Zuora and Ben Gardene.

Nearly a week elapsed before Desmond returned to ops. He was scrambled on 13 March at 11.45 a.m. leading Blue Section. As the two sections of three aircraft patrolled west of Medenine, they sighted and bounced a formation of MC202s. The two other pilots with him each made claims. Desmond manoeuvred into position to open fire on one of the MC202s, and although his cannons failed, he saw his machine gun bullets hit one of the MC202s. However, because it was unverified, it was one claim that was not awarded to him.

He had better luck a few days later on 22 March, when the newly arrived 22-year-old Acting Sqn Ldr John Stuart Taylor DFC led six Spitfires out on his first 'scramble' with the Millionaires. The son of a reverend from Suffolk, Taylor was told to 'make angels' at 12,000ft over Mareth.[19] Once in position, they spotted four ME109s 1,000ft above them, so continued climbing, looking to gain a tactical advantage over them. Each opposing formation carried on in this manner, steadily spiralling upwards with odd, half-hearted engagements taking place periodically up to 15,000ft, when they finally met each other with decisive action.

Taylor attacked one of the 109s at a 300yd range, striking its starboard wing with both machine guns and cannon fire. As pieces of the wing fell away, the plane began to dive, but Taylor lost contact with it as it went into cloud, apparently out of control.

Desmond was leading the other two pilots in Yellow Section but selected and pursued his own target as the engagement quickly became a free-for-all. He doggedly kept up his attack, closed in and hit the belligerent German at least three separate times with his machine guns. Some rounds struck the coolant system, causing the familiar white smoke trail of a mortally wounded plane. Desmond continued to pursue it and watched as his opponent's engine finally seized up. Soon the propellor stopped turning altogether, and the ME109F began to glide gently away to its end. Satisfied it was now completely incapacitated, Desmond left the enemy fighter at 4,000ft over the mountains and returned to base to claim this one as a probable. The two surviving 109s quickly made off for safety, at which point the Spitfires turned for home.

On 23 March, the squadron began to receive delivery of the new Spitfire Mk IX. Desmond managed to secure one for the sortie that morning, a scramble to cover the Gabes area. On arriving over the coast at 15,000ft, they saw eight MC202s and six or more 109s, but Desmond counted around twenty to thirty enemy fighters. This time the Spitfires were on the receiving end of the attention and were dived on by several enemy fighters with guns blazing. The Spitfires turned and broke into the attacks, and several dogfights broke out. During one of these, Desmond claimed he hit a 109, which turned out to be the second aircraft he had damaged that was not recorded. He was attacked on several occasions, yet the enemy pilots never managed to gain a decisive advantage over him. Eventually the skirmish broke up with the enemy being chased off.

From now on, there was another hectic period of almost daily scrambles resulting in large-scale dogfights. Following weeks of trying to get the Luftwaffe and Regia Aeronautica fighters to engage in a fight, it seemed the war was on again.

On 24 March, when 601 Squadron was out escorting tank-busting Kittyhawks in what was supposed to be 'the best show ever', Desmond was chased by nine ME109s. The day after that, he wrote that he saw a South African pilot chased by twelve ME109s and another one bail out. As if that wasn't enough to contend with, there was a significant amount of anti-aircraft fire coming up at them from the guns of the soldiers below. During one escort mission, the Spitfires were intercepted and shot at by American fighters.

On his third sortie of the day on 26 March, Desmond was involved in a patrol over the New Zealand infantry and the 1st Armoured Division lines. This was, he wrote, an 'amazing show. Dozens of "Kitties" straffing. Many fires. Big tank battle. At least fifty (aircraft) over Area 8 not a 109 or 202 dare come near.' From his vantage height of around 6,000ft he had the ideal view of the ground activity and not much to worry about as the enemy fighters stayed away.

As the Afrika Korps surrendered the Mareth Line on 29 March and began another stage of their retreat, the squadron flew one of the most hectic days of operations for several months, with eight separate missions being flown. Desmond himself flew on four of these sorties.

On the fourth sortie, Desmond's section (led by Sqn Ldr Taylor) were scrambled to patrol the Medenine area. Flying at 5,000ft due to the cloud base, they spotted retreating columns of enemy soldiers, tanks and trucks. Desmond wrote that the Spitfires began chasing JU-88s and 109s, but on seeing the enemy vehicles below, they immediately descended to strafe them. They set one six-wheeled half-track armoured vehicle on fire, severely damaged a tank and accidentally hit a hospital transport. The return fire from the Afrika Korps was understandably fierce, and this time it was accurate too. Desmond's Spitfire was hit in the fuselage and wing, and he was lucky to escape any serious damage.

At the end of the day, the squadron split up again as they moved forward from Bou Grara to El Hamma via Medenine Landing Ground. The Allies were advancing further along the coast of Tunisia. As March gave way to April, the only activity of note remained on the ground. The Luftwaffe again refused to meet the RAF in the air on many occasions, and whenever there were any scrambles, they often proved fruitless.

Desmond led a section of four Spitfires to join the rest of the squadron at El Hamma on 3 April. Unfortunately, his Spitfire's engine developed an internal glycol leak, which caused it to overheat and threaten to seize up. Only part way between Mareth and Gabes, with no choice but to get down as quickly as possible, Desmond made for the nearest, flattest stretch of ground he thought he could land on. As he touched down, he suddenly realised the ground was considerably rougher than it had at first appeared, but it was too late. The Spitfire's narrow undercarriage dropped into a deep rut, causing the aeroplane to ground-loop. The violence of the impact sheared both wings off and the tail section too, completely destroying the Spitfire. Desmond was lucky to walk away unhurt, admitting privately that 'I only slightly dented myself.' Again, he had stayed with a faulty Spitfire and tried to land it.

The squadron advanced again through Sfax and on to Bou Goubrine near Sousse, another airfield close to the coast, and the more welcoming sight of green grass, flowers and the sound of birds in the trees. It was not until 13 April that Desmond and the squadron saw significant action again when they intercepted forty-plus ME109s. Desmond singled one out. The German saw him and took evasive action, but the Spitfire remained fastened on his tail. He pushed the nose forward, hoping his 109, reputedly faster in a dive, would outpace the pilot behind. Desmond closed, firing intermittent bursts, but his frustration mounted as he saw his tracer rounds whizzing harmlessly past the ME109: 'I fired everything I had at it and still the thing went on. I found I could easily hold the 109 in the dive but could not shoot straight.'

It was evident – in mid-April – that Rommel now faced his last days in Africa, and there was an end in sight for the Allies as they focused their sights on capturing Tunis. Having held Cairo and recaptured Tobruk and Tripoli, retaking Tunis would mean the end of the war in North Africa. At the Casablanca conference, the army generals had committed to liberating North Africa by 15 May in order that the Allies would have time to re-equip and prepare for an invasion of Sicily in the late summer or early autumn of 1943.

On 16 April, 145 Squadron was top cover, with 92 Squadron escorting a fighter sweep of Kittyhawks. Wg Cdr Ian Richard 'Widge' Gleed led the fighter escort, staggered at different heights as usual. Neville Duke spotted a formation of around eighteen Italian SM82 transport aircraft several thousand feet below him, which he reported to Gleed. Gleed could not see them, so ordered Duke and his section in to attack. Duke shot down two Italians before he and his colleagues were themselves suddenly attacked by several FW190s and ME109s. As Duke was being chased by a few Focke Wulfs, he glanced to one side to see Gleed's wingman bail out of his burning Spitfire. Duke's attention returned to his own predicament as he was now being pursued by a FW190, and the pair of them ended up spiralling down to nearly wave-top height pulling high-g twists and turns. Duke managed to break away by pulling his Spitfire IX into a steep climb. When the Spitfires returned to base, the news was not good. Desmond knew it: 'Rich collected a helluva packet.' No one had seen Ian Gleed being shot down, but since he did not return, he was reported missing. Gleed was one of the renowned fighter leaders, having led the wing with distinction, and his loss was significant. He had been in the RAF since the war had started and had flown right through the Battles of France and Britain, receiving a DFC in November 1940 and a DSO (Distinguished Service Order) in May 1942 along the way.

On hearing the news, the AOC Desert Air Force, AVM Harry Broadhurst had to decide on Gleed's replacement. He called Brian Kingcome over from Malta, where he was then based as a squadron leader, to his office in Sfax on the Tunisian coast, about an hour's flying time away across the Mediterranean. Broadhurst was blunt in telling Kingcome that he had no choice but to appoint him as Gleed's replacement. Both were also well aware that the new position also meant a promotion because the qualifying rank for the leader of a mobile fighter wing such as 244 Wing had only recently been raised to group captain level. The short reception Kingcome received was mainly because

Broadhurst did not know him that well, though both would get on very well professionally. The now Gp Capt Kingcome would remain in the post for two years and later lead Desmond and his colleagues into battle over Italy.

While patrolling over Bou Goudrine, out at sea or over the harbour at Sousse, Desmond could see a number of German ships gathering near Tunis to the north. The situation on the ground was rather like that which had faced the British Expeditionary Force in northern France three years earlier, when they had faced being cut off, with their backs against the sea and needing an emergency evacuation. Now, in the early spring, the Panzer Army and Afrika Korps were hemmed into the Cap Bon peninsula and struggling to maintain cohesion in the face of severe pressure on two fronts. They continued a fighting retreat while what men and materiel could be spared were spirited away to Sicily.

Harassed by both the Royal Navy and US Navy warships, any German resupply or evacuation had to be done largely by air. In one instance, Ultra decrypts had given the Allies a vital tip-off about a much larger relief mission of soldiers and equipment due to take place on 18 April by air. The formation was part of *Generalmajor* Buchholz's last desperate attempt to keep the *Panzerarmee* Africa supplied and consisted of triple-engined Junkers JU-52 transport aircraft, along with larger six-engined ME323 heavy-lift aircraft that could carry vehicles.

On 18 April, three American Kittyhawk squadrons of the 57th Fighter Group accompanied by the 314th Squadron were assigned for the attack. The Spitfires of 92 Squadron and 601 Squadron flew as top cover on their second operation that day and took off at 4.15 p.m. to find and intercept the relief aircraft. The formation was spotted low over the water off the Tunisian coast. From their position above, both Desmond and Neville Duke watched as the Kittyhawks went about their grim work:

> Peering down from our cockpits occasionally we could see the Americans getting right in among the enemy, flying low over the sea. A Junkers would begin to glow, become a ball of flame, and stagger on over the water. Some went straight in, others succeeded in reaching land, only to crash and blow up. As dusk fell, we looked down to see burning aircraft glowing over an area of many square miles. It was a blood chilling sight.[20]

As the American Kittyhawks engaged the transports through, the escorting Spitfires were bounced by, Desmond recalled, a mixed formation of 12 ME109s and a few MC202s and another dogfight broke out, Desmond caught one, got in a single burst, missed, and was then attacked three times himself before returning safely to the airfield at Bou Goubrine.

That evening, Desmond noted, 'the Kitties shot down 58 JU-52s for the loss of 6' in what became known thereafter as the Palm Sunday Massacre.[21]

At the end of April, when the Millionaires met two ME109s and two Focke-Wulf 190s, Desmond had what he called 'a very nice dice' with a FW190, which was a blasé way of describing an encounter with a potentially lethal opponent. The FW190 was a new single-engined fighter that had already been in service with the Luftwaffe for nearly a year in occupied Europe but had limited deployment in North Africa and now flew across the Mediterranean from bases in Sicily.

In a similar turn of events, reports had reached the Luftwaffe squadrons of a new version of Spitfire – the Mk IX – now entering front-line service with the RAF. It was very similar in appearance to its predecessor, the Mk Vb, but an uprated Merlin engine gave it greater speed and improved handling at higher altitude. Initially, the Germans had been caught out when they had encountered the new Mk IX, thinking them to be the slower Mk Vs, and became wary of them.

This was Desmond's first noted encounter with a FW190, and while he could hold his own against a fighter that technically outclassed his own machine, he realised he still had to be on his guard because when the German flicked over into a steep turn to use the FW190's greater turning rate, he very nearly managed to turn inside him, but Desmond recognised the danger and managed to successfully break off the encounter.

The next day, on an escort mission to bombers of the American 79th Group, flying at 16,000ft, the Millionaires came across a handful of MC202 Thunderbolts. Desmond saw his colleague Llewellyn 'well and truly hit' one, which he claimed as a probable when it suffered an explosion underneath the cockpit, which sent the Italian spinning down into the sea. Desmond, who was flying as a pair leading John 'Tilly' Tilston, then saw one of the Italian 'Maccis' fly past in front of them. The angle being from a position 50° off its port side was not ideal, but Desmond aimed instinctively and let rip. Tilly recalled, 'Ibby took a poop at it and … he hit it! It was absolutely incredible. I saw it go into the sea.'[22] Desmond noted that his bullets hit 'round the port wing root and cockpit and he flicked straight into the drink'. The Thunderbolt was confirmed destroyed and, after 197 operations, was Desmond's eighth victory. As respectable an aeroplane as the Thunderbolt was, it had a nasty reputation for suddenly entering a spin when handled too violently – for example, when trying to flick roll and break away from an attacker. It had been the downfall of several Italian pilots who might otherwise have escaped.

Many of the scrambles and patrols for shipping during the first week of May resulted in no contact with the enemy, which allowed the bombers and fighter-bombers 601 Squadron escorted to go about their business without any real interference at all because most of the Axis airfields had been vacated, their planes and pilots dispersed to new airfields over in Sicily.

During a two-day period from 8 to 10 May, the Spitfires focused their efforts on escorting bomber raids on Pantelleria, a small Italian island between Tunisia and Sicily, which was home to a large aerodrome and of some importance to the Luftwaffe. Desmond participated in the early morning of 8 May and witnessed the results of the bombing, there being no enemy fighters around to worry about. 'Slap on the aerodrome. Such devastation.' The next day was a repeat: 'poor Pantelleria, so many bombs'.

From 10 May onwards, realising the end of the war in North Africa was only hours away, pilots from all squadrons, some overdue to end their tours, were desperate to get in the air right to the bitter end and see out the final victory. All over the area, squadrons were flying their last missions.

The Spitfires of 244 Wing escorted 239 Wing Kittyhawks on anti-shipping patrols and armed reconnaissance sorties.

No. 112 Squadron, 'The Sharks', flew their last sorties on 10 May, bombing enemy vehicles south of Korba.

No. 3 Squadron bombed a pier, scoring a direct hit both on it and on the building at the base of the pier, going on to strafe vehicles on the nearby road.

No. 450 Squadron, 'The Desert Harassers', attacked and bombed goods wagons in a railway siding before also attacking enemy MT hidden under trees at the side of the road.

No. 250 'Sudan' Squadron dive-bombed the last remaining enemy troops in the Cap Bon peninsula, but by now the Allied troops were so close to the enemy positions that further attacks were stopped for fear of hitting their own soldiers.[23]

The air war ended, as Neville Duke recalled, on the afternoon of 11 May 1943 when, 601, 145 and 92 Squadrons escorted American Kittyhawks around the Cap for the last time. 'When the bombs had gone down the controller called up all aircraft. "Return to base. The show is over." he said.'[24]

'Tunis is ours!' Desmond wrote. The day after, on 12 May, General Von Arnim was captured. Then the day after that, General Messe accepted the unconditional surrender of all remaining Axis forces in North Africa.

Not surprisingly, the exhausted DAF aircrew began enjoying themselves, and there were many mess parties to celebrate the postings in and out of various pilots.[25] Many hoped to return home and were disappointed when they found out they were to stay in North Africa. Those that could made use of various bases close to the coast and enjoyed bathing in the sea, relaxing and spells of leave to cities such as Tripoli, Benghazi, Alexandria and Cairo, which is where Desmond wound up on the last day of May, having hitched a lift in a Hudson alongside ACM Sir Sholto Douglas himself.

At the conclusion of his first tour, Desmond had shot down eight enemy aircraft confirmed destroyed (three Stukas, four ME109s and one MC202), four probables (all ME109s) and seven damaged (five ME109s and two JU-88s). In the space of just over eighteen months since he first began operations back in the UK, he had also received a DFC, a commission to officer rank and was now a recognised 'ace'.

Had his career ended then, he could quite happily have said he had 'a good war' and had a good raft of stories to tell his grandchildren. Instead, he would be rested for six months, starting with some leave in Cairo, before his next tour began in Italy. His summer in Egypt would see a stint of test flying, an intense period of gunnery practice and an enigmatic encounter with a beautiful Russian dancer.

CHAPTER 13

The Interlude Between Tours

Egypt
Summer 1943

Having flown 215 operational sorties, Desmond could be forgiven for not wanting to spend a day longer in North Africa when his first tour expired, but there was no indication he wanted to return home. With the war in North Africa over, his first tour of ops complete and the warmer summer weather approaching, he must have felt it was the ideal time to enjoy time off before his next tour began.

After the German surrender in May 1943, Desmond spent the remainder of the month occasionally flying a Spitfire around Tunisia. Once he flew a Lysander down the coast to Ben Gardane with some mates.

During the summer and early autumn of 1943, Desmond had four posts. He had a short stint as an instructor with 73 OTU at Abu Sueir, attended a gunnery course, flew rare marks of Spitfires on test and delivered aircraft around Allied air bases in the Middle East. The flying was more relaxed: fewer sorties, regular working hours and more free time.

Fellow instructors at the OTU included Desmond's former flight commander, Geoff Garton of 112 Squadron, who was now a squadron leader and house mate of Neville Duke – the pair shared a bungalow on the base. Duke recalled that the daily routine for many of the instructors there at the time meant they worked from dawn until midday, then had a siesta before going swimming or sailing in the Suez Canal or the Great Bitter Lake. It could have been around this time the photographs of Desmond and other pilots in their swimming costumes were taken.

The large number of fellow DAF types meant there was always good company about and usually an easy selection of friends to visit the various fleshpots and bars of Cairo with, such as Shepherd's, the Turf Club, Jimmy's Bar and the Continental.[1] It was not unusual though for some of the resting DAF pilots to resent the move to a training school. Even Neville Duke protested to his immediate superiors that he had been promised a return home by none other than the AOC himself. Regardless of his griping though, he was to remain in Egypt and, ultimately, he settled very well into his post. These were salad days for instructors and pupils alike. The opportunity to fly His Majesty's fighters in beautiful clear skies without hindrance of hostility allowed many a freedom not readily available to them in either England or Egypt in recent months. All were certain the war would soon call them again, and they would once more be in the thick of it.

Desmond did not fly at all for the first three weeks of June before he travelled across North Africa to the training school at Abu Sueir, some 80 miles away to the north-east of Cairo on the banks of the Suez Canal. He was there as a temporary instructor flying Harvards, Tomahawks and Kittyhawks, teaching the trainee pilots how to fly battle formations, fly on instruments alone and practise air combat. He stayed there for only two weeks before receiving his next posting on 5 July.

CHAPTER 14

Central Gunnery School

El Ballah, Egypt
5 July–15 September 1943

El Ballah was close to the Suez Canal, in a salt pan with very high humidity. Accommodation was, as usual, in tents. At this time of year, with the sun at its highest, the heat and flies were almost unbearable; it was not a pleasant posting. Duke wrote: 'The heat became so intense that perspiration dripped and streamed from us even while we were sitting limply; we cursed and killed thousands of flies and made sure of a daily swim either at Ismailia or in the Suez Canal.'[1]

Desmond spent the next two months at El Ballah flying a mix of Hurricanes and Spitfires on practice air gunnery sorties. Sometimes he flew a Hurricane, towing a drogue target for other pilots to shoot at; other times he was in a Spitfire or Hurricane shooting at the target being towed.

The Spitfire Mk Vs, VIIIs and IXs had, as their most common configuration, two 20mm Hispano cannon with sixty rounds each and four Browning 0.303in-calibre machine guns with 350 rounds per gun. Ten years earlier, in 1933, Sqn Ldr Ralph Sorley of the Air Ministry's Operational Requirements Branch had presented a paper to Sir Hugh Dowding, the then head of Fighter Command, on how best to arm the RAF's new fighters. His idea was to mount the eight machine guns he deemed necessary in the wings instead of in the fuselage, as the designers had originally intended.

Sorley also calculated that to put 400 rounds of machine gun bullets into the enemy plane, at a standard rate of fire of 1,000 rounds per minute for each 0.303in gun, the fighter pilot would need to give his target a 2-second 'burst'.[2] The 2-second burst would put sufficient rounds into a grouping on the target to make it unflyable, rather than necessarily blowing it right out of the sky.

Tests proved Sorley's point, and his proposal of eight Browning 0.303s became the standard armament fit for the early marks of both the Spitfire and Hurricane, all 'harmonised' at 400yds, meaning all the bullets were aimed to coincide in a reasonably compact cluster at that distance away from the attacking aircraft.

In the two years since Desmond had learnt to fly fighters in combat, things had improved in terms of the speed, performance and armament of the Spitfires and Hurricanes, as successive upgrades to these aeroplanes took place. Yet the perennial problem – perfecting the technique of aerial marksmanship – remained.

In 1934, the RAF had taken to towing aerial drogues (dummy targets) behind another aeroplane. The drogue was a 10ft-long conical 'kite' shaped like a standard windsock, open at both ends to let the air flow though. It was vividly coloured to stand out and had large diametrically opposed target circles painted on the centre of the cone. Bullet tips were dipped in marker paint so any that hit the target would leave a visible residue behind. To separate one pilot's performance from another, they would each use a different colour. There were four methods of attack laid down in the standard training syllabus that pilots had to practise: above, astern, quarter (angled off by about 45° to one side front or rear) and beam (full side on).[3]

Pilots practised these various attacks to work out where the bullets would hit with each approach. The effect of eight .303 Browning guns was devastating at close quarters, but the guns were inadequate at longer ranges against manoeuvring enemy fighters, unless a hit was registered in the engine, petrol tank or cooling system.[4]

In common with other pilots' experience of actual air-to-air combat from early 1940 onwards, opening fire at 400yds, as Sqn Ldr Sorley had calculated was the required range, was often found to be ineffective. Desmond, like the majority of fighter pilots, successfully shot down his opponent when he closed to less than half that range. Even then, scoring hits did not mean the enemy would immediately fall. The .303in bullets caused damage, but more of them were required to bring the opponent down. The introduction of 20mm cannon to the Mk V Spitfires and Mk II Hurricanes with rounds that were twice the size and weight of the .303 bullet ensured a greater likelihood of destroying the target.

The Hispano cannons were not without their own set of problems though, including freezing at altitude and frequent stoppages or jamming. As if that was not annoying enough, the spontaneous and asymmetrical stoppages in the Hispanos meant when one cannon stopped and the other continued firing, the whole balance of the plane would shift. The resulting recoil caused the aeroplane to yaw (or skid) dramatically to one side.

Desmond's logbook records that while at El Ballah he was flying as many as four sorties a day, practising his gunnery skills in either a Hurricane IIB or a Spitfire VB. The pilots flew in standard formations of between six and twelve aircraft on each sortie, looked for their towed target and took turns shooting at the drogues. Other sorties saw the pilots simulate attacks on bombers in 'cooperation flights' that enabled both fighter pilots and air gunners to practise.

Feint attacks were also carried out on fellow pilots as they practised air-to-air combat on one another, occasionally using a camera gun – a small movie camera mounted in the wing near the gun itself. It was operated by a separate switch, mounted on the control column next to the gun button, which the pilot had to press immediately before the guns were fired.

Desmond dutifully kept a record of his scores but, perhaps unusually, made no comment about how he felt he was doing:

8 July Hurricane 11 hits from 330 bullets: 3¾%.
17 July Hurricane 8 hits from 400 bullets: 2%.
19 July Hurricane 5 hits from 400 bullets: 1¼%.
19 July Hurricane 7 hits from 350 bullets: 2%.
21 July Spitfire 0 hits from 120 bullets: 0%.
22 July Spitfire 0 hits from 83 bullets: 0%.
26 July Hurricane 0 hits from 120 bullets: 0%.
26 July Hurricane 0 hits from 200 bullets: 0%.
27 July Hurricane 12 hits from 120 bullets: 10%.

29 July Spitfire 5 hits from 180 bullets: 3%.
4 August Spitfire 1 hit from 363 bullets: 0.3%.
5 August Hurricane 14 hits from 400 bullets: 9%.
1 September Spitfire 21 hits from 150 bullets: 14%.

From this, it's possible to estimate what Desmond's practice and progression looked like. By the start of July, Desmond was using more ammunition and firing longer bursts. The method was to approach the drogue at 150mph, shoot, then break away. If he fired 330 bullets, it meant Desmond had fired for a total of 4 seconds but in repetitive 1- or 2-second bursts.[5]

As Desmond tried to keep to the method of holding his fire until he was close in, then breaking away, his accuracy dropped for a time before improving by the beginning of September. These scores also show that, despite him being a recognised ace with eight confirmed victories, those victories were as much (if not more) to do with his skill in the pursuit as they were his marksmanship.

Just as there was always an element of luck in dogfighting, so too was there in gunnery school. Between 27 and 30 July, flying separate sorties against drogue targets, Desmond experienced his guns failing to fire, gun camera not working and the drogues being lost, disintegrating or, in one instance, being shot away when he hit the guide cables with cannon fire.

Up until mid-1943, Muriel could not recall having received any letters from her brother since he had left England in early 1942. All she, her sister and mother could do was scan the casualty lists in the local paper and hope and pray Desmond was alive and well. Just occasionally, as Muriel leafed diligently through the pages of *The War Illustrated* weekly magazine, she would find a picture or description of Desmond, which she would show Sarah and Molly with great excitement, then cut it out and stick it in her scrapbook.

As Desmond now had more spare time, he finally got round to writing letters home. This is from Thursday 15 July 1943:

Whatcha Muriel,
Just a line from your big brother. I have just been swimming. Wish you had been there? I could name a few of the pilots around here you would wish you had been if they had seen you. Girls are scarce! A

decent one I mean. I am lucky. I knock around with a Russian. A very beautiful blonde. (Natural too). I had the good fortune to nearly run over her one day. She is a grand type, swimming, dancing, sailing & oh well, she's o.k. Heavens though! Honestly she is smashing. Don't think I am in love though. She (sic) just a damned good pal.
Cheerio,
Desmond.

Unfortunately, the identity of this lovely young woman will forever remain a mystery. He must have met her very recently because he had only been at El Ballah for ten days. And nearly running her over was quite the introduction – had she been on the wrong side of the road, or had he?

It was certainly a whirlwind: swimming, dancing and sailing together. She would be getting plenty of attention from Desmond because if he didn't keep his eyes on her, then there were plenty of other keen-eyed pilots who would compete for her attention.

A young Russian woman in Egypt must have come from a wealthy family. Ordinary working-class people were in the factories, mines, farming cooperatives or armed forces and had little or no ability to travel. She may have been from a family of emigres, had a father who was a senior diplomat, engineer, financier or perhaps a spy. With Russia and the Soviet Union under the grip of Stalin and the repressive state police, few people made it out of the country unless someone had a significant role or purpose that could serve the Soviet state by being abroad and, more importantly, they had been granted permission to leave.

In the summer of 1942, with the Wehrmacht just 40 miles from Moscow and the very real threat of the capital falling to the Germans, institutions and factories important to the state were uprooted and moved. Armaments factories and their workers, for example, were moved in their entirety to locations east of the Ural Mountains and rebuilt. The Bolshoi Theatre School and the world-famous ballet company were evacuated. One of the dancers, Violetta Elvin (née Prokhorova), was 19 years old. Her father was an engineer and aviation pioneer, her mother a Polish actress. She and dozens of other young women and girls were collectively sent 1,500 miles away to Tashkent in Uzbekistan until it was safe to return.[6] Perhaps a woman like her came from a family that had also been given permission to leave Russia, and she ended up one day in front of Desmond's car.

This dancer was not the first young woman to have caught Desmond's attention. While working as a draughtsman before he joined up, Desmond had a girlfriend back home in Yorkshire. Joan Barras was, Muriel said, 'a lovely girl', the same age as Desmond and worked as a nurse at Wakefield hospital. Now Desmond flew Spitfires in North Africa and Joan, tending to patients on the wards in Wakefield, was far away from the 'very beautiful blonde' dancer and action girl from Russia who Desmond had now fallen for. Muriel kept the letter[7] with her other photographs and newspaper cuttings of her beloved brother and wondered if she would ever meet his new girlfriend.

Throughout his time at El Ballah, Desmond was under the tutelage of his flight commander and gunnery instructor, the renowned Canadian ace Flt Lt James Francis 'Stocky' Edwards DFM DFC. Edwards had arrived on posting to El Ballah only a week before Desmond and would remain there until 22 November.[8] Edwards' reputation preceded him, and colleagues spoke highly both of his gunnery skills and personal qualities. He taught his students the art of deflection shooting – firing at a point ahead of where the target would be, so the bullets arrived at the same time. Sometimes, to demonstrate his prowess to his pupils, Edwards would have the port side cannon of his Spitfire loaded with just nine rounds of ammunition. Taking off in pursuit of a drogue target, he would then attack it on an upside-down overhead pass and 'blow the drogue to shreds' with only two or three of those rounds.[9]

Nelson Gilboe, who flew with Edwards several times, recalled that, on the ground, Edwards was obsessed with American football and when off duty between ops would constantly try to encourage his fellow flyers to get a game of touch or flag football going, believing physical fitness was vital to keeping them alert in the air.[10] This emphasis on sport and fitness would have appealed to Desmond as well, and the two men seemed ideally matched – being of a similar build and personality. Reflecting on what made a fighter pilot, Edwards himself later commented, 'Not everyone is aggressive enough. You had to be a certain type.' But those qualities might only become clear in the air: 'you had to go up on a flight with him and see.'[11] Desmond successfully completed his course in mid-September and was sent to join a maintenance unit at Aboukir.

CHAPTER 15

103 Maintenance Unit – Test and Delivery Duties

Aboukir, Egypt
15 September–30 October 1943

Desmond was sent to Aboukir to undertake 'special flying duties', which included test flying high-altitude Spitfire Mk IXs and XIs.[1] Aboukir was located on the edge of the desert north-west of Cairo, 7 miles east along the coast from Alexandria and was home to 103 Maintenance Unit (MU). Aircraft of all types were sent here, behind the Allied lines, to be repaired and restored before being sent back to front-line service. Those that were not flown over were shipped in crates by sea to Alexandria, then delivered to the base for reassembly and testing. Though designated an MU, the pilots posted there did not just fly these newly assembled or repaired aircraft on air test but also carried out test flights on new and modified aircraft. Although he had flown several different types of aircraft already, Desmond had no direct experience of more extensive test flying. He could continue to fly more normal hours and not worry about the war for a while, but it put paid to his dalliance with the blonde Russian.

One of the first aircraft assigned to him was a Mk IX Spitfire. During his time at Aboukir, he would fly three Mk IXs on the unit, but one in particular would prove 'testing' in more ways than one. The Mk IX had been developed in urgent response primarily to the emergence of a new

German single-engined fighter, the Focke-Wulf 190. When this first appeared in the skies over France, it was mistaken for a French fighter, the Dewoitine D.520, but it soon became clear a new threat to Allied aircraft had emerged. The Spitfire was the best fighter in the RAF fleet at the time, but to beat the new FW190, it needed an upgrade.

Development work was hurriedly switched towards the necessary airframe modifications and a new variant of the Merlin engine, so that the first Mk IX was delivered for testing just five months after the FW190's appearance. At that time, the RAF was unsure exactly what capability it was dealing with in the FW190. That was until one German pilot, having been caught in a dogfight over the south-west of England, became disorientated on crossing the Bristol Channel, which he mistook for the English Channel and inadvertently landed at an RAF airfield. Thus, the brand-new fighter was delivered intact straight to the RAF, who immediately repainted it and began evaluation trials. These trials formed the basis of more detailed briefings to all fighter squadrons on the new enemy aircraft and the development work Supermarine and its subcontractors were required to do to counter the threat.

The Mk IX Spitfire was sent to the Mediterranean in early 1943, just in time to see service as the Afrika Korps was forced out of Tunisia. It even participated in the invasion of Sicily that September, so it was still a new aircraft in theatre when Desmond arrived at Aboukir. The Mk IXs Desmond was assigned to fly were still the new type of Spitfire, of course, but the ones he was to test were older Mk Vs (or even originally Mk Is) that had been taken from the production line, modified and sent off to Boscombe Down for initial trials as high-altitude interceptors. As well as the FW190, there was a new threat in the Middle East, which prompted the Spitfire IX's export and was one reason Desmond received his posting to 103 MU.

The threat emerged in the form of two Luftwaffe aircraft that flew at high altitude but in slightly different roles: one as a high-altitude bomber (the Junkers JU-86R), the other as a photo reconnaissance plane (the Junkers JU-88 D2/Trop or D4). Both were twin-engined and had distinctive rounded cockpits at the front of the fuselage. The JU-86 had carried out several daylight raids over southern England in mid-1942 while the JU-88 D4s, flying from a base in Crete, had been out photographing the Allied armies in the Middle East, especially in the run-up to the Battle of El Alamein. The RAF was naturally keen to put a stop to these aircraft.

Virtually all the fighters in the RAF's inventory in the Middle East had been assigned, if not actually optimised, to perform as either ground attack or air-to-air fighters. This meant they performed best at heights of around 25,000ft or below. Spitfires could reach higher altitudes, but their performance was subject to greater environmental influence as the resultant drops in temperature and pressure took effect the higher the aircraft climbed. To counter the Luftwaffe's high-level threat, the fighters had to be able to reach heights of 40,000–45,000ft in order to engage the enemy. This is where 103 MU played a role.

No. 103 MU kept a small flight of Spitfires, optimised for high-level interception, on readiness. Pilots like Desmond, posted out from frontline squadrons, would undertake testing and dispatch (ferrying) but would also be made available for what would today be called Quick Reaction Alert duties. At first, although the Luftwaffe high-altitude flights were infrequent, there were few successes when they did occur. The Spitfires either suffered engine failures or the guns failed to function properly. To achieve the speed and height required, the Spitfires were stripped of any unnecessary weight, including armour plating.

When assigned to intercept a high-altitude raider, two Spitfires from 103 MU worked together: one called the 'striker', one called the 'marker'– footballing analogies that would not have been lost on Desmond. The marker maintained radio contact with the ground controller, while the striker, flying several thousand feet higher and to one side, received instructions from the marker, whose job it was to guide him onto the best position from which to carry out the intercept. If the striker could not achieve a hit on the enemy, he might at least be able to force it to a lower altitude, where the marker could engage it instead.

When the trials of the Mk IX began at Boscombe Down in late 1942, the head of the Middle East Air Forces requested the high-altitude interceptor version of the Mk IX be developed and shipped out to Aboukir. In keeping with many other fighter aircraft sent out to the North African theatre, the factory standard Mk IXs needed modification in order to be suitable for effective operations in desert conditions. The Mk IXs Desmond flew were part of a batch undergoing specific 'in-theatre' development to both cope with the new environment and to counter the

103 Maintenance Unit – Test and Delivery Duties

high-altitude threat from the Luftwaffe's JU-86 and JU-88. Desmond took his first Mk IX up on Wednesday 15 September 1943 for a height test and to fly a few aerobatics to assess how it performed.

The town of Aboukir lies to the north of the landing ground from which the base took its name and is on the tip of the peninsula that forms one side of the bay into which the River Nile emerges after flowing 2,000 miles through central and eastern Africa. On either side of the bay and a short distance inland lie a handful of lakes spaced a few miles apart from each other and stretching almost 100 miles along the inner section of coast.

As Desmond took off on his first flight and ascended in a broad zigzag towards 30,000ft, he could clearly see the distinctive coastline with the hook of Aboukir's peninsula below. As he gained height, the desert began to lose its features and blur into a dusty tan colour far below. The coastline gradually thinned out and grew faint as his Spitfire climbed onwards into the blue sky. As he climbed past 20,000ft the air chilled and, with his mask snugly fastened across his face, he had already switched to breathing pure oxygen. In his rear-view mirror, he saw the Spitfire's exhaust fumes begin a thin contrail behind him, but eventually even this began to disappear. He was totally alone and far higher than he had ever been in an aircraft.

He planned to climb to around 40,000ft or above, but just then, around 25 minutes into the flight at a height of 38,000ft, the engine developed a fault and cut out. With the engine now silent, the Spitfire drifted momentarily. Soon the controls became heavy and difficult to move. Desmond was cast adrift, 7 miles high in a lifeless aircraft. The nose slipped forward as the Spitfire began its descent. As the air whooshed past the canopy at an ever-increasing speed, Desmond could hear his own breathing as he drew oxygen, chilled by the subzero temperature outside the cockpit, deep into his lungs. He looked outside. This high, miles above any clouds, the sun was intensely bright, the sky above a deep, dark blue. Far below, the light sand of the desert contrasted starkly with the rich blue sea of the Mediterranean. He could make out a fuzzy edge of the coastline and knew he was descending east towards the Suez Canal. The aeroplane's dive steepened. Still the controls felt heavy and unresponsive.

As the altimeter unwound, the needles rotating anticlockwise with increasing speed, he tried to restart the engine. The first attempt failed. Still the Spitfire fell. It was pointless trying to bail out, for two reasons:

firstly, if he could get out, he risked hitting the tailplane at high speed and, secondly, if he successfully opened the parachute, it would take several minutes to reach the ground, leaving the Spitfire to hurtle on out of control and hit God knows what, God knows where. Desmond would then risk being caught by winds that would cause him to drift further, either deeper into the desert or out to sea.

So Desmond stayed with the aircraft and kept trying to restart the engine. Eventually, as the silent Spitfire approached 20,000ft and the air density increased, he at last managed to restart the engine, ease the control column back to bring the errant Spitfire out of its dive and land safely back at Aboukir. The entire flight had lasted just an hour, of which at least half had involved him sweating in an uncontrolled descent trying to bring a faulty engine back to life. On landing, he reported the failure and handed the Spitfire over to the groundcrew to inspect, identify and repair the cause of the fault.

A week later, on Wednesday 22 September, he took Spitfire BS354 up on his first flight of what would be a total of nine flights in this particular aircraft. He was tasked with a height test and aerobatics on this sortie, and although he managed to take it all the way up to 31,000ft, the Spitfire's engine again cut out and it fell for several thousand feet before he could get it restarted and back under control. He landed safely back at Aboukir. When this Spitfire was ready to fly again, Desmond flew it a few more times in early October on aerobatic and normal local area flights without any issues. His only note was that the Mk IX was 'heavier than the Mk V' to fly.

He must have thought this particular aircraft was jinxed because two weeks later and tasked with another height test in the same aircraft, the engine cut out again. This time, he climbed to 35,500ft before the engine failed and descended without power to below 20,000ft to restart. What could have happened to make this engine keep cutting out every time Desmond took it above 30,000ft?

According to Supermarine's records, Spitfire BS354 had originally been built at the Vickers-Armstrongs (Supermarine) Woolston works at Southampton as a Mk Ia/b under one of the early contracts (fifth order, dated October 1940) and entered service around October 1942. Straight away, it went into trials at Boscombe Down in Wiltshire from November 1942.

While at Boscombe Down, it was fitted with a Merlin RM 9SM engine and was one of three aircraft undergoing trials at the same time to determine the best intercooled engine for high- and low-altitude flying. Around this time, it appears to have also undergone conversion: first to a Mk V, then to a Mk IX airframe and wing type. While all aircraft in the trial group had the same model of four-blade propellor, wing type and fuel-injected supercharger, the tests showed the engine in BS354 was inferior to the Merlin models (66 and 70) in the other two aircraft, and that engine model was dropped as a production unit.[2] At that time, the maximum service ceiling of the aircraft was recorded as 40,500ft. During December 1942, the aircraft was then trialled with a larger rudder, which made it easier to control and helped to counter the tendency for the Mk IX to swing to the left on take-off. There are no further test flights listed, and it is not known if the engine was replaced with a Merlin 61 or 70 as its sister aircraft had been, so its original engine was most likely retained before the Spitfire was finally shipped out to North Africa and ended up in Aboukir almost a year later. So, this inferior engine, fixed in a modified and ageing airframe came to form the Spitfire that left Desmond trying to figure out why he had been assigned to fly an aircraft that kept giving up on him at high altitude.

In mid-October, Desmond recorded what was a unique flight for him and quite a rare opportunity for any pilot. No. 103 MU had acquired a new Spitfire Mk XI, and he was tasked to fly it on a 'consumption test' at 30,000ft. Other than the usual particulars, he made only one other notation in his logbook: the initials 'PRU' – Photographic Reconnaissance Unarmed.

What made this unique was that the XI was produced for a very specific role, and so only very few were ever made. The entire wartime production run of the Mk XI was just 471 compared to the thousands of others such as the Mk V, VIII and IX. The photo reconnaissance Mk XI housed two cameras located in the rear fuselage, and to prevent them freezing up at high altitudes, special heaters were fitted into the camera bays, which used hot exhaust gases diverted from the engine.[3] Unfortunately for the pilot, there was no such luxury as heat. The cockpit was unpressurised, so cold air and lack of oxygen made the cockpit environment uncomfortable. The pilot had to breathe continually from a regulator until he returned below 10,000ft. After this first flight,

Desmond flew the Mk XI three more times, and it proved to be more reliable than his Mk IX, which had given him so much trouble recently.

At each stage during these flights after his engine cut, Desmond could have bailed out, but he chose not to. On every occasion he stayed with the aircraft and brought it back to land, just as he had when he had suffered engine problems during training or been hit by ME109s high above France and the English Channel or shot down at low level over the desert. In general, pilots were not obliged to stay with a faulty aircraft – given that aircraft were replaceable while they were not – but it was something many, including and especially Desmond, did.

Desmond completed his flying duties at Aboukir on 30 October. He was now to return to the front line, which had, since leaving Tunisia, advanced through Sicily and into mainland Italy. After a marathon journey across North Africa and via Sicily, which took him two days, eventually Desmond was at last back on ops and about to begin his second tour with 601 Squadron.

The situation in Italy was politically fraught. Over the preceding six months, Italy had formally surrendered and entered a brief but somewhat turbulent armistice period. Mussolini was ousted from power and imprisoned before being rescued by a German special forces unit. On 27 April 1945, while attempting to flee with his mistress, he was recognised by partisans. The pair were caught and held for two days, before being executed and strung up by the ankles from a petrol station roof.

In the interim period before Italy finally joined the Allies, those who could made their own bids for freedom. Conscripts and volunteers alike deserted the Italian armed forces to try to return home, while a large number of Allied PoWs endeavoured to escape their Italian camps before the Germans arrived to take over. The political, military and social environments were in flux, making it difficult to discern anyone's true identity or loyalty. Italy was becoming a very different country to the one that had existed under fascism and the one Desmond had imagined. But amid the danger, he would also find reward, recognition and a unique relationship, perhaps even love.

Two Spitfire Mk IXs of 241 Squadron RAF flying over mountainous terrain south of Rome a few days before the Allied landings at Anzio, 27 January 1944. Desmond was also engaged in flying such patrols around the invasion area around this time. (IWM TR 1531)

RoAF excavation team, October 2005. Leo Venieri is in the centre wearing a white cap, next to the Catholic priest of St Maria D'Angeli, Father Francesco De Lazzari, who said prayers for Desmond when his remains were found. Two places to the left of Leo, in the black jumper, is the doctor from LHU Perugia who helped identify Desmond. Also in the group are RoAF members; Assisi council staff including an assessor; Assisi's mayor; the deputy mayor of Conselice, Ravenna; LHU Perugia medical staff; and the digger drivers.

Some of the switches, dials and plates recovered from the cockpit and engine area, including a shoulder harness, October 2005. (Courtesy of Leo Venieri)

The press conference at Hotel Giotto, Assisi, 8 June 2007. L–R: Sue Raftree (MoD); General Tofi of the Italian Army; the British naval and air attaché, Cdr Shawn Steeds RN; Desmond's nephew, John; Leo Venieri (RoAF). (Author's own)

The evening I met Eugenio, 8 June 2007. He saw Desmond's Spitfire crash in 1944 and had been the first to arrive at the scene to try to help. (Author's own)

Castelnuovo, 9 June 2007. L–R: Eugenio, Dave, Judy, Liz and John meet for the first time. (Author's own)

Desmond's memorial service, Rivotorto, 9 June 2007. (Author's own)

After the ceremonies, Rivotorto, 9 June 2007. (Author's own)

The field where Desmond's Spitfire crashed. The excavation site is just right of centre. (Author's own)

Yorkshire Television crew record an interview with Eugenio. L–R: Eugenio; John Purtell of the Foreign Office, who was the translator; David Hirst; Martin. (Author's own)

Desmond's nieces and nephews visit his memorial before leaving Italy, 9 June 2007. (Author's own)

A flying tribute to Desmond. The RAF's Battle of Britain Memorial Flight Spitfire Mk LF IXe (registration MK356) at the Duxford Air Show on 3 September 2011. This aircraft flew in this colour scheme for five years, from 2007 to 2012, as a tribute to Desmond. Sadly, this same aeroplane was lost when it crashed shortly after take-off from its home at RAF Coningsby in Lincolnshire on Saturday 25 May 2024, killing the pilot, Sqn Ldr Mark Long, as a result. (Tony Hisgett/Wikimedia Commons)

The view south over the Tiber Valley from the veranda of the Hotel Giotto's bar, June 2007. In the summer of 1944, the pilots of 244 Wing used the hotel as an officers' rest centre. (Author's own)

In a room at the back of Castelnuovo's café is a display cabinet with recovered pieces of Desmond's Spitfire Mk LF IXe, 8 June 2007. (Author's own)

RoAF Museum in Fusignano, 28 July 2011. Author is on the right, next to Marco Maiani. (Author's own)

Desmond's medal collection. (Author's own)

CHAPTER 16

601 Squadron – Spitfires Over Anzio

Italy
12 November 1943–24 January 1944

Those front-line pilots who had been rested from ops after the end of the war in Tunisia and North Africa began to drift back to their new postings, many of which were in Italy. They frequently took up leadership positions on the squadrons and wings based there; their combat experience would be vital to the upcoming offensives in the Italian campaign.

Muriel knew her brother had been specifically asked to return to 601 Squadron but did not know who had made the request. The citation for Desmond's second DFC states: 'His keenness during his first tour of duty was such that his squadron requested his return.'[1] There had been two changes in leadership of the squadron and two on the wing in the six months since Desmond had been with them, not to mention losses and replacements of serving pilots. Yet, someone somewhere had kept him in mind, and he made the long journey back in mid-November 1943.

Unknown to Desmond, during the Badoglio armistice a couple of months earlier, Ray Sherk had escaped from his prison camp in central Italy when the camp's Italian guards had taken advantage of the armistice and simply walked away. Rather than wait for the Germans to take over, Ray and several others decided to head for the hills. They found shelter with the partisans and moved from village to village over several weeks until Ray made it to Allied lines. He heard 601 Squadron was now at Foggia, near the east coast, and made his way there. On arrival, Ray walked over to the mess tent, lifted the flap and called out, 'Hi, fellas. I'm back.' Faces he did not recognise looked back at him, then a voice muttered, 'And who the hell are you?' Ray returned to England a few days later and was posted to 401 Squadron to fly Spitfires over France. Desmond arrived a few days after Ray had left, unaware he had, once again, just missed meeting his Canadian mate.[2]

While Desmond had been resting from ops, 601 Squadron had followed the Allied armies over from Africa, providing air cover for them first during the invasion of Sicily, then the subsequent crossing of the Straits of Messina into the toe of Italy. From there, the Allies had moved steadily northwards, pushing the German defensive line back onto the Sangro river. The squadron now comprised over 250 men of all ranks. They had been stationed at Foggia for a little over six weeks when Desmond joined them.

Foggia is in the centre of a vast plain, almost all of which was, at that time at least, devoted to growing wheat. The land was well irrigated by many small streams and was in the lee of mountains to the far north. Communications and living conditions, albeit in tented quarters, were very good, but there were highly prevalent diseases around such as malaria (especially around Foggia itself), typhus, enteric fever and bacillary dysentery. Strict hygiene rules were observed, and every reasonable precaution taken so casualties of illness could be kept to a minimum.

The Army had taken control of Foggia town and administered the water supply point from which the various nearby military units drew their fresh water supplies. The water was purified first by adding four scoops of chlorinating powder to every 100 gallons. The Army field hygiene unit also provided a hot shower facility in Foggia for all personnel.

Food was the standard 'compo', or compound rations – mainly bully beef and hard tack biscuits with some tinned substances and sweets or chocolate – but where possible the catering staff cooked meals for everyone in a trailer-type cookhouse. Sanitation consisted of bucket-and-seat-style latrines, with about one for every twenty men. Refuse and swill were collected by the Sanitary Squad (at least that was their official title) in 45-gallon fuel drums and taken away to be buried. Individual latrines and collection drums were all supposed to have properly fitting lids to make them fly proof. Sleeping and living accommodation for the pilots was in large 180lb ridge tents, which slept four or five to each one. These, along with the administration quarters (messes, HQ, sick quarters and stores), were about a quarter of a mile (400yds) from the runway, while the different flights and maintenance sections were closer to the dispersed aircraft and much closer to the runway.[3]

On 15 October, the then CO of 601 Squadron, Sqn Ldr Stanislaw Skalski (another skilled and highly decorated pilot), left to return to England to serve as wing leader of 131 Polish Wing at Northolt, North London. The man who came in from 145 Squadron to replace Skalski was a South African fighter ace, Maj Bennie Osler DFC.[4]

Of the senior appointments, the commanding officer of 244 Wing was Gp Capt Brian Kingcome, who had taken up the post following the death of his friend Ian Gleed in Tunisia. The wing leader (a flying appointment) was Wg Cdr Wilfred G.G. Duncan-Smith.[5]

After a change in wing structure in September 1943, 92 Squadron and 417 Squadron (RCAF) joined 601 and 145 Squadrons. No. 92 Squadron was now led by the New Zealand ace Sqn Ldr Evan 'Rosie' Mackie – so nicknamed because of his rosy complexion. No. 417 Squadron was under the leadership of the tough talking, tough flying Canadian Stan Turner. Turner had been a colleague of Douglas Bader when Bader led the Canadian 242 Squadron. Turner was a Battle of Britain veteran, an expert marksman and brilliant pilot destined for higher command, but as soon as he was given charge of a wing, he was demoted again because of his habit of upsetting senior officers with his straight talking and blunt manner.[6]

Desmond's return was marred by bad weather, which held up any operational flying for three days from 8 November. As Ray had found out before him, 601 was practically a new squadron for Desmond now. They still flew the venerable Mk V Spitfires but were beginning to receive and convert to the newer and faster Mk VIII. All the pilots Desmond had known six months earlier had left. Among his former colleagues, Jerry Westenra, his former flight commander, was now in charge of 93 Squadron, part of 324 Wing based in Naples across on the west coast. Babe Whitamore was away in the Far East fighting the Japanese and would soon be promoted to squadron leader. Desmond rejoined his old flight – B Flight – but it was not quite the return he might have hoped for. When the weather cleared enough to fly a few days later, Desmond began with a few routine flights in the new Mk VIII to familiarise himself with the aircraft and the area.

That Saturday, Desmond and the other pilots in the wing attended a ceremony for the official presentation of a squadron crest to 145's CO, Sqn Ldr Lance Wade, made by the AOC AVM Harry Broadhurst, who paid tribute to Wade, who he extolled as the most successful commanding officer the squadron had ever had. Two months later, tragedy struck. Wade was killed when his single-engined Auster went into a spin during a routine flight over Foggia. 'Wildcat' Wade died leaving a reputation as the highest-scoring American ace to have served solely with the RAF, his personal tally standing at twenty-five.[7]

Desmond was ready to begin offensive operations again on 14 November, and his first taste of action took place the next morning. He was in a flight of eight Spitfires that took off immediately after dawn to patrol the Avezzano area. They spotted a train with fourteen goods wagons and several locos in the station at Avezzano and proceeded to attack them.

Desmond made five attack runs on the station against two locos and the train itself. The locomotive at the front of the goods train and one of those by the shed were both destroyed and the rest damaged, with Desmond claiming one of those destroyed.[8]

This type of mission would become a key part of the RAF's and DAF's future activity in Italy. Attacks on supply lines had been vital during the North Africa campaign of course, but the overwhelming majority of fighter-bomber attacks had been on MT. In Italy, there was an extensive railway network stretching all the way back into northern Italy, Austria and Germany, so attacks on key points all along that network, and along the road network too, would form a regular source of work for 244 Wing and other fighter-bomber units of the RAF. An added element of risk to the pilots was that many of the roads and railways wound their way through steep valleys and mountain passes, which made it more hazardous to pull away safely from an attack.

On the plus side, the pilots were now flying a faster and more manoeuvrable fighter. The Mk VIII Spitfire was superior to the Mk V in terms of both speed and handling and similar in performance to the Mk IX. Desmond chose to fly the Mk VIII type whenever he could, and it made up all but six of all the ops he flew through November and December. His experience in low-level ground attack in the Western Desert, plus recent gunnery training, saw him start to increase his score of enemy targets destroyed, which now included locomotives, goods wagons, gun emplacements and trucks.

Several ops were to patrol overhead enemy positions along the 'bombline' that ran close to the Sangro River, but these gave very little opportunity to engage with Luftwaffe fighters. On one occasion, when they did see ME109s, Desmond described how he and his section 'chased four of them but [I] could not jettison the overload tank and so failed to catch them. [I] got to within 600ft from one but was promptly "jumped" by four Spits. Bags of flak.'

By flying so low, the Spitfires were exposing themselves to more return fire from enemy flak guns positioned on hillsides or mounted on railway wagons at either end of a train, and small arms fire from any soldiers in the vicinity. Much of it was intense and often too close for comfort. Soon, as the Allied armies continued to advance, the fighter squadrons moved forward to a new base at Canne, a former Regia Aeronautica and Luftwaffe airfield.

On the morning of 10 December, the squadron was told to expect a visit from a VIP. Rumour had it Winston Churchill would again be visiting the front-line fighter squadrons of the DAF, as he had in the run-up to the battle of El Alamein. In the 24 hours leading up to the visit, senior staff officers and 'top brass' suddenly arrived at Canne from all over Italy. The Chief of the Air Staff had flown over in a Mosquito to be met by the C-in-C Mediterranean Air Command, the AOC of Mediterranean Allied Tactical Air Forces and the AOC DAF. Sadly, it was not to be. Churchill failed to arrive. The news came through a day or two later that he had, in fact, been taken seriously ill in Cairo. At the time, this was thought by Churchill's physician to be a mild heart attack, so news of it was kept quiet, because of the political ramifications at this stage of the war. It was essential Churchill remained steadfast and vital in the public eye.

Flying operations continued, and that morning the CO briefed the squadron for what was initially to be a patrol of the Ascoli-Terni sector. The formation included Desmond, Moore, George and Colyer, plus three others led by Maj Osler. The formation took off at 11.15 a.m. and headed north, parallel with the coast, then turned inland from Ascoli to approach Terni from the east. Terni is 50 miles north of Rome and marked the intersection of four main railway lines running out of the city in the four ordinal compass directions. As the Spitfires approached Terni, they spotted targets of opportunity in Terni's railway station and goods yards.

Osler instructed Desmond to keep his section 'up top' as cover. He scanned the town beneath and identified his own target – a locomotive at the head of a long train of tankers snaking out of the main terminal. Osler then assigned each pilot in his section a target area and a task. Finally, he called his section into line astern, and one by one they peeled off to attack Terni from about 4,000ft.

Desmond held his section in formation and circled over the railyards in a wide arc. He watched as Osler and the others sped headlong towards the targets below. Down on the platforms, the air-raid sirens began to wail. Civilians ran for shelter, and gunners cocked their weapons in readiness and turned to face the swooping Spitfires.

Osler's section strafed the area and destroyed two locos that were hauling fifteen petrol tankers. Osler claimed one of the locos after seeing his rounds blow it up. Desmond's section was then called down to join in. The gunners had anticipated the remaining fighters would eventually attack too, and anti-aircraft fire pock-marked the sky around the diving Spitfires as they followed Desmond. Bright-orange streaks of tracer rounds sliced past their aircraft. They would make just one pass over the railyards. At least half of the tankers were hit, and the resulting fires set every single one of the others ablaze, causing massive explosions and fuel fires. It was a spectacular result in the face of intense light-calibre anti-aircraft fire. All eight Spits fled the scene at low level, trying to dodge the flak and tracers that followed them. Desmond's aeroplane was hit in the wingtip, but he managed to return safely to Canne.

Desmond noted that '100,000 gallons of petrol [went] for a loop'. The initial assessment had been 60,000 gallons but this was revised upwards soon after and allowed 601 Squadron to chalk it up as their biggest single result up to that time.[9] Consequently, a war reporter turned up at the base and asked to speak to some of those who had taken part. Despite being the leader, Osler let Desmond describe the attack on the German freight trains.

Back home in Yorkshire, as Desmond's family prepared for their second Christmas without him, Sarah was reading the local newspaper one evening when her eye was drawn to a brief interview about a 'Harewood Officer Flying Spitfire in Italy'. After telling the girls about it, she passed it to Muriel who added the clipping to her scrapbook of Desmond's exploits. The article read:

> Flying Officer Desmond Ibbotson one of the pilots acting as top cover for the attacking aircraft said the railway yards at Terni had been pounded by our light bombers. 'When we got over we saw that sheds had been flattened, locomotives were useless hulks and well over 100 wagons were smashed up,' he continued. 'I saw the two locomotives standing detached with steam up. Our Spitfires dived in to attack, and one of the engines blew up in a great cloud of steam. The other locomotive caught fire. Next I saw our chaps strafe 15 petrol bowsers standing on the track and one after the other they went up in flames until at least eight were on fire. When we left the fires were spreading all along the line of petrol bowsers, and there was a cloud of smoke to fully 2,000ft. The enemy ground defences appeared to be taken by surprise, but there was a lot of flak as our planes made off. All our aircraft returned safely from this operation.'[10]

Rumours were circulating that the Germans were beginning to pull out from Chieti and move northwards once more to new defensive lines. Several small formations were sent up by 601 Squadron to scout out any troop or vehicle movements, engage them and report back what they saw. Soon after, it was decided to launch a raid on the area around the Sangro River just after dawn on 11 December. Four Spitfires were sent out to Chieti. The first pair flew along the coast but saw very little. They only managed to damage one vehicle. The other pair (Desmond as Blue leader and Sgt Colyer as his number two) flew on to Tollo, inland of Pescara on the east coast. Here, they chanced on a German Army camp and immediately set about strafing the vehicles, tents and soldiers. They attacked three trucks, setting one on fire and damaging two of them, before destroying another on the road west of Chieti town. But the return fire was intense, and Desmond was hit in the wingtip again as he and Colyer both made their escape at very low level.

This was the first Rhubarb Desmond had flown in Italy and was a throwback to those sorties he had flown over France with 54 Squadron when they had to race back to England at wave-top height to avoid the enemy guns. Now they were racing back to the Allied lines across fields and down valleys at tree-top height.

As December went on, the tally and type of targets mounted. On some raids, Desmond continued to lead sections as 'top cover': protection for the others who went in to attack ground targets, where he could only watch as the other Spitfires successfully shot up their targets. On other raids, Desmond did take part and was also strafing numerous trucks, motorbikes, armoured vehicles and, occasionally, a staff car.

On 22 December, Desmond flew a Mk VIII that had a Merlin 66 engine fitted. He had flown VIIIs many times, but this new engine had the wonderfully named Bendix-Stromberg two-stage injection supercharger fitted at the back of the engine, which fed more air, under pressure, into the cylinders. The petrol used by the RAF at this stage had a higher octane rating than that used for car engines. It burned more efficiently in the denser air below 10,000ft, giving greater power. As altitude increases, air density decreases, leaving proportionally less oxygen for the petrol to burn in, leading to a loss of power. To overcome this, the supercharger fed compressed air into the engine, from a scoop fitted under the chin of the Spitfire. This increased the fuel–air mix by increasing the proportion and density of air in each of the Merlin's cylinders which, when used with 100 octane petrol specially developed by Esso, enabled a significant increase in boost and horsepower at altitudes above 10,000ft.[11]

The supercharger (or 'blower' as pilots called it) kicked in automatically at altitudes over 10,000ft, with no warning, which could be quite disconcerting. The first clue was the sudden loud noise as the engine revs surged, followed immediately after by a 'kick in the pants' as the Spitfire lurched forward. That prompted Desmond's one word reaction about this flight: 'Wow!' The Merlin 66 engine was not a standard fit to the Mk VIII, but it would be to the Mk IX. Desmond's flight in this particular version was just a routine air test but it was in a Spitfire that carried the aircraft registration 'UF-Q' ('UF' denoted the squadron, 'Q' the individual aeroplane). It is notable because Desmond chose to fly this particular Spitfire whenever it was available because of its engine fit and handling. Moreover, when he was promoted to flight lieutenant, he could choose which Spitfire to fly, and therefore this would later become his personal aeroplane. Unknown to him, of course, was that sixty-three years later, when the RAF was looking for a Spitfire to fly in tribute to him, the one they chose would carry these same code letters.

There was a short break, just for Christmas Day, in part because the weather turned atrocious: pouring rain lasted the whole day. Under shelter though, spirits were high. With the officers and senior NCOs serving the other ranks, the cooks managed to present a full traditional roast dinner, and sweets, cigarettes, fruit, nuts and beer were in good supply. Each man had four bottles of beer, and there was a parcel of seventy cigarettes on each plate. Desmond was a non-smoker, but cigarettes were a tradeable currency, either round the squadron or with locals. Italian labourers, employed in the airfield workshops, were also invited along for the feast which, along with the airmen present, meant around 300 people had to be served in two sittings – served, as always at Christmas, by the officers, much to the amazement of the Italians.

With the rain easing off, operations resumed on Boxing Day with a short patrol over the nearby harbour. Desmond 'did not feel too happy with a sore head' from the previous day's festivities, and he was not the only one. A common cure for a pilot's hangover was to switch the oxygen supply from 'Normal' to '100%'. Officially, the Normal setting was for breathing regular concentrations of air when flying at altitudes of below 10,000ft. Above 10,000ft, in thinner air, aircrew switched to 100 per cent and breathed pure oxygen to ward off the potentially lethal effects of hypoxia (a lack of oxygen). In the deep chill of an Italian winter, breathing pure oxygen fed from a spherical tank in the fuselage behind his seat felt like a cold shower for the lungs and tasted sweet on the back of the throat. A couple of deep inhalations helped enrich the blood as the oxygen reached deep into the muscles. As the blood circulated round his body, and the little particles of chilled, pure oxygen reached Desmond's brain, the feeling was not one of euphoria but more of clarity of thought and relief from fatigue as the alcohol-infused fog that had settled in his head began to lift. Desmond landed feeling like he had at least brushed away the cobwebs.

The following day, the squadron sent up three separate patrols and, on the first two, destroyed six locos, damaged four, destroyed one wagon and damaged nine more and a lorry. On the last patrol, led that afternoon by Maj Osler, Desmond was part of a formation of eight sent out to scout around as far north up the eastern coast as Ancona and Porto Civitanova again.

At other times and in other places, Christmas might have seen a longer suspension in hostilities, but not in central Italy. Somewhere near Ancona, some German soldiers, their vehicles parked up to form a *laager*, or rest area, had decided to have a break and play football. Spotting the vehicles at the side of a field, Osler promptly called his men in to the attack. Dropping down to very low level, the eight Spitfires set about strafing the temporary encampment and the vehicles. Several of the footballing soldiers were caught in the blizzard of gunfire as they ran for cover. The Spitfires set a 'five-tonner' truck ablaze before turning away to attack more trains and locomotives on the railway not far away. From this, they destroyed three more locos and damaged three.

During one of the rare dry periods, the squadron was visited again by a war reporter and official photographer. The backdrop was their current base, the airfield at Canne, and all the pilots were assembled in front of Spitfire Mk VIII, No. JF485, for what was a rare photograph of the entire squadron together.

Sixty years later, as I followed Desmond's career through Italy, I came across this same photo on the Australian War Museum website and immediately recognised it. I ordered an A4-size copy and, when it arrived, took it to show Muriel.

The men are dressed anything but formally. The image shows a variety of uniforms, different pieces mixed together. All of it is standard issue clothing but much is worn in a non-standard way, the DAF way – for example, blue or green European theatre battledress jackets worn with sand-coloured desert campaign trousers. Some pilots wear flying boots; others, like Desmond, wear shoes. Many have moustaches, and almost all have their hats cocked to one side or tilted back.

As Muriel and I chatted about what I had found, we looked through her photograph album again. When I found the right picture, I carefully removed it from its corner mountings and turned it over. On the back, in slightly faded blue ink, was the official oval stamp of the War Office.

It had clearly been taken at the same time, but Muriel's copy showed the pilots being dismissed. As you might expect, there front and centre in the picture, just off the left shoulder of his CO, 'Bennie' Osler, was Desmond, still looking straight up at the camera and grinning. He looks like many of them do, relaxed, confident and smiling despite the conditions.

As happy as the pilots were at that moment, for one of them at least, it was most likely to have been the last photograph taken of him. Just two days later, on the second mission of the day, the squadron suffered another loss. Desmond's flight commander, Capt Lawrence Robertson Stuart Waugh of the SAAF, was last seen descending to attack two enemy trucks on the Avezzano–Popoli road at about 10 a.m. on 31 December. His colleagues stayed around to look for him, searching the area for as long as fuel would allow, but they could not find any trace of the aircraft.

Osler concluded that Waugh's Spitfire must have been hit by enemy gunfire and he had been compelled to force land somewhere away from the target area but still some distance from friendly lines, so he was reported as 'Missing Believed Safe'. Waugh was a popular leader and had been very well respected as a determined fighter pilot.[12] His skill and courage had earned him a DFC. But he had been shot down, and his whereabouts, and whether he was alive or dead, were unknown. His replacement as B Flight commander was Flt Lt 'Hindoo' Henderson.

The CO of 92 Squadron, the New Zealand ace Sqn Ldr Evan 'Rosie' Mackie, recalled the period between Christmas 1943 and the New Year of 1944:

> I can remember Christmas and the New Year, how cold it was, with ice and frost right down to the water's edge. Our airfield virtually ran down to the sea and our tents were not far away. I don't know how many blankets I used at night but there was a terrific weight of them – I know that! It was the only way I could keep warm.[13]

The weather closed in from the afternoon of New Year's Day 1944, with heavy snowfall across parts of the country to the north of Canne. Torrential rain and gale force winds soaked the pilots' tents wet through and blew many of them down. There were no New Year celebrations, because all personnel were engaged in 'hanging on to their effects'.[14] Overnight the squall blew itself out. The rain stopped, visibility cleared and while a brisk wind blew in, the ground dried out very quickly, and the airfield became serviceable once again.

From 3 January on, for the remainder of Desmond's second tour, the priority work of the four fighter squadrons of 244 Wing was directed towards the west and north-west of Italy. Then, in mid-January, the wing received orders to move south-west from Canne to Marcianise, north of Naples. Its task would be to provide air support to the Allied Fifth Army as it prepared to launch amphibious landings on the beaches around the coastal town of Anzio.

The geography of Italy, with the large central mountain range of the Apennines, meant ground troops were forced into hard fighting over rugged terrain, with every advantage to the defender, or onto the flat yet narrow coastal plains with little cover and softer, wetter terrain. This meant the best option for advancing the troops and keeping the momentum of Allied victory going was to send the forces round behind the German lines, by going out to sea and landing further up the coast in sufficient number to try to cut them off from reinforcements.

If successful, this would achieve two main aims: one, to leapfrog the main German defensive line, which would either enable the Allies to attack the Germans from behind or force them to retreat northwards to avoid being caught between two Allied lines of attack; two, once a beachhead was established and the Germans either destroyed, captured or forced northwards, it would enable the Allies to push for Rome and liberate a European capital city for the first time in the war.

Previous operations in Dieppe, Tunisia, Sicily and the Messina Straits had all demonstrated the need for air superiority to ensure landings were successful. Yet the war in Italy was still viewed as a 'soft' war, a drawn-out fight taking place in, as Churchill is widely believed to have described it, the 'soft underbelly of Europe'. Ask anyone who fought there, through the bitterest winter in nearly fifty years, and they would strongly disagree.

The Allied forces had struggled through the difficult mountainous terrain and unrelenting cold to make what progress they could across the frozen ground. Then, as spring came, the ground turned to thick, sticky mud. German resistance remained reliably stubborn, despite the supply problems inflicted on them by the RAF fighters shooting up their supply trucks and the combined RAF and USAAF bombing raids on railway stations, harbours and oil refineries.

The long-called-for 'second front' was still seen as being one that would be opened in northern France not in Italy. It was almost as though Italy was still the practice area, and Hitler's infamous Atlantic Wall was the real target. The build-up to it was beginning in earnest as men and materiel gathered in Britain to prepare for the Normandy landings, earmarked for some time in June 1944.

In the meantime, the landings on the western coast of Italy would not just be a major leap forward but would also tie up the German forces in defence, instead of being redeployed to the eastern or western theatres. This would help relieve a little pressure on the Soviet armies as well as slow up reinforcement of the defences in France.

Planning two such large-scale sets of amphibious landings meant the commanders of each theatre were left scrambling for equipment. For example, most of the ninety Landing Craft (Tanks) available to the Allies in the Mediterranean were kept busy ferrying troops to Italy from North Africa. Sixty-eight of them had been earmarked already for redeployment to England in December 1943, in readiness for the D-Day invasion. Therefore, Mediterranean commanders were forced to beg, steal, borrow and scrounge any type of vehicle, ship or aeroplane they could lay their hands on just to keep their operations in Italy going.[15]

The DAF fighter-bomber squadrons were moved across Italy to provide air cover and support for the Anzio landings, code name: Operation Shingle. The Millionaires now arrived at their new base, Marcianise.

At this time of year, in order to be over the patrol area for dawn, the Spitfires had to take off in complete darkness. Despite makeshift lighting, using flares along the sides of the runway, it was still hazardous.[16]

The landings at Anzio, preceded by air and sea bombardments, took place at 2 a.m. on Monday 22 January. The Allies landed at the Nettuno beaches only 30 miles south-south-east of Rome and near the small peninsula of Anzio, but well behind enemy lines. The Allied air raids of the previous few weeks on German positions behind Anzio and Nettuno had seemed to the Germans to be in support of operations taking place in the Cassino area, not a pre-invasion bombardment, and so the landings were practically unopposed from the air.

Desmond's short, repetitive annotations of 'Battle area patrol' or 'Invasion area patrol' account for almost all the ops he flew from January 1944 onwards. Even if they encountered bad weather and had to cut a patrol short, it still counted towards his tally of operational hours and, therefore, moved him closer to the end of his tour.

Given the proximity of the landings to the capital city, it is a mark of the determination and fighting resilience of the German Army that it would take the Allies until early June, well over four more months, to liberate Rome.

As soon as dawn broke on 23 January, a large force of Allied fighters was in the air – 601 Squadron sent up ten Spitfires, including Desmond, over the landing area first. Patrols rotated through the day. Despite the air cover, 601 had nothing to report since the Luftwaffe failed to put in a show of any kind.

In Desmond's logbook, there is nothing to distinguish 24 January from any other day of routine patrols. He just noted that he flew the operation but was 'recalled [due to] bad weather' after only 15 minutes. But a couple of pages further on is an entry I have never seen in anyone else's logbook. It was a terse message, with a distinctly legal tone about it, handwritten by Maj Osler. Muriel had never heard about it, nor had Desmond mentioned it.

Major Osler briefed his pilots early on the morning of Wednesday 24 January for a patrol over the Nettuno landing beaches. The squadron would put up eight Spitfires for the operation, flying in two sections of four. Osler would lead Red Section with Colyer, Sgt Henderson and Sgt Ross. Desmond was chosen to lead Blue Section, with Cy Yarnell flying as his number two. Lt Wearne and Flt Sgt George made up the second pair in Blue Section. Take-off was planned for 8.35 a.m.

Approaching the hold point, which was about two-thirds down the main runway, they lined up to complete their checks before moving onto the runway for take-off. The CO led his wingman out, turning towards the end of the remaining one-third of runway. At the end, they turned round as normal in order to have the full length of runway to get airborne. They took off in pairs, one Spitfire on each side of the runway centreline, the wingman set slightly back from his leader. As Osler and Colyer roared past, the second pair in Red Section, Henderson and Ross, taxied out, turned at the end and prepared for take-off. Ross went first. Henderson paused, then pushed his throttle forward to full power.

Desmond saw a Spitfire pass in front of him, then radioed Cy Yarnell and told him to follow him out and eased the throttle forward. He glanced up to the far end of the runway and saw Ross lifting off, wheels slowly ascending into the wings. Believing the complete section had taken off, he crossed the centreline, kicked the rudder to his right to make the turn and simultaneously moved the throttle forward again. However, Desmond wasn't paying attention. He did not realise that 'Red 4', Sgt Henderson, was actually still on the runway and making his take-off run directly towards him at that very moment. The rules of the air are quite clear: aircraft taking off have priority over those taxiing, and those landing have priority over all others, whether in the circuit or on the ground. That's how it was then and how it remains today.

Henderson's Spitfire was, by now, travelling at around 80mph and accelerating up towards take-off speed, and Desmond was directly in its path. Henderson eased the nose forward to lift the tailwheel off the runway and, in the dim early morning light, saw the familiar shape of another Spitfire fill his windscreen. By the time either pilot realised that a collision was imminent, it was too late. Desmond shouted, 'Oh shit!', ducked his head and braced for the inevitable impact.

There was a hard 'thump' followed by the high-pitched scream of scraping metal. Desmond's Spitfire spun round abruptly, banged down hard on the ground and came to a stop, leaning sharply to one side. As the noise subsided, he realised he was alive, but still strapped into the cockpit. Whether in the air or on the ground, a pilot's worst nightmare is fire; being trapped in a burning aircraft is a horrible way to die.[17]

Desmond tried to collect his thoughts and act rationally. Using his left hand, he pulled the throttle back, cut the fuel feed and switched the engine off, while simultaneously using his right hand to undo both his seat harness and parachute straps. He had left the canopy slightly open for just such an event, despite the freezing winter air the propellor had been blowing in. The canopy frame was still intact, and the hood slid back easily.

Desmond scrambled out of the cockpit and onto the ground just beneath. Stumbling away from the wreck, he turned to check the Spitfire. His once graceful-looking aeroplane was now bent and broken. The starboard wing had sheared off just outboard of the cannon, collapsing the undercarriage on that side. The propellor was missing a couple of blades, having detached and spun off as they hit the ground at about 1,000rpm and left deep gouges on their departure. Henderson's Spitfire had also clipped and bent the entire tailplane of Desmond's Spitfire as it passed by, before coming to rest flat on its belly a few yards ahead. Desmond realised Henderson's canopy was still shut. Then he heard the roar of the other Spitfires' engines in the near distance. Desmond ran to the holding point. Yarnell saw him approaching, pulled the throttle to 'idle' and slid his canopy back. He unclipped his mask and yelled out,

'You okay, Ibby?!'

'Yes, fine!' Desmond shouted back. He ran round the tip of Yarnell's wing, jumped up the wing root and crouched at the cockpit. Cy asked if Henderson was okay. Desmond turned and watched the canopy slide back slowly on the pancaked Spitfire off to his right. Desmond told Cy to take his section and continue the patrol. He would catch them up in another Spitfire soon. Desmond then stepped off the back of the wing and ran over to Henderson's Spitfire from where a head was now slowly emerging.

Yarnell clipped his mask back onto his helmet, rebriefed Wearne and George and they took off for the Anzio area. Desmond reached Henderson's cockpit just in time to give him a helping hand out. Henderson took it and stepped over the side.

Desmond just said, 'Are you all right?' 'I think so,' said Henderson. As they began to walk away Henderson apologised, 'I'm sorry, Sir. I just didn't see you till the last second, and you were just so close I couldn't get out of the way.' 'Look, I'm afraid it was my fault,' said Desmond before ushering Henderson off to get a checkup. Desmond ran towards the line of Spitfires that were standing ready. Some of the groundcrew had begun to run towards the wrecked Spitfires. Desmond shouted at them to turn back and get another one warmed up as Henderson walked off towards the medical tent.[18]

Desmond found a spare Spitfire and took off just 15 minutes later. He caught up with the remaining six aircraft and continued the operation, heading for Nettuno. However, as he approached the patrol area, the weather worsened, and the Spitfires had to be called back early. Desmond never so much as hinted at having had a serious collision with another aircraft in his logbook, or even that he was delayed taking off – just a brief note that the bad weather cut the operation short.

When the pilots landed and Osler heard what had happened, he had no choice but to formally investigate the matter. In the past, when

Desmond had crashed (as opposed to being shot down) or had an accident, it had been the result of a technical failure with the aircraft. This was the first time he had caused an accident with another aeroplane. It showed what could happen if he allowed his keenness and overconfidence to get the better of him. Desmond faced another 'carpeting', or 'one-way conversation', with the CO. Only this time, he knew this was his fault and disciplinary action would surely follow.

CHAPTER 17

601 Squadron – Final Victories

Italy
24 January–30 March 1944

When Osler had completed his investigation, received reports back from the engineers on the extent of the damage to the Spitfires and spoken to the pilots involved, he wrote up the outcome and the endorsement in Desmond's logbook. Desmond's Spitfire that day was JF754:

> F/O D. Ibbotson. DFC. At Marcianise L.G. on 24.1.44 through gross carelessness damaged His Majesty's aircraft Spitfire JF754 and JF780 in that he taxied out on to the runway preparatory to take off in front of another aircraft already taking off.

Signed M.S. Osler Major DFC Officer Commanding 601 Squadron.

The wording of the endorsement laid the blame squarely on Desmond and his 'gross carelessness'. He had been too keen to get airborne and, at a critical moment, just not looked where he was going. It was fortunate that neither Desmond nor anyone else had been seriously injured or killed. Although the Spitfires were full of fuel and ammunition, if they had been carrying 250lb bombs when the crash happened, the outcome might have been very different, causing casualties and putting the runway out of action at a time when the armies landing at Anzio were reliant on air support to establish their beachhead.

The squadron had a lot of work to do, and Desmond was a very experienced pilot and promising leader, but even so, Osler was obliged to apply service discipline appropriately. Desmond did not fly the day after the accident, but he did resume normal operations after that. His experiences during operations in the desert had taught him that even when you were knocked about a bit, shot down, crash-landed or even had bullets pinging round the cockpit, it could have happened to anyone. Indeed, in North Africa it had happened to nearly everyone. The prevailing attitude was, get back to work and carry on. Humour and alcohol were readily available if you needed an outlet, but otherwise any self-pity was rarely entertained.

The Luftwaffe had as many problems with the weather as the Allies did, and the pilots up on escort missions to 'delouse' the Allied bombers only saw the ME109s and FW190s at a distance. The Luftwaffe had diverted squadrons away to shore up the eastern front as the Soviet Red Army advanced. The squadrons left had less-experienced pilots in them and they were less keen to stay around and fight.

Just after his accident, Desmond was part of a twelve-aircraft formation for an early afternoon patrol. Maj Osler led three sections of four Spitfires – Red, Blue and Pink. Desmond was number two to the CO in Red Section (kept where Osler could see him), with the Belgian André Eid and Desmond's flight commander, Hindoo Henderson, leading the other two sections respectively. They patrolled the beaches at Nettuno at heights between 4,000 and 20,000ft without incident. Then an ME109 was seen in the Cisterna area diving in from 10,000ft. The fighter may have spotted the formation above. No sooner had Desmond seen it than it did a 180° turn, at which point Desmond left his section and gave chase. He was joined in the pursuit by four Kittyhawks. He wrote later, 'The [109] dived into its own ack-ack so I let the Kitties continue the chase.' But that was not all. As Desmond got to about a 1,000yd range from the ME109, he saw another aircraft away on his starboard side. Thinking this was also an enemy fighter, he turned with it, ready to get into a position from which he could open fire. The fatter nose housing a single engine, the squared-off wingtips and teardrop canopy made the fighter look, from a distance, to be a German FW190, but as Desmond closed on it, thumb hovering over the 'fire' button, he could see the stars and stripes on the top of the wings and realised it was an American P-47 Thunderbolt.[1] At that, he broke off the attack and climbed to rejoin the CO's section. Only a few days later, he intercepted and nearly shot down an American Mustang.

In early February, the Luftwaffe was finally up in sufficient numbers for Desmond to get the fight he had been itching for. Over the course of several days, the Luftwaffe had been causing a nuisance to the Allies with raids on the shipping in the bay, including the first ever use of guided bombs flown by radio control from the twin-engined bombers that launched them.

Among the other squadrons active on 7 February, eight Spitfires from 601 were scrambled at just after 2.30 p.m. This time Flt Lt W.B. Hay led Red Section with 'Pete' Pote as his wingman. Desmond and Cy Yarnell (newly promoted to flight lieutenant) were paired with each other again as Reds 3 and 4 respectively. Sgt Henderson, Sticky, Tilly and Flt Sgt Parker followed on as numbers 5 to 8.

They were to patrol at between 13,000 and 20,500ft. As they reached their base height, they saw three sections of four FW190s above them at 17,000ft, flying in line abreast formation and slightly stepped up. The Germans then began to dive down at the Allied shipping moored in the bay below, and two bombs were seen to burst in the sea as a result. Hay ordered his Spitfires to engage, and one by one they banked over and followed him down towards the FW190s. As they did so, the British and American guns on the ships and on the beachhead beneath opened up on them too.

Nevertheless, the Spitfires managed to split up the enemy formation. In the ensuing dogfight, Desmond and Cy Yarnell each claimed an FW190 as damaged.[2] It was the first time in nearly ten months since Desmond had made any claim against an enemy fighter, and the 'friendly fire' they received back was unwelcome. Desmond wrote, '12 FW190s bombed. Gave chase & only got a damaged. Our own flak was terrific how the hell they expect Spits to cope I don't know.' During this time, the DAF squadrons suffered a spate of engine failures and forced-landings. Shortly after they had intercepted the FW190s, another patrol had been over the Nettuno beaches when Sgt Henderson suffered an engine failure. Mistaking a field with white edging near the beach to be Nettuno airstrip, he made to land there but realised too late it was just a farmer's field and ended up belly landing his Spitfire in it.

Henderson's engine failure came on the back of several the wing had experienced over recent days, including Desmond's. The spate of such incidents caused real and deep concern among the squadron commanders, engineering officers and pilots, because it was a problem not unique to any unit or particular aircraft. The 244 Wing staff began to suspect the fuel supplies had been sabotaged, so ordered detailed assessments to be carried out. The results of these inspections led them to believe some foreign matter, possibly copper sulphate, had been introduced into the petrol, which then caused the engines to cut out at random.

Although the British and American armies handled the delivery of the petrol from ship and transport aircraft to the landing grounds, the squadrons used Italian locals as additional labour to help refuel the aircraft. The problem was found to be most severe on 417 Squadron, so its aircraft were temporarily grounded while their tanks were emptied and cleaned and the petrol bowsers given the same treatment. As word spread, it emerged that the Spitfire VIIIs and IXs of 324 Wing were also experiencing the same problems, with the result that 111 Squadron aircraft were also grounded for inspections, tests and remedial maintenance work.[3]

Two days later, with this operational crisis threatening to severely disrupt the air support available to the beleaguered troops in the Anzio beachhead, more experts flew out from Rolls-Royce in England, to carry out further petrol tests and assess the foreign matter found on previous inspections.

Leading the team of inspectors was Ronnie Harker. Two years earlier Harker had test flown a new American fighter, the P-51 Mustang, at Duxford. To improve its performance above 15,000ft, he came up with the idea of fitting a Rolls-Royce Merlin engine instead of the American Allison. The result was utterly transformative, and the Mustang became one of the finest all-round fighters of the whole war. When fitted with long-range drop tanks as well, the Mustang became the first fighter to be able to escort American bombers all the way to Berlin and back.[4]

After examining the troublesome Merlins in Italy, Harker declared the mysterious substance to be rust not copper sulphate and that there was nothing wrong with the Rolls-Royce engines themselves. What was happening was that the squadrons were using old fuel, which had been decanted into equally old drums, where it was being contaminated with rust or other particulate matter. When the Merlin engines developed maximum power for a lengthy period, this particulate matter smeared the sensitive plug points, thus causing a complete bank of cylinders to cut out,[5] the engine to fail and pilots like poor old Sgt Henderson to end up in a random field, miles from base.

The unfortunate result was that the mechanics on the ground now had to change the plugs after every mission flown by each and every Spitfire. This significantly reduced the problem almost immediately. In the meantime, consignments of petrol started to be vetted before being dispatched to the squadrons in sealed drums. Upon arrival it was 'chammied' (filtered) twice more before it reached a Spitfire's fuel tank. Though the view taken on suspected sabotage waned, the wing staff took no chances. They ordered extra guards to be put on the airfield day and night and raised the alert level to the highest state.[6]

Despite these efforts, problems still occasionally continued to affect pilots in the wing. Whatever the fuel and engine problems, support missions still had to be flown. Desmond experienced three engine failures during this period but was fortunate not to have to make forced- or crash-landings.

During February and March, Desmond flew almost continuously and consistently in one particular Spitfire, a Mk VIII (registration JG164), UF-Q. He was flying it when he shot down his last enemy fighters of the war. He was flying it when Vesuvius erupted and he saw the volcano spread its massive ash clouds over the Bay of Naples and, perhaps to prove he actually was a Spitfire pilot and not just another pilot 'shooting a line', he flew it when he met a young WAAF who, unlike his other girlfriends, would be with him for the rest of his short life.

The last of Desmond's victories came in February and March. Throughout these weeks, whether escorting large formations of Allied bombers, or strafing enemy vehicles, gun emplacements or even an army barracks on one occasion, the Spitfires of 601 Squadron had to contend with very heavy barrages of flak. This came from both the German and the Allied forces. Through inexperience, fear or poor aircraft recognition skills, the friendly forces Desmond and his mates were trying to protect were too often the ones also trying to shoot them down. Some of Desmond's notes highlight the problem: 'Terrific flak, awful bombing, 4 bombers shot down by FLAK! 5 'chutes seen', 'Tour of Italy and flak!', 'Recce battle area for M/T Flak!', 'Flak! 5 bombers hit, 1 bale [sic]out.'

The anti-aircraft fire ranged from light machine guns carried by soldiers to medium-calibre guns mounted on decks and vehicles to heavy guns. These included the infamous and deadly 88mm, which sent shells upwards of 6 miles to explode in a thin smoky cloud of steel shrapnel balls, at the same altitude as the bombers and escorting fighters.

In a period of less than a week, Desmond noted several of his colleagues were hit by flak and forced to take to their parachutes. Two of them went down over the Mediterranean and were eventually rescued by an Air Sea Rescue launch.

On 19 February, a section of five aircraft from A Flight (designated 'White Section') along with five from B Flight (designated 'Black Section') took off at 9.10 a.m. to patrol over Nettuno at 14,000ft. They were protecting a formation of forty-eight B-25 Mitchell bombers that were coming in over the coast heading for Genzano di Roma, a small lakeside town 15 miles to the north of Nettuno and halfway to Rome. Desmond was leading both the formation of ten Spitfires and Black Section, with Cy Yarnell as his wingman. At 10 a.m. Desmond was radioed by control, who reported enemy aircraft over Velletri preparing to attack Anzio. The ground controller ordered the Spitfires to the Anzio area. Desmond radioed back and told control he wasn't on that mission and was instead escorting a formation of bombers to Genzano. But control insisted and again ordered him there.

As the seconds ticked by and the Spitfires continued north, Desmond faced a difficult choice. The others in the formation were all listening in. What should he do? The new orders were a change to the original mission, but the wing was, after all, tasked with air cover for the ground forces in the beachhead area – and the troops were likely going to come under air attack in a few minutes. Diverting a formation of ten Spitfires already in the air meant the enemy could be intercepted and soldiers on the ground spared. But leaving the bombers meant they would be vulnerable, and recent losses had been higher than normal. It was not unknown for a small section of enemy fighters to try to draw the fighter escort away, leaving the bombers open to attack from a second, larger enemy fighter formation. Either way, Desmond's decision would now mean disobeying orders. But which ones?

As they drew nearer to the Anzio area, Desmond caught sight of the formation of B-25s they were to rendezvous with, a few thousand feet below them crossing the coast. There were also nine enemy aircraft flying above them at 17,000ft.

Desmond decided to stay with the bombers and fly with them to the target area. He watched as the Germans manoeuvred into position, then dived to attack them. Desmond ordered White Section to keep their position close to the bombers. He then called the rest of Black Section, which had the height advantage as top cover, to intercept the German fighters. These were a mix of ME109s, FW190s and Italian MC202 Thunderbolts repainted in Luftwaffe colours.

As the Spitfires peeled off into line astern of Desmond and raced headlong towards the enemy, one of the B-25 bombers managed to shoot down one of the German fighters. A tense fight followed. Desmond's six Spitfires engaged the fifteen enemy fighters as they fought to get the bombers through to their objective.

Desmond first attacked a FW190, but when he realised he was up against a very capable pilot and couldn't hold him, he broke away. He was then attacked by three Italian MC202 Thunderbolts, but when *they* realised Desmond could handle his Spitfire, they too disengaged and headed north. Desmond sensed he now had the upper hand and set off after them, leaving Cy Yarnell behind. Desmond pursued the Italian Thunderbolts as far north as Rome before they dived away, showing no further interest in fighting. Over the radio, he could hear the rest of Black Section were being kept busy too, calling out to each other as the melee of fighters tried to out-manoeuvre each other and shoot their opponent down. Sticky was tackling three Germans by himself as Hindoo was scrapping with a Focke-Wulf, which broke away. Hindoo re-engaged and attacked a 109 from ¼ astern firing from a 300yd range. His bullets struck the German fighter on the wing roots close to the cockpit. A panel came off, and the 109's engine began to pour out black smoke. Hindoo claimed it as damaged.

Desmond was now below 3,000ft and turned back towards the bombers which, as they neared their target, were being attacked again by four of the German fighters and attracting intense anti-aircraft fire from the guns beneath them.

On the way, Desmond spotted a German truck and decided to turn and strafe it. He dropped down to tree-top level and gave it one pass. His bullets hit the truck's fuel tank, and it burst into flames. Satisfied he had at least hit one target, Desmond began to climb back to rejoin the main battle above him.

As he did so, he spotted six enemy aircraft flying south-east over hill tops. The leader of the enemy group saw a single Spitfire flying a roughly parallel course and decided it would be easy meat, so the Germans turned towards Desmond and made to attack him. Desmond watched as they made their approach. Turning in to face them too soon could be fatal. He let them line up ready to attack him and waited. The lead ME109 began his dive towards Desmond, but he misjudged his speed and his bullets raced past Desmond's canopy. In a split second the 109 had overshot him and swept past the Spitfire.

Now the hunter became the hunted. Desmond simultaneously pushed the throttle forward, rolled the Spitfire hard over to manoeuvre in behind and follow the ME109 down in a dive. Without looking, his thumb moved the selector button to 'cannon and machine gun' on the top of the control column. Adjusting his position with instinctive touches of his hands and feet, Desmond concentrated on the little orange reticule in the gunsight and watched it slowly swing a fraction past the nose of the ME109. Desmond was 40° astern of the 109 now, and he pressed the 'fire' button hard to release a short but intense burst from just a 100yd range. Desmond's aim was spot on. The bullets hit the German plane in the engine and round the cockpit, sending pieces of metal airframe scattering into the slipstream and ricocheting off Desmond's aeroplane. There were strikes around the cockpit ahead too, and the 109 began to roll its wings level but was still descending. The stricken fighter's undercarriage came down, but the aircraft carried on down, trailing smoke, then caught fire. Desmond saw it crash in flames in a wood north-west of Anzio. He checked the sky around him and glanced in his rear-view mirror. There were no more ME109s to be seen. There were no more Spitfires either. Desmond radioed the rest of Black Section, turned south and made for Marcianise.[7]

Despite the ongoing problems with contaminated petrol, 601 Squadron proudly recorded that it was the best-performing squadron in the wing, having flown the highest number of operational hours

(851.5). In fact, the squadron pilots had flown more hours over the skies of Italy in any one month than they had actually flown during the Battle of Britain nearly four years earlier. Among its other statistics, the squadron claimed to have achieved a record for serviceability of its aircraft (95 per cent), destroyed 240,000 gallons of fuel, destroyed 125 vehicles (plus 104 damaged), destroyed twenty-nine locomotives and damaged thirty-four.[8]

In terms of aerial victories, the squadron only claimed eight aircraft in total during February (four destroyed and four damaged). Apart from Maj Osler, who claimed two destroyed, the best-performing pilots were Desmond and his flight commander, Flt Lt W.R. 'Hindoo' Henderson, who each claimed one destroyed and one damaged.

The patrols over Anzio continued when the weather allowed, and the Allied armies continued to advance slowly out from the beachhead. On 7 March, eight Spitfires in two sections of four aircraft took off at 8 a.m. The lead pair was Hindoo Henderson (the formation leader and leader of Red Section) and the Canadian Fg Off 'Tommy' Thomas, who was his number two. Capt F.J.M. Meaker was Red 3 and Lt J.E. Sharpe was Red 4 (both SAAF). Desmond was Blue leader, with Pete Pote his wingman. Blue 3 was the Belgian Flt Sgt André Eid who, as a newcomer to the squadron three months earlier, had shot down their 200th enemy fighter, then in late February had been shot down and bailed out. His wingman (Blue 4) was the Australian Flt Sgt Alan Simpson.

The Spitfires arrived at their patrol area over Anzio and climbed to 14,000ft to begin their work watching for the enemy. Minutes later, the ground controller reported over the radio that they had identified bandits at 20,000ft. Hindoo ordered the formation up to 21,000ft to gain height advantage in anticipation of an imminent encounter. The other seven Spitfire pilots listened in quietly to the voices over their radio, following their leader's instructions, manoeuvring under the guidance of the controller until Henderson had made visual contact with the enemy and could take over the tactical decisions. Almost as soon as they reached the intended height, they spotted over ten ME109s and FW190s flying line astern in pairs – just as they began to dive, passing under the Spitfires, heading for Anzio and their targets in the Allied beachhead.

Hindoo radioed the ground controller that he now had the bandits in sight and immediately called the Spitfires in to the attack. In turn, they half-rolled at 1-second intervals and began their dives. They must have been spotted, though. Hindoo was leading and was some distance ahead of his wingman as he concentrated on trying to attack the enemy fighters, with Tommy following behind him. Tommy then saw two FW190s slide onto Hindoo's tail. Tommy called out a warning to his leader over the radio and Hindoo took immediate and violent evasive action by making a steep climbing turn. Just at this critical moment, at a height of 16,000ft, Thomas lost sight of his leader, partly as a result of the manoeuvre but also because his windscreen misted over as a result of the g-force as he too pulled into a steep climb trying to catch his leader. When he regained sight of the aircraft ahead of him, Tommy could see the two FW190s, but there was no sign of Hindoo. Tommy was then forced to defend himself as the two 190s attacked him. He could not outrun them. Instead, he turned to face one of the FW190s and made a head-on attack. As he opened fire, he saw cannon- and machine-gun strikes in the enemy's engine and pieces fall off. The FW190 dived away and was last seen trailing white smoke. Tommy claimed this one as damaged. About 2 minutes later, Tommy heard Hindoo over the radio, giving his position as being over the Anzio area and saying that he 'had got one'. Then enemy aircraft were again encountered and a dogfight took place over Cori, to the north of Anzio.

While Hindoo and Tommy and the other pair in Red Section were scrapping, Desmond and Pete were dealing with their own battles. Desmond tried to get on the tail of an ME109, firing at it from 30° astern but missed. He stayed with it and closed to within 300yds, firing at it again from ¼ astern. This time he got it. Pieces began to fall off the airframe, and seconds later the ME109 exploded in mid-air.

But Desmond was still being chased. He tried to avoid the explosion in front of him, turned to engage another ME109 passing in front of him and steepened his dive. Within a few seconds, Desmond had lined himself up behind the enemy for a second time, giving the Messerschmitt a full burst. His rounds struck the airframe, and pieces began to fall off. This time the ME109 poured black oil and smoke from the engine and, through the smoke and debris, Desmond continued to follow it down. He last saw the 109 at 6,000ft, spiralling down to earth but, because he did not see the end of it, he could only claim it as a probable.'[9]

On re-forming, Red Section found Hindoo was missing and there was no reply from him over the radio. Those pilots who landed at Nettuno, including André Eid and Alan Simpson, met a few soldiers who reported they had seen a pilot bail out over the Lepini Hills at the time of the combat. The Army further reported another pilot bailing out over Carocetto. Desmond simply noted that Hindoo had bailed out but gave no indication as to where it might have been. Hope remained that he had parachuted to safety. Sometimes when one of the Spitfire pilots had bailed out, their colleagues were able to note the position and, especially over the sea, stay behind and circle the area to guide rescuers in. Others had made it back with the help of Allied soldiers, and Desmond knew from his own experience in the desert that a pilot could return after a few days spent evading capture.

The end result of these battles then was three 109s destroyed, one probable and one damaged, in return for the loss of Hindoo Henderson. When the Millionaires put forward their combat reports, the conclusion from Wing HQ was that these 'very aggressive' Messerschmitts were part of a new crack *Gruppe* (a Luftwaffe wing) that had moved to a base in the Viterbo area approximately 50 miles north-west of Rome.[10]

It was these expert Luftwaffe pilots who provided the stiff competition for the DAF fighters and who would continue to do so as the armies pushed on towards Rome. During the next few days, Desmond notched up his 300th operational flight.

On 13 March, Maj Malcolm Osler was posted to Advanced DAF HQ. In his place came a former 601 flight commander, now a squadron leader, John Hamilton Nicholls DFC, who had served with the Millionaires at the same time as Desmond during the El Alamein and Tunisia campaigns.

In the meantime, William Raymond 'Hindoo' Henderson was now listed as 'Missing in Action' following the dogfight over the Cori area near the Anzio beachhead.[11] Desmond was promoted to flight lieutenant and given command of B Flight. It was a bittersweet moment given what had happened to Hindoo and, before him, Capt Waugh.

Although Desmond never mentioned it in his logbook, this was still a significant step in his career. His mate Cy Yarnell was already a flight lieutenant and perhaps should have been given command of the flight instead. But Desmond had more flying hours, wider experience and was now a 'double ace' with ten confirmed enemy destroyed and a DFC. He had shown himself to be a decisive and competent section leader, willing to follow (and occasionally break) orders. He had developed a keen eye for aerial combat and was well respected among his fellow pilots. Desmond was not far off completing his second tour now and, on paper at least, could soon be up for command of his own squadron. But, at 22 years of age, he was still considered too young.

As usual, a party was held in the officers' mess to celebrate the promotions, departing colleagues and new arrivals and, alongside the presence of senior officers including Gp Capt Brian Kingcome and Wg Cdr Stan Turner, a fair number of nurses had turned up from a nearby Canadian (military) hospital to enjoy the dancing and drinking too.[12]

The day after, the Australian Flt Lt A.J. Radcliffe was formally posted from 145 Squadron (based just across the airfield) to take over command of 601 Squadron's A Flight in place of Flt Lt W.B. Hay. Hay had received a promotion to squadron leader and was himself sent across the airfield at Marcianise to command 417 Squadron (RCAF).[13] He would later be sent to command the former DAF Training Flight, 5 Refresher Flying Unit, and, in the summer, become Desmond's commanding officer.

The daily operations for Desmond and the squadron were not noticeably interrupted by the eruption of Mount Vesuvius, which exploded into life on 17 March for the first time in seventy-two years. Eyewitnesses said the noise of the explosions sounded exactly like artillery fire. The eruptions sent huge clouds of ash and rock thousands of feet into the air, with smaller fountains and flows of lava following. The Americans evacuated men and whatever equipment they could carry from Pompeii airfield in Poggiomarino, a few miles east from the base of the volcano, but the 340th Bomb Group based there lost almost eighty-eight B-25 bombers.[14] The eruptions and clouds of ash continued for days afterwards, and all aircraft had to divert around them. Marcianise lay 15 miles to the north and was, for the most part, unaffected.

On 18 March, the first patrols over the Cassino battle area began in support of the first offensive to try to overcome the German positions on and around the mountain sides. Cassino, some 60 miles due east of Anzio, overlooked the plains from an extremely well-defended and commanding location. The battles to try to take this fortress-like basilica atop the extinct volcano came to be a byword for the Allied campaign to liberate Italy itself.

Desmond soon claimed his first victory as a flight commander, which would also turn out to be the last confirmed victory of his career. It happened during a dawn patrol on 20 March, when 601 sent up a formation of twelve Spitfires to patrol the Anzio beachhead. Capt Meaker led Yellow Section and the formation as a whole. Desmond led Red Section, with Pete Pote his number two. Cy Yarnell was Red 3 and Sgt Holton Red 4. Fg Off Davidson led Blue Section.

When the Spitfires reached 22,000ft, they saw forty plus[15] 109s and FW 190s flying below them at 18,000ft with a further eight[16] flying as top cover above them at 25,000ft. The enemy fighters were all flying southwest, away from the patrol area. Despite intelligence reports that there was a crack *Gruppe* of German squadrons in the area, the opportunity for fights was reducing. Many German pilots turned for home when they saw any Spitfires, meaning the Millionaires were left frustratedly scratching around for any targets they could find. Today though, the Germans were not going to turn and run.

Capt Meaker told Desmond to take Red Section and climb to engage the 109s 3,000ft above – the idea being to keep the German top cover occupied and off the backs of Blue and Yellow Sections, who would keep a careful eye on the more than forty enemy fighters in the main formation at 18,000ft.

However, the flak batteries around Anzio opened up again, making it more difficult for the Spitfires to intercept the main formation. As black clouds of smoke puffed out around and below them, sending steel shrapnel balls everywhere, Meaker decided to make his move and called the Spitfires in to the attack. The main German formation spotted their attackers, scattered and a huge dogfight began. But Desmond could do nothing about it and continued climbing Red Section, heading for 25,000ft.

As Desmond's section prepared to intercept the German top cover, they too broke away and began to dive back north towards Rome. Desmond and Red Section followed them down, but then he saw an ME109 flying parallel to him at approximately 16,000ft. He decided to engage it and broke formation. When he was 45° from the port side of the ME109, Desmond gave it a half-second burst with his guns, but the German instantly half-rolled and dived to try to escape.

Desmond gave chase, pushing the throttle forward. The Merlin 66 roared again as he half-rolled onto his back, pulled the stick back hard and accelerated his own Spitfire into a headlong dive after the ME109. Once more, Desmond had left his wingman (this time Pete Pote) behind, along with Cy Yarnell and his wingman, Sgt Holton. They would all just have to fend for themselves. He was committed and fully focused on the target. The angular, ugly shape of the Messerschmitt with large black crosses on the wings contrasted with the deep blue of the Mediterranean beneath.

The ME109 was not an elegantly streamlined aeroplane at all. It was as though the Germans had taken an expensive, sleek design, then sawn bits off the nose, tailplane, canopy and wingtips to save money. As this particular ME109 turned to head inland, Desmond could see the pilot looking around, trying to work out where the Spitfire was. Slowly the fighter in front grew ever larger in Desmond's gunsight. Once more the orange dot began to creep slowly across the centreline of the ME109, then onto its nose. Desmond could hear his own breathing louder and faster now, above the staccato chatter in his headset as his colleagues far above him faced their own opponents. As his thumb hovered over the 'fire' button, he checked his rear-view mirror. There was another ME109 on his tail. Desmond was about to be attacked from behind, sandwiched between two German fighters, all three in a near-vertical dive at over 300 knots. But because Desmond still had the first German ahead of him, now fully in his sights, he stuck with him. He was less than 200yds away now, about 2 seconds away from firing.

As he closed to around 100yds, Desmond gave his enemy another half-second burst from the starboard quarter with his guns. The intermittent lines of orange tracer rounds streaked out ahead, and the bullets hit home. But still the German continued to dive earthwards, seemingly undeterred by the strikes on his own aeroplane.

Desmond's bullets had hit the 109's engine and oil began to pour out, followed by thick black smoke. It continued diving down and made no attempt to pull out. The pilot did not bail out, and the Messerschmitt smashed straight into the ground, not far from the German lines.

The second 109 chasing Desmond had not given up and shot past him as they turned away. But the speed and momentum of Desmond's own dive meant he was still racing earthwards and faced the same fate as the first German if he wasn't careful. Desmond pulled back hard on the control column, almost blacking out due to the excessive g-force, which was draining the blood down his body into his legs. As he pulled out of the dive with only a few hundred feet to spare, the pursuing German turned away and headed north. Desmond did not follow him. As he levelled off and turned south, the familiar voice of the ground controller, who had witnessed the dogfight, called over the radio to him: 'Good show!' After a short time, Desmond spotted a loose barrage balloon, probably from an Allied ship in the bay that had strayed from its moorings. He shot it down in flames before finally heading home.[17]

Despite the huge dogfight that had taken place, Spitfires in Yellow and Blue Sections did not shoot any opponents down. Fortunately, though, they suffered no losses either. Soon after he landed and returned to dispersal, the groundcrew refuelled and re-armed the Spitfire. Then they took out the paint tins and painted another swastika on the side of Desmond's Spitfire. The ME109 was his eleventh confirmed victory.

CHAPTER 18

601 Squadron and the WAAFs

Italy
31 March–30 July 1944

At the end of March 1944, the Advanced Headquarters of the Mediterranean Allied Air Forces (MAAF) relocated to Caserta Palace, just 5 minutes away from Marcianise. This was welcome news because it meant impromptu visits not just by senior officers but also various officers of the Women's Auxiliary Air Force (WAAF). The women who visited the officers' mess were taken on walks out to see Vesuvius as it continued to grumble and spit its fiery ash into the air. At night, the pilots and their new friends walked out to see the lower lava streams.

The WAAFs who now arrived at Caserta had previously been in North Africa, waiting along with the rest of the HQ staff for things to stabilise sufficiently in Italy until suitable accommodation could be found. The seventeenth-century palace, which now had its own airfield close by, was the ideal place. HQ could be entirely accommodated within the palace grounds rather than close to a city centre, and the large airfield at Marcianise meant staff and senior officers could travel in and out more efficiently.

Among the young women on the HQ staff was one in particular who believed pilots always threw the best parties and who always enjoyed their company. Being based a few miles north of Naples meant she would also be able to indulge another of her interests: travel. With the front now a hundred miles or more to the north, Naples and the renowned holiday spots along the Amalfi coast were no more than half a day's travel away, and with summer on the horizon, it would be the ideal opportunity to explore the area.

That particular woman was Patsy Jensen. Her new posting offered the best of both worlds: mildly interesting yet routine work with a tinge of danger, coupled with the prospect of an even more interesting social life to follow.

Desmond too found his work a little routine now. The patrols and bomber escort missions continued almost daily, with only occasional interruptions due to bad weather or shockingly bad visibility, in part due to the activities of Vesuvius. While his colleagues still had encounters with the enemy, most of these (and there were only a notable handful) were increasingly ground attack and strafing runs at German troops, guns and vehicles. Even the sightings of enemy fighters were dwindling, as the Luftwaffe was steadily drained of experienced pilots to send to the home and eastern fronts. As the Allied armies sought to both capture Monte Cassino and push on towards Rome, preparations were being finalised for the invasion of northern France in the early summer.

Over the next two months, Desmond clocked up another sixty ops, all but five of which were in his own personal Spitfire Mk VIII, 'UF-Q'. On three of these ops, his Spitfire's engine failed, but he again stayed in the aeroplane and managed to bring the fighter back safely. On one of these occasions his engine started leaking glycol coolant, and he landed at Anzio.

Perhaps, as the Allied armies continued to advance, and the Luftwaffe failed to show the willingness to fight much anymore, Desmond began to have a sense that he would come through his final tour unscathed. Although his ability and enthusiasm for the fight seemed undiminished, when this tour ended, he knew there would be another rest period, probably for six months, then what?

Realistically, another short post as a flight commander, then maybe his own squadron, maybe in France or maybe closer to home if the rumoured invasion were to actually go ahead. When he was with 54 Squadron, Desmond had gone north to Castletown in Scotland, while the more experienced pilots had been sent out to Australia and the Pacific Islands to fight the Japanese. That was nearly two and a half years ago, and he was now one of the more experienced pilots who could be selected for service in the Far East himself.

On Thursday 25 May, Desmond was due to lead a squadron operation from its new base at Venafro, close to Monte Cassino, escorting American bombers on a raid over the Cassino/Rapido area, but his Spitfire developed engine trouble, and he had to stand down. Instead, Desmond borrowed Gp Capt Brian Kingcome's own single-engine, two-seat Auster and flew down to Marcianise by himself for the presentation of his second DFC, which had been formally announced two days earlier in the *London Gazette*. It was a 'well earned' award that recognised his 'outstanding courage and determination on operations against the enemy'.[1] During the Second World War, 20,354 DFCs were awarded but just 1,550 (or 7.5 per cent) of this number were second awards.[2]

As was customary for senior officers when assigned their own light aircraft for the purpose of visiting other squadrons and attending staff meetings, Kingcome had his initials, BK, painted on the fuselage as identification code letters. Unusually, this Auster was painted white rather than camouflage.

This was also the day when Patsy and Desmond met. Patsy had been at Caserta for just over six weeks. Working in the signals section of MAAF HQ, Patsy had been aware of the arrangements being made, as many of the messages would have passed through her office, if not across her own desk.

As various aeroplanes arrived carrying mostly senior officers and high-ranking air staff, Patsy recognised the white Auster of the 244 Wing CO among them but was surprised when a shorter, dark-haired, young junior officer got out instead of the tall, slender figure of Brian Kingcome and made his way to the operations building. Who was this upstart who had arrived in the group captain's personal aircraft?

The photo taken of his award shows Desmond receiving the medal from Sir Sholto Douglas in the company of AVM Sir Arthur 'Mary' Coningham and AVM Harry Broadhurst, all of whom are standing in front of a Mosquito fighter-bomber. At the same time as Desmond received his bar, Neville Duke, the then CO of 145 Squadron, received his second bar to his DFC. After the ceremony, Desmond returned to Venafro, where the gusty winds he encountered on landing meant he nearly broke the Auster when he touched down.

On 31 May it was Brian Kingcome's birthday, and he was leaving to go to RAF Staff College in Haifa. Command of 244 Wing, at Kingcome's recommendation, went to his Wing Commander Flying, Hugh 'Cocky' Dundas. There had been changes in command of the squadrons in the wing too, with many former colleagues who had flown together in the Battles of France and Britain now reunited, so the changes and awards of medals and promotions called for a major party. To host the wing's biggest social event, an abandoned farmhouse near the Wing HQ was commandeered, and five separate bars established – one tended by each squadron and the fifth tended by Wing HQ:

> Each vied to outdo the other in the potency of its drink such that after a sip of some potions one felt the only thing to do was to call out the fire tender. The loft had been turned into a very suave honky tonk, where the band of 18 Squadron churned out hot jive. The SMO (Senior Medical Officer) who pulled the strings, brewed the brews, and superintended the luscious buffet certainly made a wizard job of it.[3]

Desmond returned to operations and for the next few weeks mainly flew patrols over Anzio and bomber escort sorties.

Patsy had overcome several obstacles to end up in Italy, among them rejection at interview for an overseas posting and what would now be classed at least as sexual harassment and probably actual assault in today's working environment. While working in the typing pool at Bomber Command HQ, High Wycombe, a squadron leader called her into his office to 'take a letter'. Patsy sat poised and listened carefully. But as he finished, terrified of interrupting him, she confessed she had not written anything down. The senior officer told her not to worry then 'complimented [her] on her teeth, patted her on the head then, as [she] made to leave the office pulled her across the desk and planted a smacking kiss'.[4]

Patsy was born in the UK but, thanks to her father's work, which resulted in postings overseas, grew up with her ex-pat friend, Delphine Rawlins, in Brazil. 'Patsy' was a childhood nickname, but her Christian name was Rosemary. Her surname, Jensen, was inherited from her Danish grandfather and her father, Jens Jensen, who had also married an Englishwoman. The Jensens and Rawlins families were friends, and Patsy spent several years abroad before her father moved the family back to Britain in the mid-1930s and built their home at Camberley in Surrey. At the outbreak of war, Patsy and Delphine (who had also returned to the UK by then) had originally dashed off to the recruiting office in Aldershot to enlist, hoping their enthusiasm and lying about their ages would see them through. Instead, they had been kindly told to 'go away and grow a bit more'. Next, they tried to join the First Aid Nursing Yeomanry (FANY), which was, Patsy explained, 'a prestigious relic of the First World War – whose glamorous female despatch riders now traversed the country on motorbikes or chauffeured the staff cars of famous generals – a highly desirable lifestyle. However, there were no open arms, and we were once again unwanted.'[5]

Aged 16 at the time and her attempts to enlist thwarted, Patsy took her mother's advice and enrolled at a local secretarial college attached to the Farnborough convent, taking courses in typing and shorthand. Eventually, in June 1940, Patsy and Delphine both joined the WAAF. After completing their induction, Patsy was selected for three weeks of training in Codes and Ciphers (C&C) at the C&C school at Headington near Oxford. Courses were usually evenly split: twelve men and twelve women. According to the Air Ministry, candidates had to be 'officer type; steady; reliable; reticent; if possible able to use a typewriter and willing to undertake office work of a somewhat tedious nature'.[6] On successful completion of her tests, Patsy was commissioned into the Administrative and Special Duties Branch as an Assistant Section Officer, a rank given exclusively to women that was equivalent to pilot officer in the RAF and served only to emphasise the rule that women could not be pilots in the RAF.

Patsy's first posting was to No. 5 Group HQ Bomber Command at Grantham. The group's squadrons were based at Doncaster, Finningley, Hemswell, Lindholme, Scampton and Waddington.[7] Delphine was posted as a radar operator to RAF Digby. Neither Digby nor Grantham were far from Lincoln, and there she met up with Colin Rawlins, Delphine's brother, who had also joined the RAF, earned his pilot's wings and was flying twin-engined Handley Page Hampden bombers for 144 Squadron based at Hemswell, to the north of Lincoln. Patsy and Colin became close and tentatively began a relationship, which had to be kept secret due to strict regulations about 'fraternising'.

Eight months later, on the night of 11–12 May 1941 Patsy was on duty in the C&C office and, being bored, ventured down to the ops room to see what was going on. The huge blackboards fastened to each wall showed the details of each squadron, the aircraft number, times of departure and if they had landed or not. One of the intelligence officers present approached Patsy (having presumably seen her before with Colin) pointed to one line on the board and told her, 'I'm afraid that that missing plane is your friend ...' Patsy immediately returned to her lodgings, borrowed her landlady's car and went to break the news to Delphine. There was nothing Patsy or Delphine could do, except wait for news.

Colin's Hampden had participated in a raid on the port city Bremen. It was a relatively small raid comprising a mixed force of Hampdens, Whitleys and Manchesters. Of the eighty-one bombers sent out, thirty-one were Hampdens. Colin's was the only Hampden, and indeed the only aircraft, lost on that night's raid.

Colin Guy Champion Rawlins was born on 5 June 1919 in London and, like Patsy, had travelled widely. He spent his childhood in Pernambuco (now Recife) and Rio de Janeiro. His mother died when he was barely 5 years old, so he and Delphine were sent to live in South Africa with relatives for two years. He eventually returned to the UK and attended Oxford University. While there he joined the University Air Squadron before being called up to join the RAF.

After training, he began his first tour with 144 Squadron at Hemswell. The period from mid-August to December 1940 was busy and saw him fly missions over occupied northern France, notably against German invasion barges assembling in the Channel ports during the late summer and early autumn of 1940. Following the completion of his first tour, at the age of 21 and a flying officer, he was awarded the DFC in February 1941 and rested.[8] It was during this break from operations that Colin met up with Patsy again.

He wanted to return to his old unit, and he did so in May 1941, this time as a flight lieutenant and flight commander before being quickly promoted to the rank of acting squadron leader. The raid on 11–12 May was only his second operation of this tour. They took off at 10.55 p.m. and arrived over the initial point of Dummer See (a large lake to the south-west of Bremen), ready to begin the run-in from around 15,000ft, gliding down to around 10,000ft to drop their bombs at just after 2 a.m. Visibility was excellent owing to the bright moon and clear skies over the city. While the searchlights and anti-aircraft guns were active with both light and heavy ack-ack accurate to height, they managed to miss all the other bombers during their attacks and departed to the north, making their way home. It was during the return leg from Bremen that Colin's aircraft was intercepted and shot down over Holland by a Luftwaffe ME110 night fighter.[9]

Patsy remained at Grantham for a year, followed by a year working at the School of Technical Training at RAF Weeton near Blackpool, but she remained determined to be as close to front-line operations as possible. She applied for postings overseas, was knocked back at her first interview and, after a few months at Redcar and intermittent holding posts, was sent to RAF Kirkwall in the Orkneys instead in June 1943. At her second interview in London, she was accepted and sent back to RAF Weeton in early 1944 with orders to collect her overseas kit, then board a troopship from Liverpool to an unknown destination.

Patsy was fluent in French, having spent nearly three years in a sanatorium in Switzerland from the age of about 8, and it was only when she befriended a young French officer on board the troopship, whose regiment was on its way to North Africa, that she found out their destination was Tunis. Arriving there on 3 March, she and the other WAAFs made their way to La Marsa, a small seaside town, to begin her posting at MAAF HQ, British North African Forces.

Very soon after arriving though, Patsy fell ill with non-amoebic dysentery and was transferred to the nearest army hospital, where she stayed for over three weeks until the end of March 1944. By then the war and her HQ had moved on without her, so she left North Africa for Italy, hitching a lift in an American Dakota across the Mediterranean to an air base at Capodichino near Naples. From there, she hitch-hiked out of the city to the MAAF HQ (then located at Caserta Palace, north of Naples).

Patsy shared billets with other WAAFs in an old farmhouse with a walled garden whose adjacent stables had been converted to a shower block. As a teenager, she had learnt to ride and, when off duty, was permitted by the Army to ride its service horses round the vast and sprawling palace grounds. Using a 48-hour leave pass, she would hitch a lift north as close as possible to the Allied front lines, which then lay just south of Rome, to see what was happening. At this stage of the war, the Allies were preparing to strike at Monte Cassino, around 60 miles to the north of Caserta. Despite the pleasant surroundings and grand buildings, Patsy found her work monotonous but was keenly aware of its importance:

> The cypher room was up a long winding stone staircase from one of the four palace courtyards, where we worked mainly on coding/de-coding machines on a four-watch system. Surprisingly, our door was not locked or guarded, and every morning Italian women cleaners would enter, accompanied by an RAF guard, to sweep up and stuff into sacks the yards of discarded white tape, then taken for destruction. Ever a query-er, this seemed incredibly lax, I queried the system with a security officer, pointing out the ease with which sweepers could pocket the small and highly secret drums of our machines. (These, drums, the very heart of the coding system, were reset daily). This lack of security was in great contrast to the American code room next door, whose only communication was via an impersonal hand through a hatch. We regarded the Americans as being rather over-security minded, and one was wary when approaching their sentries (I heard that an airman had been shot by a trigger-happy guard), but they were undoubtedly correct in their code-room security.[10]

The Allies advanced on, then captured, Rome on 5 June – the first capital city to be recaptured in occupied Europe and, because it was the only capital city in 1944–45 where Hitler did not demand a fight to the death, was spared significant destruction. This joyous occasion was immediately overshadowed though by the D-Day landings in Normandy 24 hours later.[11]

Patsy had studied Latin at Westonbirt School and was keen to visit Rome following the liberation. She travelled there possibly in the company of the pilots of 244 Wing. A photograph taken around that time, dated 8 June, shows Spitfire pilot Johnny Gasson (SAAF) walking alongside Desmond, Patsy and 'Doc' Thomas as they pass the MAAF mess tents at Caserta. The wing's padre, Reverend (Sqn Ldr) Aston, organised trips into Rome to give everybody the opportunity to visit St Peter's Basilica in the Vatican. About twenty men left each day, and it was said these and many other service personnel of all nations were received by Pope Pius XII.[12] Fellow Spitfire ace Wilfred Duncan-Smith visited the city at the time too and noted:

In Rome the crowds spilled across the streets, throwing flowers into our vehicles and offering us great hospitality. Roman priorities did not seem to have changed, however. While [his friend and fellow Spitfire pilot] Barrie was kissing a dark-eyed damsel a hand removed his camera from the jeep.[13]

Since leaving England two years earlier, Desmond had barely had any opportunity to go sightseeing. A few days later, he flew his own Spitfire IX over to the only Allied airfield near Rome, Fabrica (officially called Fabrica-di-Roma) located some 30 miles north-west of the city.

Desmond was up flying patrols again on the evening of 16 June when he led a section of six out on an offensive patrol over the Chiusa–Arezzo–Perugia area, just as the battle was focusing on the Assisi–Perugia area, through which the Germans were now retreating.[14]

On 17 June, the squadron moved again, from Littorio to Fabrica landing ground. The convoy of trucks passed down roads littered with the burnt-out, bullet-riddled wrecks of dozens of German cars, motorbikes and trucks.

Ground attack patrols by the squadron had been stepped up in support of the Allies advancing through the towns of Spoleto and Foligno and up the country roads to Assisi and Perugia. British troops advanced into the outskirts of Perugia by 18 June. Following heavy rain for two days and the German withdrawal on the night of 20–21 June, Perugia finally fell to the two British motorised infantry brigades (61st and 1st Guards).[15] To this day, the citizens of Assisi continue to celebrate their liberation day on 19 June, Perugia on 21 June. Sometimes, the two anniversaries combine for one special commemoration.

With the liberation of Perugia town came the acquisition of a substantial forward airbase at St Egidio – a former Italian and Luftwaffe airfield. It had a single concrete runway with turning circles at each end, taxiways, hangars and the full array of buildings. The front line soon moved north again to Arezzo before falling roughly on a line stretching almost coast to coast from Pisa to Rimini in early July.

Desmond next saw Patsy on 21 June. Patsy remembered this very well because it was her first flight in an Auster, and it was her first with Desmond as the pilot. Any opportunity Patsy had, she persuaded the usually friendly pilots to let her sit up front in the cockpit and have a go at the controls herself. She even once managed to hitch from Bari to Foggia and flew back to Marcianise in a twin-engined Mosquito.

The Taylorcraft Auster Mk Is were simple little monoplanes with a distinctive high-wing. They had an engine with a tenth of the horsepower of a Spitfire and had less than a tenth of the glamour too but, although slow and ungainly, they were functional. They were primarily used to spot targets for ground troops and call in fire support from artillery batteries. Their slow speed, stability in the air and good downward visibility made them ideal for this purpose. Elsewhere, they were used by RAF commanders for communication flights between dispersed squadrons in the field. Desmond arranged to borrow the group captain's personal Auster again to fly himself and Patsy from Rome down to MAAF HQ.

They took off from the airfield at Fabrica and, once out over the sea, Desmond trimmed the aircraft out so it would maintain a straight and level attitude in flight and offered Patsy a go at the controls. She said yes without hesitation. The cockpit of an Auster is only slightly roomier than that of a Spitfire. The pilot sits up front, offset to the left and the passenger sits slightly behind and to the right, so quite how they managed to swap seats without knocking any of the controls in mid-air is a guess – but it obviously involved getting very close to each other! It helped that they were both under 5ft 6in, slender and not wearing parachutes.

With Patsy now at the controls and following Desmond's instructions, they headed south along the coast near Littoria. Patsy described the view through the canopy as she 'played pilot: looking shoreward, we saw the white devastation of the bombed holiday villas along the coast road. [The view] was of mile upon mile of completely ruined, white, dusty, seaside towns.'[16] They continued south towards Nettuno – the closest airfield to Anzio.

However, on turning inland, they suddenly encountered unexpected turbulence. There was only one thing for it: to swap seats again. As the little aeroplane began bucking and dipping left and right as the rising currents of air buffeted the wings and airframe, shaking them as though they were two peas in a tin, Patsy described what followed as an 'undignified scramble. Never had pilot and passenger swapped at such speed in such a confined space [and it was] achieved in record time.'[17]

Flustered and laughing at their near miss, they made their way gingerly a little way inland to Nettuno, where they refuelled and had a break before taking off again, this time heading further south on to MAAF HQ. For this leg of the journey, Desmond directed the little Auster further inland towards Venafro and over the Monte Cassino battlefield.

Earlier that year, seated at her desk taking dozens of messages from the urgent to the mundane in those high-ceilinged rooms of the ornate palace, Patsy had heard about the development of the battle as it gathered both pace and ferocity. From time to time on her solo travels towards the front line, she had seen truckloads of smiling and whistling soldiers pass her on their way north to the fighting. On one occasion, she had climbed the banking at the side of a road to watch troops of the 6th South African Armoured Division go by. As she exchanged waves with them, she had wondered how many of those 'grinning dust-covered heroes' would ever return. Now, several weeks later on a hot June day, as she flew over the remains of a battle that had accounted for over 60,000 lives between both sides, she looked down and remarked on the strange sight of 'the once green fields [below being] covered with thousands of red earth splodges – as if the ground had measles'. She pondered on the likelihood that some of those men she had waved at in days past were those same red splodges.[18] As they flew on to Venafro, Desmond pointed out one or two other landmarks he had used when flying his Spitfire around the area.

About 20 minutes later, they touched down at Marcianise. After a meal and a few drinks in the mess, they made their way back to their separate quarters, where Desmond spent the night. When they recalled that first flight together, Patsy wrote about what she had seen and the seat swapping. Desmond simply noted that 'Patsy can fly too ...' This was the first time he had encountered a woman who was not just interested in flying but who could actually take the controls and handle the plane herself. When one of the predecessors to the RAF, the RFC, was formed, pilot recruits were taken from the officer ranks of the Army. The old adage for selection was, 'If you can ride a horse, then you can fly an aeroplane,' and Patsy, who was a keen and competent horsewoman, had just proven the truth of this saying. Patsy's interest in flying was one thing. Her sense of fun and have-a-go approach to life struck a chord with Desmond because she was just the sort of woman he had grown up with and enjoyed being around. She was also pretty, chatty (in a well-spoken way) and easy company.

The next day, back at Fabrica, Desmond took his first flight in a silver Mk IX Spitfire (EN475) 'a shiny silver SPIT! [which did] 403mph (computed at 22,000ft)'. This was only the second time he had written about an aircraft in capital letters. The first was three years earlier when, after finishing training, he learnt he was being posted to 'SPITS!' Now, after hundreds of hours on Spits, his breath had been taken away again. This one did not just look sleek and fast as it stood on the apron glinting in the sunshine, looking like a prototype with its all-metal finish; it *was* fast.

The visits with Patsy became regular and more frequent. Every few days, in between the remaining operations he was flying to complete his tour, which involved primarily dive-bombing roads and junctions with 500lb bombs, Desmond borrowed an aeroplane and took himself off to Marcianise and MAAF HQ, which was at most a 40-minute flight away. He had no work to do there, no course to attend and there are no official reasons recorded for his trips. Sometimes he flew his personal silver Spitfire (JG164 then, later MJ250); other times he borrowed the group captain's Auster. On one occasion, because the squadron was training a section of Fleet Air Arm pilots on temporary detachment from their carriers, he borrowed one of their Seafires – the navalised version of the Spitfire VB.[19] He felt he now had the freedom to visit whenever he had a few hours off duty. As a flight commander, no one was going to question too much where he went or who he saw, but a few of his friends on the squadron could guess. Especially when Desmond took off on his own last thing in the evening after operations had finished for the day and returned at 6 a.m. the following morning.

The timing of Desmond's visits to Marcianise – recorded in his logbook and the squadron's operational record book – fit in with the alternating shift pattern that Patsy worked. When working night shifts, there was usually a bed available where duty officers could sleep if there was little or no message traffic coming in. Patsy found that, being somewhat significantly closer to the front line, the routine at MAAF HQ was different:

> Caserta was a very busy station where we were up all night. I certainly worked hard and conscientiously when on duty – an on-going round of four by eight hour shifts followed by 24 hours off – but when off, as shown by this story, we played. Twenty-four hours, for instance, was time enough to hitch a ride down to Naples and on to Sorrento

– where the RAF had taken over the Hotel Coccumella [sic] as an officers' rest camp – or for me to visit 244 (Fighter) Wing.[20]

Photographs reveal the pair visited Naples, Sorrento and Assisi together (the latter several times), scrounging lifts in trucks or any passing vehicle on the road that had room. In a few of the images, Patsy is seen with a dog on a lead – probably one of several kept by the wing. She noted:

> The CO of 244 Wing at the time was Group Captain 'Cocky' Dundas. 'Cocky' had a litter of puppies. Back at Caserta, the head medico in Italy, an Air-Vice Marshal, had decreed that, as an anti-rabies precaution, all station dogs were to be destroyed. Hearing this and realising what a morale-blaster it would be, I'd passed on my fears to [Sir John] Slessor at a party. I was told later by a man who attended the daily War Briefings that Slessor had thumped the table and said 'Gentlemen, dogs!' and the AVM's ruling was revoked! I consider that saving the puppies was my most useful contribution to the war effort …

Patsy and Desmond shared a love of dogs, both having grown up with or around them. When travelling around Naples, Patsy took 'Peter' with her and Desmond, while on other trips they took 'Piltzie'. When out walking near Santa Maria degli Angeli later that summer, Desmond was snapped holding one of the puppies.

There are a few photos that appear in both Patsy's and Muriel's albums which, taken together, confirm their locations. The first two are of a group of 601 Squadron pilots seated at a rough-and-ready table made from what appears to be the side of a large packing crate. The flyers are sitting around in various styles of chair – randomly acquired from their travels – eating and chatting in the sunshine. There are Italian cypress trees in the middle background and looming mountains in the distance. The version in Muriel's album shows Desmond in the left of the scene, wearing sunglasses and in animated conversation with Cy Yarnell. Patsy's picture, taken at the same time, did not show Desmond. Others in Muriel's album are captioned simply 'summer 1944', while the same ones in Patsy's album are dated.

The strictures of war and limited availability of photographic equipment and materials to the public made photography difficult. Yet Patsy, who was herself photographed by no less than Cecil Beaton while she was working at 5 Group HQ in Grantham, was keen to document her wartime adventures. She captured the places she went, the people she met and always seemed able to acquire film and get it developed.

But just as she managed to capture the scenes with very few people and vehicles around and houses and streets seemingly intact, she wrote of the everyday dangers that were present away from the front of the lens: the black marketeering that went on, the bribery of Military Police guards, the prostitution that was 'rife in Naples' and how her Italian maid who cleaned the barrack room in Caserta asked her for birth-control medicine to prevent an unwanted pregnancy by her some-time boyfriend. Even when she saw the funny side of changing seats mid-air with Desmond as they flew down to Marcianise, she witnessed the bombed-out white-stone ruins of the villages below, some that she had passed through when hitching rides in military vehicles. Walking through a remote village once on the way to Bari, she felt an uneasy presence watching her as though waiting to exact their pent-up revenge, despite the fact she was an officer in uniform of the then Allied liberating forces.

Desmond and Patsy became fast friends and companions during that summer. For her part, Patsy was drawn to pilots simply because they made good company and knew how to have a party. They were, almost by definition, outgoing, confident young men, opportunists and (to varying degrees, of course) risk-takers. She admitted that she herself shared the pilots' view to life: 'work hard, party hard'.

She was also acutely aware of the fighting going on in the area stretching from the Anzio beachhead inland to Monte Cassino and across to the east coast. In her office, she would be handling the message traffic sent between RAF units and hearing aircraft droning overhead heading out on operations. She was well aware of the risks the pilots took, the danger they faced and how that affected their attitude to life.

For Desmond, it was his first notably serious relationship (certainly his first since meeting the Russian dancer the year before). For Patsy, it was her first notable relationship away from Colin – a relationship that had stalled in 1941 before it had properly begun. Patsy had several friends on 244 Wing, but Desmond was the only one she flew with regularly, and the one who appears most in her photos.

She writes, 'I had several friends in the Wing and [as they moved forward ... I would occasionally follow]. Apart from reaching them by hitching, my logbook records airfields flown to such as: Fabrica, Littorio, Nettuno and Perugia.'[21] Yet, while she notes having taken flights on 3 July and, much later, on 6 October in a Harvard trainer, she does not mention she was actually taking these trips to different airfields just with Desmond.

Whether Patsy saw Desmond as a safe and trustworthy friend among a group of women-hungry young pilots or as a more intimate companion is not known. She writes opaquely of her closest relationships during this period of her life and keeps her truest feelings hidden. The photographs she took hint at what she took care not to write down.

The squadron was released from operations on 23 July and arranged transport for all personnel to Perugia, Assisi and Lake Trasimeno. Desmond extended this and had another two days off at least. On 25 July, the whole wing was stood down to prepare for and receive a visit from King George VI, who was touring the Italian front in the company of General Oliver Leese (who had replaced Montgomery as head of the Eighth Army) and AVM Dickson.

Desmond flew his final operation in the mid-afternoon of 26 July when, leading one of two sections of four aircraft, he attacked a building believed to be a Wehrmacht headquarters a few miles south of Rignano. The Spitfires approached from 12,000ft, dived on the target, releasing their bombs at 1,000ft. They scored two direct hits and put the remaining six bombs in the target area. They then proceeded to shoot up the buildings and three vehicles parked nearby before heading home.

When Desmond ended his second tour, there was another huge combined party to celebrate everyone's end of tours, awarding of medals and promotions. The squadron had been stood down again on 29 July, and Desmond wanted to go to the party being held that Friday night, which the wing had organised at the Hotel Giotto in Assisi – then commandeered by the RAF as an officers' rest centre. After dinner, its large basement dining room was turned over to serve as a bar and dance floor. Verandas on the floor above faced south overlooking the broad valley below and functioned as quieter spots for a drink and space to relax away from the increasingly drunk and noisy pilots dancing away in the basement.

Desmond was on a high. He had survived a tough time on flying operations to complete his second tour unscathed, received a bar to his

DFC, a promotion and was a double ace. With his experience and background, he could have been in line for some choice postings or even command of his own squadron after a rest period. He might have been in a position to ask one of the senior officers he knew for a favour or two to get a good one. All he could do though was wait for confirmation of his next assignment, but Desmond knew if he had to leave Italy, it would be a wrench.

Dancing and drinking that warm summer night away among friends and females was probably the closest he ever got to attending a VE Day party as the DAF band played jive on the stage. One of the officers present at the party wrote later:

> Special late passes had been provided by the Town Mayor for various popsies of not very exceptional beauty who to varying degrees of disappointment, were of the 'haut' rather than the 'demi monde'. Their scruples did not deter them, however, from toting away as much of the buffet as they could cram into their handbags. Two, who sneaked in without passes, spent the night in the 'cooler' when the MPs [Military Police] caught them. We wondered what the nuns in the adjacent convent made of the strains of 'St Louis Blues' and such like which floated out till eleven o'clock. Also what other inhabitants made of it when certain members of the Wing strutted through the deserted streets chanting the 'Horst Wessel' and 'Deutschland Uber Alles!'[22]

CHAPTER 19

No. 5 Refresher Flying Unit

31 July–18 November 1944

Back home, Muriel was preparing for her wedding to Jim Richardson, a young, newly commissioned Army officer. He had been sent home to the UK for officer training after serving on the front line near Monte Cassino, shortly before the main offensive began. Muriel had invited Desmond to the wedding too and was hoping he would be able to travel back to attend the ceremony. Years later, Muriel still did not know why Desmond had not come home; it may have been because Desmond had received notice that his new instructor posting would be effective from Saturday 7 August.[1]

Desmond flew to Marcianise again on 3 August, returning the day after. Although formally serving with at No. 5 Refresher Flying Unit (RFU) from 7 August, Desmond travelled overland south from Perugia to Marcianise to meet up with Patsy. From there they both caught a flight from Marcianise to Siena in a DC-3 Dakota. They spent two days sightseeing there before travelling overland again from Siena to Rome (probably the airfield at Fabrico) on 9 August and taking a return flight in another DC-3 Dakota back to Marcianise. From 9 August to 12 September Desmond did not fly and instead took a month's leave, much of which he spent with Patsy. She had photos of them in Assisi dated 7 September.

There are two photos of them taken later on a beach and in front of a hotel, when they stayed at the officers' rest camp at (La) Cocumella.

The hotel is built on the top of a steep cliff near Sorrento, overlooking the bay. It had then, and still has, access to its own private beach nestled in a sheltered cove at the foot of the cliffs, accessed by a series of narrow stone steps cut into the rock face.

The two of them photographed each other enjoying the sunshine and the privacy afforded by the surroundings. Desmond is, in one picture, larking about posing in his swimming trunks, and in the other laid back in a uniform shirt and shorts, relaxing on a small sundeck at the bottom of the cliffs. Desmond took a photo of Patsy as she perched on the side of one of the rowing boats beached on the sand, her right hand outstretched resting on the one to the front of her to balance herself, while her bare feet dangle lazily off the side of the boat, her toes just dipping into the sand.

Desmond travelled to Loreto airfield, located on the Adriatic coast halfway between Ancona to the north and the port town of Civitanova to the south, on 12 September to begin his next posting at 5 RFU as an instructor and flight commander. A good mate from 601 Squadron, Alan Radcliffe, was already there as A Flight commander, and arriving on the same day as Desmond to begin instructor duties was another mate from 601 Squadron, Fg Off Mitch Hammet.

Desmond also knew the CFI, Sqn Ldr William B. Hay, because they had flown together under Maj Osler in the autumn and winter of 1943–44. Desmond had been a flying officer on B Flight, while Hay had been a flight lieutenant in charge of A Flight. Then Desmond received his promotion and took command of B Flight. In March 1944, Hay, who was another of the Americans flying in the RCAF, had been granted a promotion and left 601's A Flight to take command of No. 417 Squadron. After just three months or so in that role, Hay was then posted to No. 5 RFU. He brought with him a big black dog called Nick.[2]

The RFU was a cross between an OTU and a gunnery school. It served as an intermediary flying school for experienced pilots returning to the front line after a spell of non-operational duties, pilots of mixed experience who were joining to rebuild a squadron or a squadron that was re-equipping or converting to a new type of fighter. The syllabus focused on formation flying, aerobatics, tail chasing, bombing and strafing.[3] Desmond had already flown with this unit two years earlier in Egypt when it had been the DAF Training Flight. Back then,

No. 5 Refresher Flying Unit

he was a sergeant converting to Kittyhawks. Now he was back teaching the same course.

Desmond began flying duties on 14 September and took an old Spitfire Mk V (Charlie 4) as his own for the next few days. On 15 September, he was assigned as flight commander of C Flight in place of Capt R.K. Hall (SAAF), who left to return to South Africa.[4]

From 17 September, and throughout the rest of the month, Desmond then used Spitfire VB 'Charlie 2' as his own. After he had finished his instructional sortie on Tuesday 19 September, he flew 'C2' across to Marcianise again to visit Patsy before returning to Loreto the following day to teach a trainee how to conduct bombing in a Spitfire. After he finished, he had the chance to take his first and only flight in a Mustang P-51 fighter, which lasted 45 minutes, and he found it to be an 'excellent aircraft'. P-51D Mustangs – equipped with the Packard Merlin engines built under licence in the USA – were just beginning to replace the Kittyhawks of 239 Wing, now based at Jesi airfield approximately 20 miles north-west of Loreto.

Shortly after this, the CO, Wg Cdr Charles Overton, received instructions to prepare the squadron to move around 80 miles inland to Perugia on 24 September. Perugia was a well-equipped airfield with concrete hardstandings and tarmacked runway and taxiways, and the move was completed by mid-afternoon the following day. However, the move made it more difficult to get the fuel needed for flying through from the supply dump at Arezzo to continue the normal training schedule. This was mainly due to a lack of transport and the distance to the dump, which was around 20 miles away to the north, almost halfway to Florence. To add to the demand for fuel, 11 Squadron SAAF now arrived to begin their conversion training to fly Kittyhawks under the instruction of 5 RFU.

Although Desmond flew the odd sortie over the next couple of days with students, the weather closed in again, considerably restricting the normal flying programme. Instead, the pilots went off to explore Assisi and use the facilities at the Hotel Giotto.

The heavy rain continued over the next few days into early October, marring the normal routine of things. Conditions on the base were poor to say the least, with the men living in tents; the aircraft were parked on the field as there were insufficient concreted areas to house them all on the base.

On 2 October, Flt Lt Leitch was tasked with leading a flight of five Spitfires from C Flight out on a training flight. As their flight commander, Desmond should have taken this group out, but he was still away, having spent the previous night over in Marcianise. When he finally did return to base, the CO informed him the flight were overdue from their sortie. Put another way, they had gone missing and nobody had heard from them. As this group was technically Desmond's responsibility, he was tasked with going out and finding them! He took a spare Kittyhawk and set off to look for them. He headed east and was up for 45 minutes searching before putting down at Foiano airstrip halfway between Siena and Perugia. Desmond eventually found C Flight safely ensconced at Castiglione airfield on the shores of Lake Trasimeno, where they had decided to land after running into bad weather. As there are high mountains to the western side of the lake between Castiglione and Perugia, this was probably a wise move. What they had not done, though, was let anyone know! Desmond flew back to Perugia, relieved to have found his missing pilots. Eventually, the pilots flew back to Perugia.

Lake Trasimeno is Italy's fourth largest lake and is bounded by eight different *comuni*, or municipalities. Although the area had been territorially disputed and fought over for centuries, it is now a tourist destination, but in 1944 the RAF was using the lake as a bombing range, and the students of 5 RFU regularly practised dive-bombing and strafing runs over the water. Despite there being a well-established fishing industry on the lake, targets would be towed out onto the water for the pilots to aim at. Then, when the RAF had finished for the day, some of the locals went out to collect the dead fish that had risen to the surface from the exploding bombs.

On 6 October, Desmond flew a Harvard down to Marcianise with Patsy as passenger. Despite the poor weather through the following weeks, Desmond and Patsy continued to see each other regularly. He made these flights in a Harvard on 6, 8, 15, 19 and 23 October. A violent storm blew in on 7 October and flooded many of the pilots' tents; by 9 October it had caused much flooding across the whole camp. The bad weather in the region continued and was clearly causing the RAF problems at airfields right across Umbria and Tuscany. As Perugia was a reasonably large airfield with a hard tarmacked runway, well-constructed taxiways, dispersals and hangars, the only option was to fly a few aircraft in from outlying airstrips that were getting bogged out. These included thirty-two Spitfires of 7 Wing SAAF, followed by twenty twin-engined Bostons and several Baltimore bombers.

Perugia airfield was feeling the strain of such a high number of aircraft using the base and was gradually succumbing to the torrential rain. In mid-October some twenty-nine local Italian labourers had to be drafted in to begin repair work to the taxiways and runway. The officers' main concerns during this period in October and through into November were the problems caused to the aerodrome facilities (runways, taxiways, control facilities and tentage) and flying training programme through the severe bad weather, which only let up for a day or two at any one time over these few weeks. Subsidence following heavy rainfall caused large craters to appear at certain points in the runway surface, meaning repairs were ongoing for a day or two each time and caused the airfield to be shut down and declared unserviceable on at least two subsequent occasions in early to mid-November while repairs were carried out. Also of concern were the frequency and severity of a spate of accidents and near misses during training flights which, on more occasions than was expected, resulted in the complete loss of both aeroplane and pilot. During October the accident rate was about two per week.

In the first week of October, Sgts Law and Fox were killed flying into Lake Trasimeno.[5] Then, on 16 and 17 October, two RFU students were nearly killed when they hit trees and power lines while practising low flying. On 19 October, a Kittyhawk pilot crashed his fighter when caught by a gust of crosswind on landing at Perugia. The day after, another pilot – this time in a Spitfire from 5 RFU – tried to make an emergency landing at Castiglione but misjudged his approach and crashed on overshooting the end of the runway. On 30 October, Sgt Coulson survived a crash near Grutti, which resulted in his Spitfire being written off. Finally, on 31 October, in a period of excellent weather, Flt Sgt Swales crashed his Spitfire on Perugia's runway but escaped serious injury. On each occasion, the squadron engineering officer, Fg Off James, attended the scene to recover the pilot and wreckage.

Desmond flew down to Marcianise to spend six days in Naples from 23 to 29 October. He celebrated his 23rd birthday there on 25 October.

He met up with Patsy and they went around Naples together – a photo of the pair together is dated 24 October 1944. He reported back for flying duties as usual at the end of the month, but early November saw heavy rain and fog stop any flying from Perugia for several days in the first week.

Patsy then travelled up to Assisi in early November, and the last known pictures taken of Desmond show him and Patsy outside the Basilica di St Francesco in the autumn sunshine. One is dated 6 November 1944 and shows Desmond sitting on the wall at the top of the steps overlooking the main courtyard. He doesn't even seem aware the photo is being taken and is absentmindedly fiddling with his own camera. Another photo shows him at the foot of the steps in the piazza, jokingly striking a pose and pretending to gaze off into the distance.

The day after, Desmond returned to instructor duty at Perugia and took Spitfire 'Charlie 1' up on a routine 30-minute air test with no problems. He did the same on 8 November in 'Charlie 3' – again, no problems.

In the second week of November, Desmond flew, on average, one sortie a day, using for the most part Spitfire 'Charlie 5', even though the heavy and regular rain continued to disrupt the usual run of training. It was getting much colder, and snow fell for the first time on the surrounding mountains on 10 November. It then picked up a little to allow flying over the next three days, but on 14 November the heavy rain started again, washing out the flying programme completely and causing more problems on the runway to the extent that from the late afternoon of 15 November, the airfield was shut again for two more days to allow repairs to the runway to be made. For the staff of 5 RFU the current course of students had managed to complete their training and the students for the next course arrived in on Friday 17 November. These factors would account for Desmond's lack of flying in these few days rather than any more leave, because from 14 to 18 November inclusive he did not fly at all. By now, Desmond was due to make another of his regular trips to Marcianise.

Then, after five days of instructing and a break of five more days due to bad weather, he took 'Charlie 7' up on Sunday 19 November for another air test. He had never flown this particular aircraft before, and he probably followed the same route he had with the other Spits.

It was the last flight he ever took.

CHAPTER 20

5 RFU – Final Flight

St Egidio Airfield, Perugia
19 November 1944

The morning of Sunday 19 November starts cold and fair, but quite misty. Flying is temporarily suspended to see if the mist will clear. Yet again, the instructors and students are restless, kicking their heels, itching to get flying again. Later that afternoon, it does clear, and flying can resume.

A new course is starting tomorrow, and the aircraft that have been in for servicing while the weather was poor are to be returned to the flight line for use by the training school. A new plane is also being flown in. The pilot, Flt Sgt Gregory, is bringing in a Spitfire Mk IX (No. EN446) to land, misjudges the approach and crashes on the runway. Fortunately, he causes more damage to the plane than to himself. Soon after, another pilot, 2nd Lt G.D. Doveton, is taxiing out in a different Spitfire Mk IX (No. JL364) when he collides with a jeep.[1] The day is not going well so far.

Desmond decides to take out one of the Mk IXs that needs an air test. This one is a clipped-wing version. Fast and highly manoeuvrable, the Spitfire Mk LF IXe is a delight to fly and good at low level with a high rate of roll, making it ideal for ground attack and air-to-air fighting. The fuel tanks are full, and there is a full complement of ammunition, although this is not needed today. As the autumn days are getting shorter and the light will soon begin to fade, this will probably be the last flight of the day.

The Spitfire is Charlie 7 (No. MH614), and it isn't Desmond's usual plane. He's flown virtually all the other aircraft in the flight already: usually either Charlie 2, 4 or 5, with just one sortie each in Charlie 1, 3, 9 and 11 – but never this one. Perhaps that is why he has chosen it. Back when he was on 601 Squadron they had the 'long-wing' types. This is a 'clippy' and just that little bit different. Flights like this one (a routine post-servicing test) are carried out, like a test drive, just to make sure the work done by the mechanics is satisfactory.

Desmond is wearing his regular uniform: battledress jacket, trousers and black shoes. His only flying kit is a leather helmet, gloves and a parachute. He won't be out for long, so doesn't bother with a flying suit or boots. As instructors, they don't get that high or cold for that long, and shoes will give him better feel on the rudder controls. A good deal of the training is at the lower levels, that is below 10,000ft. He signs the RAF Form 700 to take responsibility for the aircraft at around 3 p.m., having already given himself a few minutes to check over the aircraft's particulars, what work was done on it, any minor faults still present that won't affect the Spitfire getting into the air or behaving normally, and any comments the flight line mechanics may have made. He heads towards his Spitfire and walks around it, carrying out the usual checks on the airframe, wing tanks and guns, control surfaces and tyres – just to make sure there are no obvious faults such as fastenings or filler caps undone, no tyre wear or 'creep' and free movement of the ailerons, rudder and elevators. Then he takes his parachute off the wing and wriggles into the harness, does up the straps, steps up onto the port wing root and gets into the cockpit. One of the two attendant airmen helps him strap himself into the bucket seat, then steps off the wing. Desmond pulls his helmet onto his head, snuggles his ears into the radio earphones and does up the chinstrap. He plugs his R/T lead into the socket at the side of his seat and starts going through the checklist for start-up. When he's ready, he looks around to the side and front of the aircraft, signals to the groundcrew he's going to start the engine and calls, 'Contact'. The generator whines as it draws power from the auxiliary starter to turn the prop shaft. Very slowly, the propellor blades start to turn. Then there is a cough, followed by another and then a surge as the Merlin 66 catches and roars into life. As it kicks in, Desmond gives it a touch of throttle to make sure the Spit's happily running on its own, and the airman steps forward to remove the generator plug from the side of the engine. The aeroplane now idling on its own power, Desmond waves the chocks away and draws the canopy shut to keep out the noise and cold draught.

Now he releases the brakes, gives the Spitfire a touch more throttle and begins to taxi out to the northern end of the runway, zigzagging from side to side as he does so, so he can see forward of the Spitfire's long, raised nose. Once at the hold point, he does his last set of ground checks, is given the green light from the black-and-white-chequered control caravan at the edge of the taxiway and rolls forward onto the runway. He adds a touch of power to counteract the friction and pushes his right foot on the rudder pedal to swing the aircraft round to the right so he can line up dead on the centreline of the runway. As he straightens up, he applies the brake by using the lever on the control column. Now the last 'pre-take-off' checks follow, but he knows them all off by heart anyway — just the odd one or two different actions from the Mk V, but still he calls them out to himself: trimming tabs (elevator one notch down, rudder fully right); propellor (speed control lever fully forward); fuel cocks (main tank ON, drop tank OFF, rear fuselage OFF, main tanks booster pump ON); flaps (UP); supercharger switch (auto-normal position and red light out) and, finally, carburettor air intake filter control (closed).[2]

Everything is fine. There is nothing else in the air or taxiing across the runway, so he slowly but insistently pushes the throttle lever fully forward and releases the brakes as the engine reaches around 75 per cent power, continuing to push the throttle fully forward to maximum in one smooth motion. Now the nimble little fighter starts to roll forward again, very quickly gathering speed. The aeroplane comes to life in one easy, smooth movement, charging inexorably forward. Desmond keeps his left hand on the throttle and right hand on the stick, ready to guide the fighter into the air. He can feel the Merlin's power coursing through the whole airframe, recognising the sounds and vibrations instinctively, subconsciously attuned to whether it all feels right — hardly surprising given he has accumulated over 600 flying hours in Spitfires alone.

As the propellor washes the air back along the fuselage and tail, the Spitfire begins, ever so slightly, to try to swing to the left. At the same time Desmond applies right rudder to counter the movement and is so used to it now, there is not even a twitch in the tail to show he has done it. Keeping it running nicely down the centreline, the tail comes up and, in a few seconds or so, around the 100–110 knot mark on the airspeed indicator, depending on the wind, the Spit wants to be off and flying. The lightest touch of 'back-pressure' on the stick and the wheels are off the tarmac.

Suddenly the rumbling and heavy vibration echoing through the cockpit is gone. In less than 20 seconds, the plane is in smooth air. It's time to bring the undercarriage up – dab the wheel brakes to stop the wheels spinning as they come up and watch for the indicator lights. Listen carefully and you can just perhaps hear the wheels travel home and lock themselves away one by one. Already, there are a few more knots of airspeed coming on as a result. Take-off time will be logged as 3.10 p.m. Now Desmond settles the fighter into a steady climb and heads beyond the airfield boundaries, to the south initially, following the extended line of the runway and looking towards the mountains in the far distance. The airfield recedes beneath him. The good weather gives him a distinct visual horizon by which to judge his manoeuvres, the first of which is a gentle climbing turn to the left, to head eastwards towards Foligno.

It is a beautiful day. The wind isn't gusty or harsh, and the sunlight begins to fill the cockpit, light reflecting off the dial glasses on the instrument panel every so often. The air in the cockpit chills as Desmond climbs the Spitfire up to about 3,000ft and heads down the wide valley where the River Tevere (Tiber) and its tributary, the River Chiascio, meet. Assisi is clearly visible off the left wing, its huge basilica perched proudly on the end of the ridge, ivory-coloured walls gleaming in the sunshine and snow-capped, rounded mountain tops behind. He can appreciate the building again from the air. It is no longer just a navigation marker. Instead, it is where he spent time relaxing with Patsy as they explored the courtyards and cloisters only a few days ago. That summer they had walked miles together, around the towns and along the paths through fields and woods. Monte Subasio stands just to the east and to the rear of Assisi, 4,000ft high and imposing, its grass-green summit now dusted lightly with snow. All the trees, except the firs and pines, that surround the lower slopes are shedding their brown leaves. Winter is coming. Christmas is only a month away.

Foligno, directly to the south-east of Perugia at the neck of the valley and some way off the Spitfire's nose, is not quite yet visible, but smoke is rising from chimneys up ahead – that must be it. The air outside is still cold and getting slightly colder but still everything appears normal. It's a shame Desmond can't do any aerobatics on this flight, but it's only a check flight. He just has to make sure all the rivets and panels stay in place and there are no strange noises or leaks coming from anywhere.

It's 10 minutes into the flight now and still the Merlin growls happily away to itself. There's even the chance to look around below for a few seconds to see what is going on, if anything – nothing except the odd vehicle, mainly army trucks. Habit compels Desmond to scan the instrument panel at regular intervals. 'Look outside for 75 per cent of the time, inside only 25 per cent,' his instructor had said, way back when he was a student. A skilled pilot needs even less time to look at the instruments. He knows just where to look on the panel and what the warning signs are. He doesn't always need to know the actual readings; just the general position of the needle on the dial tells him whether everything is all right. Moreover, a pilot of Desmond's experience can feel the aeroplane by instinct and intuition. Desmond is very attuned to it. He listens for changes in engine noise, unfamiliar noises and even the sound of the air around him as it passes over and around the cockpit. He looks alternately between the far middle and near distance, his eyes focusing on anything of a different shape or movement – a little black dot in the distance, perhaps. His fingers and hands can sense the subtle movements of the Spitfire and how it feels as it cruises along effortlessly at nearly 250mph, occasionally dipping a fraction or bucking with the rise, fall and movement of the air. But today all is clear. There are no clouds around, so there are still no particularly strong gusts or downdraughts.

As he approaches the outskirts of Foligno, Desmond decides to turn around and head for home. He looks out into the sky ahead and beyond, then around, then out to the edge of the wing, which he then dips to initiate the turn. He does it all naturally, coordinating the subtle adjustments made by his right hand using the control column, with his left hand adjusting the throttle as required during the turn. He fixes the nose correctly against the horizon in front, then looks into the turn, focusing his attention to the side again to check the reference point he is turning towards and where he wants to roll out. As the Spitfire noses round towards Perugia, then to Assisi, he rolls the wings level with the estimated end of the runway just to one side of the nose. That will mark the start of the downwind leg and the point at which he will enter the circuit to bring the Spitfire home again. He completes a loop or two – nothing demanding – and levels off on the same heading. Now he readjusts the trim for pitch slightly and relaxes again. The Spitfire is back practically flying itself now, and about 15 minutes of flying time has elapsed. Perugia airfield is no more than 10 minutes away; St Maria d'Angeli is approaching off to the right of the nose. Desmond is straight and level at nearly 2,500ft, and there are no indications anything is about to go wrong. Until now.

At this point, something in the flight changes. The Spitfire's nose drops forward as it enters a dive. The engine noise turns from a smooth, regular growl into a whine: a rising insistent pitch as though it's going to attack a target below. But there is no target. There is no reason to dive – no low flying, no reason to show off – not today. This is just an air test.

As Desmond passes the 2,000ft mark on the altimeter, there is very little time left to do something if he needs to get out. But whatever is happening, the dive cannot be corrected. If anything, it is getting worse and now seems irretrievable. Down and down goes the fighter, gathering more and more speed all the time. The engine pitch rising all the time, the needle on the airspeed indicator goes round faster, winding round the dial clockwise as the altimeter unwinds anticlockwise at almost the same alarming rate. Both dials are acting as though they are in free fall. Come on, little Spit. Come on, pull out. If it does respond, he will be very low and very fast. But at least he would be near straight and level again. Just a few seconds into the dive and Desmond is now too low to bail out. What options he has are running out fast, evaporating in the final seconds of flight. Now he is below 1,000ft. It has to be a forced-landing, but the less response there is, the harder the landing will be. There is no choice. Just a couple of hundred feet left, less than 2 seconds at this speed. Still no response. Nothing. The Spitfire is locked in its dive and, in his last view outside of that tiny cockpit, all Desmond can see is the dark blur of bare brown earth. There's a loud scrape: he's hit a treetop. Immediately this is followed by a loud and violent explosion. The Spitfire, still two-thirds full of fuel and loaded with ammunition is effectively a bomb. Travelling at around 200mph, it smashes headlong into a remote Italian field. Desmond is killed instantly.

There was no radio message, no call for help.

Nobody knew where he was, and nobody, it seems, saw what happened.

He was 23.

PART 3

The Aftermath

The Family and Two Burial Sites for One Man

CHAPTER 21

The Aftermath

Castelnuovo, Italy
19 November 1944–May 1945

As the thump of the explosion fell to silence, and the plume of thick, black, oily smoke rose above the field, some of those who were in farmhouses nearby, or about a mile away in the closest village, Castelnuovo, were roused to action and headed for the scene.

While the basilica at Assisi, on the edge of the ridge, can be seen from the airfield on the eastern horizon, the field where the Spitfire came down and nearby village cannot. They lie across the plain, on flat land to the south-east, so are not visible from Perugia airfield.

Perhaps off-duty officers on the balcony of the Hotel Giotto looking out across the fields to the south-east heard the aeroplane hit the ground and, seeing a rising column of smoke suspected an accident and contacted a squadron at Perugia.

It was possibly this that triggered the single-engined Auster spotter plane to be sent out. It arrived over the scene shortly after. The pilot could see a group of civilians now gathered around the scattered wreckage. A few of them looked up to watch the Auster as it circled overhead, wondering if it intended to land. The pilot focused his attention on the deep, dark hole beneath him and the pockets of fire surrounding it. He noted the location on a map and radioed back to base. He lingered a minute or so longer to ensure there was nothing else to report and the location he had given was accurate, then turned away and flew back to Perugia. The villagers turned their attention back to the scene in front of them.

The RAF began to act on the message confirming a downed aeroplane. An Army major was assigned to take charge on site. He took with him a field ambulance, a truck and several soldiers with rifles to guard the site. When they arrived, it was clear there was no hope of finding the pilot – at least, not in the wreckage, but also because there was no evidence of a parachute. No parachute meant the pilot was probably still inside when the plane hit the ground. In the expression of today, this was now no longer a rescue operation; it was a recovery operation.[1]

Having done what they could (most of), the Army contingent left the scene as dusk fell, leaving behind a handful of soldiers to guard the site. They returned the following day, Monday, to organise the excavation and removal of the wrecked Spitfire. The wings and tailplane could be retrieved more easily as they were on the ground, but bringing up the remainder of the fuselage was going to take a lot longer. The work began as soon as they arrived, but it took a further two days of digging, shoring and lifting to complete the retrieval. On Wednesday 22 November, the 5 RFU adjutant recorded, 'The remains of Flt. Lt. D. Ibbotson were recovered after digging to a depth of approx. 20 feet.'[2]

The news was now passed quickly through the formal channels from the squadron. The CO and Desmond's friend, Sqn Ldr Hay, notified Wing and MAAF HQ, who notified the Air Ministry in London. They sent a telegram stating that he was 'missing believed killed in accident to aircraft Spitfire 9 MH614 on 19-11-44'.[3] One copy went to Desmond's parents, the second copy to Nurse Joan Barras at St Luke's Hospital, Bradford. The telegram arrived at his grandma's post office in Harewood just two days later and was received by his sister Muriel. At the time, Desmond's mother, Sarah, who ran the post office, was ill in hospital. Muriel had to go and tell her the sad news. This was followed very soon after by a second telegram confirming Desmond as 'previously missing on 19-11-44, now killed on active service. Body recovered o/seas.'[4]

Having been formally identified during the week, on Sunday 26 November, a week after Desmond had been killed, Padre Savage from No. 5 General Hospital conducted a church service and burial at the British Military Cemetery on the outskirts of Assisi.[5] There are no records or photographs of his funeral service, so just who among his friends and colleagues attended is not known. Perhaps Patsy was there, along with a few of his mates from 601 and 112 Squadrons who had heard the news. It had been around six months since Desmond had last seen any of them, and they were now based 60 miles away at Fano on the Adriatic coast, following the steadily advancing front line.[6] Perhaps a few of those left from his desert days made it in time for the funeral.

On Monday morning, 27 November, Capt C. Sinclair of 11 Squadron SAAF was formally assigned the task of investigating Desmond's crash.[7] Sinclair's squadron had previously flown Spitfires, but its pilots were ordered to retrain on the Kittyhawk under the tutelage of instructors at 5 RFU, including Desmond.

It was certainly unusual for an outsider from another squadron to be appointed to investigate an accident, but Capt Sinclair was one of two flight commanders and a senior pilot on 11 Squadron. While the task of investigating the cause of Desmond's accident landed on Sinclair's desk may owe more to the simple exigencies of war and availability of suitably qualified staff, Sinclair would have known Desmond personally and received his advice as both a pilot and flight commander. The two would have worked together to develop the training programme, and Desmond would have kept Sinclair updated with the progress of the trainees under his command until they completed their conversion course on the last day of October.[8]

Capt Sinclair was the last known official to view the wreck and remains of Desmond's Spitfire. With the formalities of such an investigation having been completed, the hole was refilled, the ground levelled and handed back to the Cavallucci family. It was reploughed and replanted in time for the following year's harvest. Sinclair completed his report, filled in the covering form to return to the Air Ministry and gave the order for the recovered wreckage, piled in the corner of a hangar, to be disposed of. Sinclair and the remainder of his squadron finally moved to Pontedera near Pisa in mid-December 1944 and carried on with the war until it ended in Europe on 8 May 1945.[9]

Following Desmond's death and the end of the war, Patsy went through her collection of photographs and sent all but a handful of images of herself and Desmond to Sarah in Yorkshire. Some time after Colin Rawlins' Hampden bomber had gone missing, Patsy and

Delphine learnt that Colin was finally, as she put it, 'safely in the bag'. His Hampden bomber had been intercepted and shot down by a night fighter in May 1941. Of the four crew on board, Colin and his navigator survived; the two gunners were killed. Colin had managed to bail out but did so at very low altitude. The result was that he landed heavily and broke his ankle – somewhat hampering any escape attempt he may have wanted to make. He was captured by the Germans and taken to the German naval hospital at Alkmaar, 20 miles north of Amsterdam in occupied Holland. He remained there for three months, recuperating before being taken to Frankfurt for further interrogation, then onward to the first of several PoW camps before finally ending up at Stalag Luft III near Sagan – the camp made famous by the book and film *The Great Escape*. Colin was one of hundreds of RAF PoWs repatriated to the UK from Germany as part of Operation Exodus in 1945.

Patsy remained in the Middle East working in C&C and continued to blag flights whenever she could. After the end of the war in Europe, and hearing news of Colin's repatriation, she managed to return to the UK for a few weeks' leave with Colin before returning to Egypt. A few months later, she telegraphed Colin to say she had been offered another posting elsewhere in the Middle East. She asked whether she should come back instead – the implication being a future together. He telegraphed back, 'yes'. In 1946, Patsy returned from the Middle East, was demobbed, married Colin and raised three children including a son, Rob.

Desmond's story began to pass slowly into history. He became a footnote in the official records, remembered and missed only by his family and a handful of close friends.

CHAPTER 22

Sarah Remembers Desmond – The Way to the Stars

Harewood, West Yorkshire
1945–50

Desmond's flying logbooks were sent from the RAF Central Repository to Sarah's home in Harewood almost two years after his death.

The film *The Way to the Stars* was released in 1945, before she received them and after the war in Europe had ended. The title is a play on the words of the RAF motto, *Per Ardua Ad Astra* ('Through adversity to the stars'). This particular film opens with the camera tracking around a fictional disused airfield, which had been fully operational during the Battle of Britain. It tells the story through the eyes of one RAF pilot, Plt Off Peter Penrose. He had been part of a group of pilots who had started the war together on the same squadron but had gradually fallen victim to the aerial fighting during the summer of 1940. The story includes the entry of America into the war and shows the change from Britain 'fighting alone' to flying joint bomber raids with the Americans over occupied Europe.

The narrative recounts the effects this had on the squadron's personnel and the local civilians. At a time when there was great social change, celebration at the end of the war and servicemen returning home, this film was a timely reflection on what service personnel, families and the country had just been through. Based on Terrence Rattigan's play *Flare Path*, it deals with the sense of loss and deep grief that others were feeling for those loved ones who had flown with the RAF and were never going to come home.

The film uses one of John Pudney's poems to express the sense of loss that many may have been feeling. That poem is called 'For Johnny' and is read by the character Peter Penrose, played by John Mills, in a scene where he recites the verse to a young wife whose husband had been killed. The British Film Institute's description of the film notes that 'it also puts into relief the film's main focus – Penrose's development from callow youth into a burnt-out, emotionally detached pilot, and his eventual return to life and love'.[1]

Of course, Desmond could not, like the fictional Penrose, return to life and love. But the poem would help comfort Sarah as she read the story of Desmond's career through the text of his logbooks and reflected on the life of her only son.

Although unfamiliar with the meaning of many of the notes, as she turned each page, Sarah could recognise her son's voice in the longer entries about what had happened or what he had seen. First came his doubts and understatements, the dream of flying a Spitfire – achieved in the summer of 1941 – then his escape from the Afrika Korps in the Egyptian desert in 1942, his surprise at enjoying a dogfight with an Italian pilot, to feeling hungover on Boxing Day 1943 and flying someone called Patsy around in the summer of 1944. She could follow the growth of her son from a teenager with no previous flying ability to a professional Spitfire pilot, leader and instructor. She could also see the names of those he had known, mates who had 'bailed out' were 'missing', then perhaps 'found safe, but badly wounded', 'got clobbered' or 'collected a helluva packet', until his own fate, 'crashed'.

When she watched *The Way to the Stars*, the poem used clearly struck a poignant note with Sarah; she transcribed the text of it onto a slip of paper and stuck it into the back of Desmond's second logbook. The words would have reminded her that she was not the only one who had lost a close relative to the vagaries of war and RAF operations, where men left base and were never heard from again. Unfortunately, Sarah had no answers. All she could do was hope the accident that killed him was instantaneous and that he felt no pain.

However, there were the ever-present questions of why and how the accident had happened. How could someone so experienced and competent have come to such a sudden and unexpected end?

After the war, British aviation stood tall. The industry was a world leader by some margin. The Spitfires, along with most of the propellor-driven aeroplanes that had proliferated in the war years, were retired, scrapped or sold off to air forces overseas such as Israel and Greece. These venerable servants had been replaced by jet-engined fighters and bombers. As the RAF pilots demobbed, they took up civilian flying posts as commercial airline pilots or company test pilots for the likes of Avro, Hawker, Bristol and Supermarine. The exploits of former fighter aces such as John Derry, John 'Cats Eyes' Cunningham and Neville Duke made headline news, and they became household names once more, as test pilots who set world records as they flew higher and faster than ever before in modern jet aircraft.

In September 1952, John Derry was demonstrating a prototype twin-engine jet aircraft (the de Havilland DH-110, forerunner to the Royal Navy's Sea Vixen) at the Farnborough Air Show. He had broken the sound barrier by executing a high-speed dive, pulled out at 1,000–1,500ft, then began a high-speed circuit of the airfield. As he turned towards the crowd line, at about 400ft, the aircraft suddenly broke up mid-air, killing both crew (Derry and his observer, Anthony Richards) instantly, with the debris scattering among the crowd below and in front, causing twenty-nine fatalities and many more injured.[2]

The whole tragedy was caught on newsreel and handheld cameras, a very visible demonstration of the dangers and risks inherent in test flying. It is likely that, as a result of seeing and reading about such accidents, as well as the fact the last entry in Desmond's logbook read 'Air Test', Sarah, Muriel and Molly came to understand Desmond's death as an accident that happened to him while out test flying a Spitfire.

CHAPTER 23

Sarah Visits Desmond's Grave

Assisi, Italy
1950

It was not until I interviewed Desmond's niece, the daughter of his younger sister, Molly, in 2016 that I came across another strand of their family's story. Some years earlier, Muriel and Molly had fallen out, causing a rift between the two sisters. But the discovery of Desmond and his Spitfire, and the subsequent newspaper article, had forced the sisters to confront their memories of the loss of their brother. Not surprisingly, this brought some uncomfortable emotions to the fore.

By the time of the ceremony in Italy, the sisters were in touch again. Molly's only daughter, Jayne, now lived near Ilkley. After the family handed over Desmond's medals and memorabilia to the Yorkshire Air Museum, I arranged to interview her about Desmond to see what the view had been from Molly's side of the family.

I expected to hear the same stories about Desmond that I had heard from Muriel, but that was not necessarily the case. Molly had a clear memory of being in the family post office one day in late 1944. This was after Muriel had already received the telegrams and told Sarah about Desmond's fatality. Sarah had by then returned home from the hospital to convalesce when a parcel arrived addressed to Sarah.

It was wrapped in thick brown paper and tied crossways with thin binding string.

The formal handwriting style, official government department stamps and title, 'Mrs H. Ibbotson', dampened the light heart with which she might otherwise have opened the bundle. Inside were one or two personal items of Desmond's clothing, the largest and most significant of which was the battledress jacket he had been wearing on 19 November.

Sarah took the parcel through to the kitchen at the back of the house and opened it on the table. As she lifted the jacket up, she could see, as it unfurled, the two thin blue parallel stripes on each epaulette denoting Desmond's rank. Just above the left breast pocket were the faded silver wings. Between the wings and the top of the pocket were a sequence of coloured ribbons. On the left side of these ribbons was a diagonal-striped purple and white ribbon with a rosette on it, signifying the award of two DFCs. The original colours were tarnished in places, stained deeply by the rich, dark smears of blood that had penetrated the fibres.

Whoever had gathered the jacket and other items together had not considered the impact this might have on his family. Molly, then just a young girl, stood between the kitchen and the shop front of the post office. She watched her mother open the package and start to cry, Muriel next to her.

The jacket was not the only thing to be returned from Italy. Around the same time, a letter and photographs were sent to Sarah. The covering letter, which no longer survives, was from Patsy. Sarah took these precious photographs and placed them carefully in an album with those of her own.

The album was detailed, valuable and utterly personal, filling in many gaps in Sarah's knowledge about Desmond's life in the RAF after he had left England for North Africa just over two years earlier. But Sarah had other questions. Where had he been in the days before the crash? The letter and photographs allowed Sarah to put a face to Patsy's name, but she didn't really know who she was and what she had meant to Desmond. What was their relationship to each other? Would they have got married and returned to England to start a family? And who were the other pilots shown alongside Desmond? Would they still be around? Did they survive, and would anyone be able to tell her how he died?

Sometime after she had received the telegram of Desmond's death, the then Imperial War Graves Commission (now the Commonwealth War Graves Commission) sent Sarah an official letter and brief guide as to which cemetery Desmond had been buried in. The cemetery site itself had only been laid down in September 1944, two months before Desmond's death.

Six months after these items arrived, the war in Europe ended, followed three months later by the end of the war in the Far East. All over the country, for another twelve months or more, those who had been in the armed forces were demobbed. The country was shattered though. The economy had been given over to total war, and the population had to adjust to a new reality, as well as the continuation of rationing and austerity. It took another five years of working and saving before Sarah had enough money to travel to Italy to find where her son had been killed. By then, she had divorced Horace and begun a new life. She would make the long trip across the ruins of Europe to see for herself where Desmond had been living and walk the same ground he had done in the final days and weeks of his life, to see the same views he had seen, be where he had been.

During our discussion, Jayne produced a photo album. In among the copies of photos I had already seen were others I had not – ones that were unique to Molly. One of them was of Sarah with a small group of unidentified people. They were all gathered round a small café-style table outside. I looked carefully at the photo. In the background were the distinctive tall stone arches of the basilica in Assisi. Sarah was in the middle of the photo, looking different but still recognisable. Middle age had thickened her limbs and waist a little. Her hair was still dark and waved in the 1940s style but was lifted and curled away from her face. She was looking to the camera through thick-rimmed, round-lensed glasses and wore a short-sleeved, knee-length patterned tea dress, which led me to think the photo must have been taken on a late spring or early summer day.

It was dated 1950. The photo meant Sarah had managed to travel to Italy at around Easter time, alone, to find Desmond's final resting place. I had walked close to the spot where the photo was taken several times when I had been there, and indeed had taken photos from the nearby

Piazza Inferiore di San Francesco, where the broad pavement curves back on itself to continue up the slope to the front of the basilica.

I had been there to try to see exactly where Desmond and Patsy had stood when they had visited the basilica in early November 1944. Clearly, Sarah had seen those same photos and also endeavoured to see for herself where her son had been.

When she arrived, Sarah explored the town on foot. The narrow streets meant the town, positioned as it had been since the early middle ages high up on the natural elbow of a ridge, had no militarily useful purpose except as a rest area and observation post but, with the houses and other buildings stepped up and stretching their walls to the very edge of the valley sides, the Germans soon realised they could not dig in, drive tanks or armoured vehicles through the steep, narrow streets nor park any heavy artillery up there. Even the observation posts were moved out into the surrounding fields and woods to overlook the valley and roads below. This meant that, as the Allies had advanced, the Germans had withdrawn and left almost everything intact.

The photo shows Sarah with two female companions and a dark-haired, slim male sitting on a wooden chair in front of the three women. He and the woman standing to his left shoulder look to be locals and are perhaps the hotel owners. The woman in the middle of the group is also unidentified but seems to have a more English than Mediterranean complexion. These could be the people who helped her locate the military cemetery and Desmond's grave.

Walking through the wrought iron entrance gate of the cemetery on what was a fine and sunny day, Sarah would have had the impression of what all such Commonwealth cemeteries in Europe strive to achieve, that of a well-tended English country garden. Approaching the middle of spring, with the scent of roses, tulips and cypress in the air, it would have been all she could have hoped under the circumstances: that Desmond's final resting place was in such a scene of tranquillity.

There is one other photograph of her visit to Assisi. It shows a terracotta vase of flowers in front of Desmond's headstone. Nobody appears by the graveside, so it must have been taken by Sarah herself. In the vase, there are three white roses that stand above the accompanying tulips. There is something touchingly significant about this:

she had chosen three white Yorkshire roses – one each, from his mum and two sisters.

No doubt Sarah wondered what Desmond and Patsy had talked about as they paused here to take photos on the last sunny day of November 1944. Were they romantically involved? Was that why he hadn't come home that summer after his tour had ended? It would be hard not to fall in love with an attractive, intelligent young woman as they spent more time together in this ancient little hilltop town deep in the Umbrian countryside.

Sarah left for England a few days later and never returned to Assisi. In making this trip, Sarah had not only kept her promise, but she had also laid the foundations for the stories she would pass on in future to Muriel, Molly and her grandchildren. No one knew then that Desmond had not finished revealing his side of the story.

CHAPTER 24

Muriel Remembers Desmond's Death

Preston, Lancashire
September 2003

When I first met Muriel, I was not aware of her brother. In fact, I didn't initially go to visit her – it was her husband, Jim, who I was interested in talking to. Jim and my mum belonged to the village bowling club. On the evening of 9 September, Mum was sat on a bench by the green waiting for her turn. Jim Richardson sat down next to her and struck up a conversation, the most significant part of which was the phrase 'Do you know it's sixty years ago today since I went ashore at Salerno?' My mum listened as Jim described wading ashore as part of the landing forces as the Germans fired at them.

At that time, I had returned from university and lived at home with my parents. When I heard of their conversation, I telephoned Jim, explained how I had always been interested in military history (especially the Second World War) and asked if I could talk to him about his experiences. He agreed and we arranged to meet.

I interviewed Jim twice and, before I left after the end of the last session, Muriel arrived home. We chatted briefly and, as I made to leave, I mentioned the picture on the wall by the door to the kitchen and asked who it was.

'Oh, that's my brother Desmond,' she said.

The portrait, which showed just his head and shoulders, was printed on a china plate mounted on a wall bracket. The glaze made the colours, particularly that of his blue RAF uniform, richer. I mentioned the pilot's wings and asked what type of aircraft he flew.

'He was a Spitfire pilot,' Muriel replied.

'Wow. Is he still around?' I asked.

'No,' Muriel replied, 'he was killed in 1944.'

'What happened to him?' I asked, thinking he may have been shot down in a dogfight.

'He was killed test flying a Spitfire in Italy.'

'Would you mind if I researched his story?' I asked.

She was wiping up a spill on the side of the sink as she made tea. She stopped and looked ahead of her out of the window into the darkness outside. Her reply has stuck with me ever since:

'No, as long as you don't go muck-raking.'

We arranged to meet again, and she explained that what memorabilia there was left from Desmond's career had been divided between her two sons. One had the medals, the other the logbooks. Her eldest son, John, lived in Yorkshire, so seeing the medals should be straightforward. Her youngest son, David, lived in Australia, which made it more difficult. However, she told me there was a plan for both sons to visit her in the near future, so we could view the logbooks then.

I met Muriel again a few weeks later and looked through the logbooks. They were showing signs of age and water damage. The hardback covers were thick, dark-blue with patches of Sellotape on the spines. Inside, the pages seemed untouched. I held the spine of each logbook and carefully turned a few pages together, looking for key dates in both his life and the war. I turned to the last page, eager to see a clue about his last flight. There was precious little. The final entry read:

19 Nov 44– Spitfire C7– Air Test– :20– crashed.

Desmond normally completed an air test in 30 minutes. This flight lasted only 20 minutes. The details were written and signed by his Canadian friend and 5 RFU's CFI, Sqn Ldr W.B. Hay.

Underneath the handwritten entry is a bureaucratic stamp, in capital letters and red ink: 'Killed on active service', with another red oval stamp underneath from the RAF Depository and the date written in the centre. It was a sad, formal conclusion to the career of one of the RAF's best pilots, just an anonymous official mark at the end of a page. The logbook was closed, then packed along with other possessions and sent back to the UK.

When the Air Ministry notified Sarah and the family, the news arrived a month after Desmond's 23rd birthday and a month before Christmas. Later still, some of his possessions arrived. These included a collection of photographs of Desmond and various friends, followed by his flying jacket and medals. Then, nearly two years later, his logbooks arrived. Not all these items came through official channels though. The photographs, for example, came from a young woman named Patsy, who had clearly known Desmond very well. What made it difficult to trace this young woman though was that, according to Muriel, she was Danish, and there was no known address for her. Oh, and Patsy was not her real name.

Canne, Italy, 9 December 1943. No. 601 Squadron pilots with Spitfire Mk VIII JF485. On the top (sliding off the engine cowling) is Sgt John 'Tilly' Tilston (RAF). Ibby is fourth from right (light trousers, looking at the camera). On his left is Flt Sgt 'Dickie' Stickney (RAF); on his right is Flt Lt Sandy Kallio (USAAF). Fourth from left, front row (officer's hat, light trousers, flying boots, looking to the camera) is Flt Lt Peter 'Tommy' Thompson (RAF). The OC Major Malcolm 'Bennie' Osler (SAAF) is ninth from left (with light shoulder flashes on a battledress jacket and peak cap). Belgian André Eid is at the far left. Third from left, front row (light trousers) is Flt Lt 'Doc' Thomas, the squadron medical officer. (Air Ministry Crown Copyright/Ibbotson family album)

Muriel, March/April 1944, Yorkshire. (Ibbotson family album)

No. 244 Wing leaders at Triolo LG, near San Severo, Italy (L–R): Sqn Ldr P. Stanley 'Stan' Turner, OC of 417 Squadron; Sqn Ldr Peter Harry 'Hunk' Humphreys, CO of 92 Squadron; Wg Cdr Wilfred G.G. Duncan-Smith; Gp Cpt C. Brian F. Kingcome, CO 244 Wing; Sqn Ldr Lance C. Wade, CO of 145 Squadron; and Maj Malcolm 'Bennie' S. Osler (SAAF), CO 601 Squadron RAF. (Piemags/ww2archive/Alamy stock photo)

'Flt Lt Ibbotson of Yorkshire' in a Mk IX Spitfire, Italy, May 1944. Desmond's watch is now in the RoAF Museum. (IWM CNA2827)

Desmond receives the bar to his DFC, 25 May 1944. L–R: AVM Coningham, Desmond, ACM Sholto Douglas, AVM Broadhurst, unknown staff officer. (Ibbotson family album)

Desmond in flying gear, taken by Patsy, summer 1944. This is one of two of him in her memoir. (Rosemary Rawlins' family album)

Photo of Patsy taken by Ibby while hitching back to Naples, summer 1944. (Ibbotson family album)

No. 601 Squadron at Venafro (L–R): Ibby, Flt Lt Cy Yarnell (RCAF), Doc Thomas. (Ibbotson family album)

Pilots of 601 Squadron, 244 Wing, Venafro (near Cassino), summer 1944. This is Patsy's photo – minus Desmond – found in her memoir in 2015. (Rosemary Rawlins' family album)

Desmond and John 'Tilly' Tilston outside what is possibly the MAAF mess tent, summer 1944. (Ibbotson family album)

L–R: Johnny Gasson (SAAF Spitfire pilot), Ibby, Patsy and Doc Thomas walk past the MAAF mess tent, Casserta, 8 June 1944. (Ibbotson family album)

Ibby at Sorrento, summer 1944.
(Ibbotson family album)

Ibby at Sorrento, summer 1944.
(Ibbotson family album)

Patsy, taken by Ibby at Sorrento, summer 1944. (Ibbotson family album)

Ibby near Santa Maria degli Angeli, summer 1944. (Ibbotson family album)

Ibby and Patsy Jensen with Peter the dog, Naples, 24 October 1944. (Ibbotson family album)

Taken by Patsy and titled 'Ibby outside St Francis Church Assisi. 6 November 1944', this was sent with other photos to Desmond's family after his death. He is wearing the RAF battledress jacket he was wearing when he was killed on 19 November 1944 and that was sent to his home in Harewood. (Ibbotson family album)

Excerpts from unknown local press reports (1941–44) from Muriel's scrapbook of Desmond's career and death. (Author's collection)

Desmond's grave at Rivotorto cemetery when visited by his mum Sarah in 1950. (Ibbotson family album)

Sarah Ibbotson (left) and friends in Assisi, Italy, 1950. (Ibbotson family album)

October 2005, Castelnuovo. This recovered identification plate shows Spitfire MH614 was assembled at Castle Bromwich near Birmingham as part of contract no. 981687-39-C.23(c) from 28 May 1942. (Courtesy of Leo Venieri)

A plate from the cockpit or engine area, October 2005. (Courtesy of Leo Venieri)

Hotel Giotto, Assisi, 8 June 2007. L–R: Bruno Cavallucci, author, Leo Venieri of RoAF. (Author's own)

The author at Desmond's memorial, the field near Castelnuovo, 8 June 2007. (Author's own)

Desmond's artefacts displayed in the RoAF Museum, Fusignano, Italy, 28 July 2011. (Author's own)

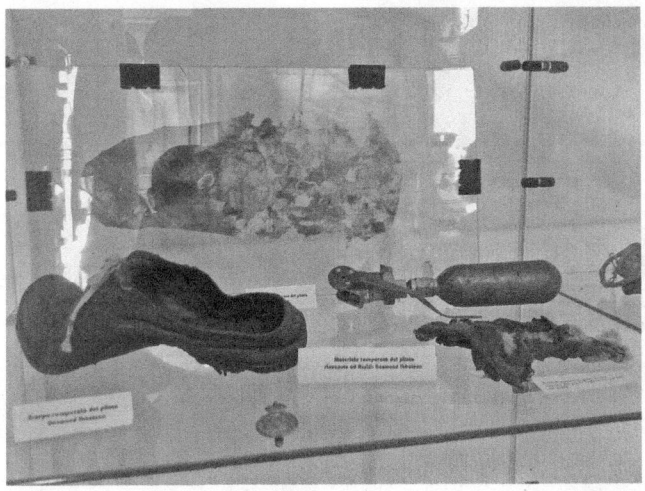

Desmond's artefacts in the RoAF Museum, Fusignano, 28 July 2011. (Author's own)

A flare pistol among Desmond's artefacts on display in the RoAF Museum, Fusignano, 28 July 2011. (Author's own)

Instruments: a bullet and metal identity plates from Desmond's Spitfire, on display in the RoAF Museum, Fusignano, 28 July 2011. (Author's own)

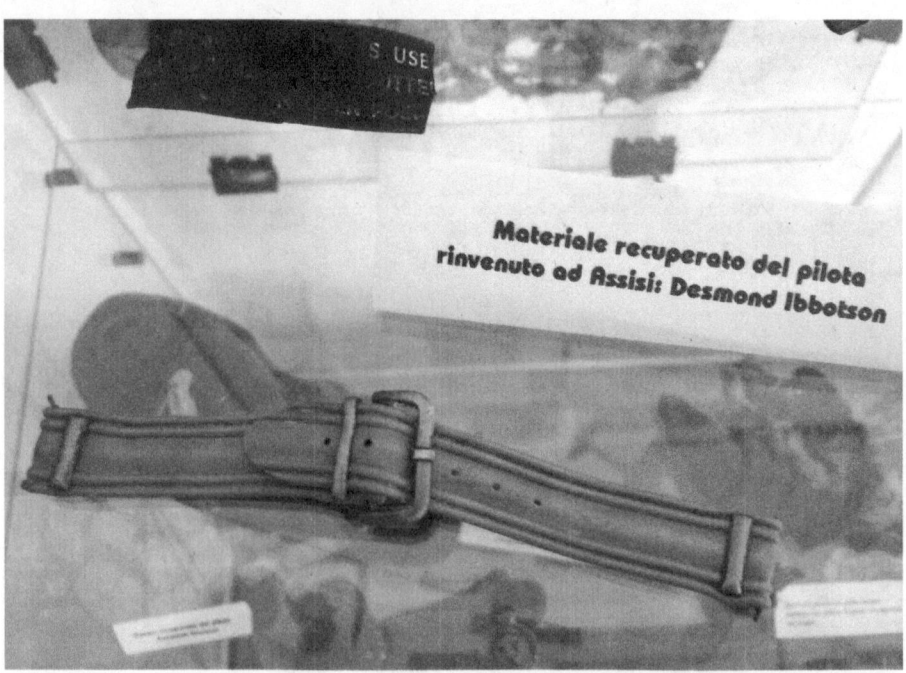

Desmond's watch strap in the RoAF Museum, Fusignano, 28 July 2011. The team claim to have identified him, in part, by comparing it with the strap seen in the IWM photograph of him being strapped into a Mk IX Spitfire in May 1944. (Author's own)

IN GRATEFUL MEMORY OF
DESMOND IBBOTSON
OF THIS PARISH
ALSO OF JOHN DURLEY AND
HERBERT ALLEN YOUNG
CONNECTED WITH THIS PARISH
WHO GAVE THEIR LIVES IN
THE WAR 1939 — 1945

Greater love hath no man than this, that a man lay down his life for his friends.

Desmond's memorial plaque in All Saints' Church, Harewood, 31 January 2016. (Author's own)

CHAPTER 25

The Re-Excavation of Desmond's Spitfire

Castelnuovo, Italy
2005

In 2011, on another visit to Italy, I interviewed Marco Maiani of RoAF, and he explained how the team had come to excavate Desmond's Spitfire in 2005.[1]

Many years after Desmond's crash, a former ENEL (Italian National Electricity Board) worker, Luigi Malizia, was working in a field near Castelnuovo repairing electrical equipment with a colleague, Mario Boscini Vitali. Mario told him:

> On a Sunday in November 1944, an English fighter plane had engine trouble and crashed around here. The pilot was unable to bail out and so he remained aboard the plane. According to somebody the aircraft was six or seven metres underground.

They finished the job and moved on, but Luigi remembered the story and decided to research it. He found other testimonies of an aircraft crash in a field close to where they had been working, and suggestions that the remnants of the plane may still be there. One old local farmer, Carlo Ferroni, showed Luigi the location of the crash. Carlo told him:

> I remember very well hearing the rumble of an aircraft engine. Suddenly, the engine lost power and I saw it falling to the ground with a dreadful crash followed by an unreal silence. The plane, with the engine which had cut out, flew over an oak and then crashed. Surely, the aircraft is still underground. I think that only the pilot was taken away, but the plane should still be there.

Luigi contacted the owner of the field, Bruno Cavallucci. Bruno, who was a young boy in 1944, said, 'It was an afternoon at the end of November, I was doing my homework when, 200 metres away, I heard an aircraft's engine rumbling and then losing power. After that, a big crash. From the window I saw fire and smoke, then nothing more.'

After that, Luigi contacted Bruno Barbini, the director of the local newspaper *Il Rubino* (*The Ruby*), and local journalist Mario Cicogna. Rather than publish the story straight away, Barbini decided to approach RoAF to carry out further investigation.

On Sunday 25 September 2005, Uliano Dalmonte, a member of RoAF and president of the Ravenna Civil Protection Coordination, began a superficial exploration in the field where the various accounts had said the crash happened.

Not long after he started, Uliano found several pieces of aircraft wreckage. Then, the team proceeded to carry out more detailed research using powerful metal detectors and ground-penetrating radar. This led to the RoAF president, Leo Venieri, and the board of directors informing Bruno Barbini of *The Ruby* that the group wanted to do a new survey in the middle of October 2005. Word spread among the surrounding area, and the Pro Loco[2] association and some local entrepreneurs asked to participate.

Around the same time, Mario Cicogna found another testimony that was then published in the *Corriere dell'Umbria* (a regional newspaper). It was from Domenico, Bruno Cavallucci's uncle, who had been 19 years old at the time of the events. Domenico reported:

> I was following the manoeuvres of some English fighter planes that were following the example of the fallen airplane ... I don't remember from who, but I knew that the crashed aircraft was flown by a Flying Instructor. He was doing a nose-dive demonstration. I then heard the

irregularity of the engine and saw the loss of altitude: it has been a flash, but the memory is still non-fading.

On Saturday 15 October 2005 a team of RoAF surveyors, using two vans of the Civil Protection, arrived on site with several detectors. The main task was to identify the target for the excavation, near the road Via del Paradiso between Castelnuovo and Rivotorto. Due to the presence of superficial metal scraps, which could disturb the detectors (so giving false readings), the team had to clean up the area. It was during that operation that many more small finds were found, including 20mm bullets, a piece of the engine block, parts of the fuselage and pieces of the wings. Furthermore, with the ground-penetrating radar, it was possible to see the biggest object could be as much as 7m below the ground.

Two weeks later, on the morning of Saturday 29 October, at 4.30 a.m., around fifteen members of RoAF drove west from the Fusignano region to St Maria d'Angeli to meet the local government official from Assisi Town Hall, Alderman Emiliano Zibetti, and the mayor of Assisi, Dr Giorgio Bartolini, for a briefing on the day's planned excavation work. The dig would also be attended by volunteers from the Assisi branch of the Red Cross.

The group met in the Hotel Moderno situated directly opposite Assisi railway station. From there, the team proceeded to the crash site a few miles south, near Castelnuovo, and began to set up. Prior to the team entering the field, a large tree at the side of the field, as close as possible to the radar signal that indicated the location of whatever was left of the Spitfire, had been cut down so the tracked excavators could access the field with minimal disturbance.

The excavation work began around 9 a.m., and an hour later, at 10.10 a.m., the propellor gearbox, an ear cup and part of the headphone set were found, along with several other pieces of wreckage. The headphone and ear cup were originally contained in the leather flying helmet the pilot was wearing. There would have been an oxygen mask fastened to the front of the helmet, which would have fitted snugly around the pilot's nose and mouth. The mask would have contained the radio microphone with a little toggle button on the front of the nosepiece, allowing the pilot to talk to other aircraft or the ground, but it had gone.

Each object found was carefully removed from the claggy soil and lifted to the surface for cleaning and identification. The finds were then dried, bagged, tagged and placed in plastic storage crates. Eventually, these artefacts would be taken back to the RoAF Museum in Fusignano and displayed. The excavation continued. Each scoop of earth was carefully removed, turned and dropped to one side to be sifted, so the work was done at a slow pace.

The statements given by those who had witnessed the Spitfire's final dive were consistent in saying it was a single-engined fighter that had crashed, and the pilot had not got out. It was not known at that stage who the pilot might be and if any remains would be found. All known aircrew killed in this area had been recovered and were buried in the nearest military cemetery at Rivotorto.

At 2.10 p.m., the digger reached a depth of between 5 and 6m. It was here they found what was left of the cockpit area, with some remains of the pilot's lower body still in it. This was not an intact structure with a body still strapped to the seat as one might imagine. The devastating forces released on impact, the initial recovery excavation done in 1944, backfilling and the effect of time and erosion on the pieces left had all taken their toll. What the team were able to locate were just fragments of the original aircraft and its unknown occupant. That said, anything that had survived and could be cleaned up might hold vital clues to the identity of the pilot. If they were able to get to the engine, that too might hold a clue as to the cause of the crash.

The first human remains found included hairs, the jawbone and traces of clotted blood. Then the mask, the other ear cup, a small metal plate and a leather flying glove were found. Given the depth they were now working to, the team had to change excavators for one with a longer arm.

The fragments of the pilot's remains were examined by a pathologist. Work paused as the remains were gathered together and blessed by the priest of Santa Maria degli Angeli, Father Francesco De Lazzari, who said in prayer, 'Receive him with you, o' Lord, this unfortunate child after having fought on our land.'

Work continued into the evening, the digging illuminated by halogen flashlights. With the last scoops of earth came two large blocks of metal, which included the engine, the nacelle, the tail wheel, two small gas cylinders and some other personal items of clothing including a pair of shoes (one containing a sock and foot), shirt and a few shreds of material.

At 8 p.m., satisfied they had exhausted the contents of the excavation, the team stopped digging, refilled the huge hole and retired to the Hotel Moderno for dinner and discussion of what they had unearthed. The question was, if they had found the remains of a pilot, who was he? There were no identity tags and nothing on any remnants of clothing or footwear to indicate who it might be, or even his rank.

On an earlier visit to Assisi, one of the RoAF team, with Leo Venieri, decided to stop at the military cemetery at Rivotorto on the way home before travelling back to Romagna. He looked down the list of those interred there guessing that, although they had found a few remains, they had not pulled out a whole body, which meant the pilot could already have been buried in the cemetery. This fitted with something one of the eyewitnesses had said in their testimony: they had seen the recovery team in 1944 take part of the pilot out before they filled the excavation back in. This also meant one pilot, whoever he was, had in effect had two places of burial.

The Air Finders team pulled together a list of five or six possible aircrew by rank and date of death in the region who were buried in the cemetery and narrowed that list down to three possible candidates through reference to units based in the area at the time.

On the Italians' final list were:

1. Air Cpl G.L. Duncan (8 Squadron SAAF, died 23 September 1944, aged 19)
2. LAC John Henry Seddon (2771 Squadron, RAF Regiment, died 18 September 1944, age unknown)
3. Desmond Ibbotson

John Seddon was not a qualified pilot, so it could not have been him. What RoAF did not know was that I had been investigating Desmond's story from the archival perspective for some time. Broadband was still in its relative infancy, as were mobile phones. I had to travel into town and use a time-slotted computer in the public library.

Internet searches eventually led to me seeing messages from Assisi on the BBC commemorative website soon after, but there were no contact details. RoAF were able to confirm that it was a Spitfire they had found, and they believed the pilot was Desmond. I had confirmed which unit he had been flying with at the time, where he was based, the date of his crash and the location of his military grave.

Both sides had answers to the other's questions but could not contact each other to let them know. A few days later, I received email messages from two people wanting to know more and asking if I knew anything about Desmond. I wanted to bring the two sides together to close the story, to find out the truth about this mysterious discovery and let Muriel finally, properly, lay her brother to rest. The problem was my contacts were both working in the media, and Desmond's family wanted no media interest. As my time on the library computer ran out, I drafted a short email in response and wondered if I should press 'save' or 'send'.

CHAPTER 26

Digging for the Truth

England
2005–07

Following my initial interviews with Muriel in late 2003, I spent the next two and a half years rummaging through archives, reading books, tracking down veterans and researching the story. At that stage, nothing was showing up about Desmond's time with 601 Squadron in November 1944. Then, when the family received his logbooks from Muriel's son David on a visit from his home in Australia, I could begin to fill in some of the missing pieces of the story. It was 2004 before I found details of his time with 5 RFU filed in the National Archives in Kew and could then check the unit records.

As the squadron records and Desmond's own notes brought me closer to understanding how Desmond had spent his final days, it was tempting to envisage the possibility that, while out on his own, he had perhaps been shot down. It seemed only right that a dashing Spitfire pilot would have been brought down in a blaze of glory. It looked like it would be an easy trip or two to the National Archives in Kew, look up the remaining RAF records, maybe find a photo in the Imperial War Museum and that would be that. Of course, that is not how things turned out.

During one of my early visits, Muriel showed me a photo, from her own album, of Desmond's grave. She was standing behind his headstone with some of her own family, her children then in their late twenties or early thirties. It was a small colour image with tints that suggested it had been taken in the late 1970s.

Muriel explained it had been taken when John, his wife, Liz, and two daughters had taken her and Jim with them on a driving holiday to Tuscany. They had crossed into Umbria to visit Assisi and Desmond's grave. Serving as a signaller, Jim and his unit had fought their way from the beaches at Salerno up the mainland to Monte Cassino before he was transferred out only a few days before the infamous main offensive by the Allies to force the Germans off the mountain top began. That posting home to begin officer training had almost certainly saved Jim's life: a short time later, his unit was in the thick of the fighting when it started. The records and Desmond's own logbook both revealed he had been in action in the skies over Monte Cassino too. During our evening chats in 2003, Muriel and I speculated that Jim may have seen her brother in action over the area but never realised it.

From the image in that ageing photograph, I could make out a hedge just behind where the family stood and in the far distance the dominating and distinctive landmark of the Basilica of St Francis. I thought at the time that it would be a fitting end to the story to visit the grave and photograph the same view.

In 2005, to coincide with the sixtieth anniversary of the end of the Second World War, the BBC launched a commemorative website to collate and display people's personal memories from that period. In November 2005, while searching the messages and stories posted on that site, I came across a new one. It read: 'We believe to have found the Spitfire belonging to Capitano Desmond Ibbotson.' They were appealing for information from anyone who had knowledge of the pilot, his family or his background. The message contained a link to the group's website in Italy.

Along with the message were two photographs of people in a muddy brown field. In the near foreground stood a group of about a dozen people in front of a mechanical digger. What most caught my attention though was the background to the picture. In the distance beyond the hedgerow was that unforgettable image of the Basilica of St Francis again.

The similarity in perspective of this photograph compared with the one Muriel had shown me was striking. It was as though the same person had taken two photographs standing on the same viewing line south of the basilica.

From just these two pictures it was unclear: had the excavators dug up his grave, or had they dug up someone else's Spitfire by mistake? Either way, I thought, something was not right. Desmond had been found dead, in the cockpit of his Spitfire and buried over sixty years ago in the cemetery nearby, so it couldn't be him, could it? They may have found his Spitfire, but his actual grave was only a few hundred yards away. Surely, they knew that? The thought then occurred to me: if Desmond was in the Spitfire, just who had been buried in his military grave in 1944?

As I struggled to make contact with the Italian excavators, Muriel's words echoed in my mind. Particularly her cautionary phrase about 'muck-raking'. It carried a sense that investigating Desmond's life could be perhaps ignoble or salacious. Of course, she and Molly had grown up with Desmond and knew him as only sisters could – all his good and bad traits, what made him tick. She had lived with the memory of him all her life, and she was understandably concerned his reputation should not be tarnished.

Muriel was always kind and obliging with her time and answered my questions honestly. But when it came to the actual details of Desmond's time based near Perugia and his last flight, she knew virtually nothing. All she could tell me was that it had been a test flight.

Clearly, from the winter of 1944 onwards, the sketchy information Muriel's mum, Sarah, had been given by the Air Ministry, along with the eventual return of Desmond's belongings, began to crystalise into a story about their brother's wartime service that Muriel and Molly and their families would tell and retell to friends and relatives over the years. These few facts, from swooping his Spitfire low over Harewood House and the village, to pursuing both German fighters and blonde dancers in the Egyptian desert, to shooting up troop trains and aeroplanes in Italy, to receiving two DFCs, were all rounded off by his fatal crash. His last resting place was a marked grave in a military cemetery that was coincidentally less than 100 miles away from where Muriel's husband, Jim, had himself been fighting that same year Desmond died. These were part of the fixed, reliable markers in both time and geography by which the family could remember him and retell those same stories.

Then, years later, after a series of coincidences, along I came with an interest in finding out what had happened to him, and those markers looked set to change. As much as Muriel was willing to help retell Desmond's story, with caveats and concerns, I sought to reassure her that I was simply attempting to explain how he had earned his medals and how he had come to be where he lay. Up until December 2005, I had no inkling of what would be found; the wreckage of his Spitfire in a field some distance from his grave followed sometime later by the news the remains of her beloved brother were believed to have been found in the wreckage. At that stage though, I contacted Muriel to let her know I had found some more information about Desmond's Spitfire. We met briefly before and after Christmas as I continued to interview her about Desmond, and we discussed the messages and photographs I had downloaded from the RoAF website.

After leaving a couple of messages on the BBC website to try to contact RoAF and inform them I was researching Desmond's story from the archives in this country, I had received a couple of emails from a BBC producer and a journalist, Nick Pisa, wanting to know more – specifically if I was a family member or could tell them who was. Muriel and John made it clear they did not want media interest. I agreed and emailed that message back to the producer and to Nick and felt the matter was settled. The BBC politely agreed and withdrew.

In the spring of 2006, Nick decided to run a story about Desmond for a tabloid newspaper. He was a freelance journalist based in Rome and had taken the basic story of how a team of Italian amateur archaeologists with a love of Second World War history had uncovered the remains of both an iconic British fighter plane – a Spitfire – along with the remains of the ace who had flown it. The headline included a tenuous link to another renowned figure of the war – Erwin Rommel – saying Desmond had 'taken tea with the Desert Fox'.

The piece, which ran in the *Daily Mail* on 1 April 2006, was a positive summary of Desmond's life. But the fact Desmond's story had appeared in the national press at all caused considerable surprise and consternation for Muriel and the family. I tried to reassure them the press were just trying to flush out the family. There were key details we knew that the press did not. But the family could not stay hidden for long.

A few months after the story broke, in early 2007, I agreed to meet with Muriel and John again. The appointed evening arrived, and we all gathered in the front room to talk through what had been found. The story had turned from an opportunity to research a unique military career to the discovery of a loved one found where they were not supposed to be.

John sat on his father's old chair; Muriel was in her usual armchair and me on the sofa. I began by talking about my most recent record finds, about the last unit Desmond had flown with, which had not been 601 Squadron as originally thought. Then, as the paperwork began to sprawl across the table, I tentatively raised the topic of the probable discovery of Desmond's Spitfire – how a team of aviation archaeologists had dug up a remote field and pulled out bits of wreckage ... and some human remains that were thought to be Desmond's.

I passed over a couple of A4-sized photographs that showed the team and their diggers in the field, the large terracotta-coloured hole that had been excavated, its edges neatly squared off by the blade of the digging machine's bucket.

Muriel talked of how she had visited her brother's grave and of feeling shocked that there could be some of Desmond's remains still present at the crash site. Muriel's generation had been brought up to respect authority and take the government and its various departments, agencies and staff at their word. To hear the burial of a loved one had not actually been properly carried out was difficult to take in. For Muriel and Jim, it was important that things were done properly. They could be forgiven for feeling upset, though they only showed the true depth of their feelings to their closest family.

The records stated the original excavation in 1944 had dug down 20ft to retrieve Desmond. Muriel studied the photographs quietly as John and I discussed why the wreckage had been so deep.

'What's that?' Muriel asked pointing at a small coloured object in the centre of one of the pictures.

'Let me look,' said John, motioning for the picture. 'It's a plant pot,' he said, after a few seconds.

'Well, what's it doing there?' she asked.

'I think that's where they found some remains,' I said quietly.

Of course, the excavation team had not found Desmond's body intact, but there was a natural inclination to feel that it actually was him, still clothed and strapped into the Spitfire's cockpit. Then another question arose: why then was Desmond not fully recovered in 1944? To try to answer that, I would have to wait until June 2007, when I would meet someone who would throw the story in another direction altogether. However, there was a more pressing issue at hand now.

CHAPTER 27

Desmond's Story Emerges

England
April 2007

In spring 2007, when visiting John and his wife, Liz, for lunch at their home in Yorkshire to discuss Desmond's story and the latest news from the RAF, John leant over the dining room table as Liz cleared the main course plates away and asked if I wanted to travel to Italy to attend Desmond's reinterment.

John explained that since Nick Pisa's article had appeared in the *Daily Mail* just over a year earlier, the family had been in touch with the RAF. The need to calm further press speculation had meant the family had discussed the situation and agreed they had to either rule Desmond out of the picture or confirm that they were indeed his remains and his Spitfire. In agreeing to submit to that process, there was obviously going to be more media interest that needed careful handling, so John had made contact with a reporter for ITV Yorkshire, David Hirst. The broadcaster/broadcast company would now have exclusive access to the family and their journey to the ceremony that was being planned by the RAF.

I was surprised at the change of approach. I had always avoided contact with the media out of respect for the family's privacy. The two approaches made to me some months earlier had been politely declined, and the people I had emailed had not attempted to pursue any further contact with me. I had not approached anybody else in the media to discuss the story either.

I happily accepted John's invitation to meet them in Italy. I would be able to pay my respects to Desmond and see the end of this story in a fitting way. I would also research the area where he had spent his past days, and to try to work out where some of the photos I had acquired had been taken.

My great uncle Jack had been a signaller in the 2/5th battalion East Lancashire Regiment during the First World War, and I visited his grave in France for the first time in 2001. Since then, I have visited many military cemeteries in the UK, France, Belgium, North Africa and Italy and always found I learnt something from them, however small – often something about the area around which the fighting had taken place.

Wherever it is located, a CWGC military cemetery has a standard layout. The entrance is a wrought iron gate set in a low-walled perimeter. Inside the grounds, a stone cross with a bronze sword in its centre faces a large rectangular altar stone (the Stone of Remembrance) to represent the first biblical sacrifice: that of Abraham's only son to honour God. Symbolically, each family had given their son's life (and they were, in the main, men) in the defence of their country. Their remains were then laid out in individual graves as though on parade, facing towards the cross. Fabian Ware, head of the IWGC, explicitly wanted a standard headstone, applicable to the British and Commonwealth dead of all ranks and all branches of the service; death in war was the great leveller. The sacrifice was the same: each soldier, sailor or airman had given their life in the service of their country.[1]

In reality, while many bodies were recovered and laid to rest in an individually named grave, many thousands were known to have been killed but their remains never found or, if there were body parts found, never able to be identified. These tragic cases, young men whose mortal remains had been lost on the battlefield, perhaps forever, became the missing. Where sufficient remains were found but the body could not be identified, they were buried in the cemetery but given the title 'A Soldier of the Great War/Second World War – Known unto God'. Of course, one cannot help but note how young the majority of casualties were, many aged between 18 and 25, and Desmond falls right in that band too. The average age of the infantry soldier in the Second World War was 22. Desmond was 23.

Desmond's Story Emerges

In the intervening months since we had last met, John explained the Ministry of Defence had also been in touch. Its team of specialist researchers, the so called War Detectives[2] had begun the simultaneous processes to consider the remains found by the RoAF excavators and try to identify any surviving family members. The lead researcher in Desmond's case was Sue Raftree. Through service and census records, she had managed to trace Desmond's next of kin, Muriel, and approached her to request their cooperation (including, if necessary, taking DNA samples) in certifying the remains of the pilot as being those of Desmond. Sue later explained that in wartime conditions, given the likely causes of death, only a few key elements were required for a marked burial, and this included a relatively small amount of a victim's body.

A few weeks later, in early June, I flew out to Italy alone a couple of days ahead of the ceremony. I was excited to be in Italy for the first time in my life and tried to imagine how Desmond had felt about it. In 1943, he may have been excited to be going back to his old squadron and to a new country, but he was inevitably going back to the fighting. The break he had enjoyed in the Suez and Aboukir area was over. He had been certified fit for active duty again and had managed to keep his hand in flying Spitfires. He was ready to honour the trust his squadron had placed in him when they asked for him to return. The pace of life on ops was very different to a rest period. The camaraderie was different: faster, edgier. The flying was addictive: exciting and dangerous in equal amounts.

I arrived in Italy on Thursday 7 June 2007 amid high humidity and intermittent sunshine. At Perugia railway station, I picked up my hire car, navigated my way out of the city in a sudden hailstorm and headed south for Assisi. About two-thirds of the way there, having left the hailstorm behind, I rounded a wide corner, and there was the entrance to Perugia airfield. I pulled over. Two large concrete gateposts stood before me; the steel lettering spelled out St Egidio.

Driving past the rest of the airfield's western perimeter, the road led right past the end of the main runway and continued through several villages as it followed the gently undulating landscape. About 20 minutes south of St Egidio, I rounded another bend part way up a little hill and was met with a stunning view of the Basilica of St Francis perched on the edge of the ridge that overlooked the town of Assisi behind and beneath it.

In the foreground were small olive groves and fields of yellowing wheat. The sky above was a shimmering turquoise. Beyond the old town of Assisi, rising above the back of the basilica, was the large green hump of Monte Subasio. A couple of miles down the road, I turned south to St Maria d'Angeli and my hotel. I was exhausted but excited in equal measure. After checking in, I decided to take a drive around to get a feel for the area and try to find for myself the site where Desmond's Spitfire had been dug up, and his final resting place. The following morning, I attended the press conference in the Hotel Giotto or, as it had been in summer 1944, the officers' rest centre.

CHAPTER 28

Desmond is Laid to Rest

Rivotorto Military Cemetery
Assisi, Italy
Saturday 9 June 2007

At Friday afternoon's press conference, I had met David Hirst and Martin, a TV crew from Yorkshire Television who were covering Desmond's story and the family's journey to Italy. We had swapped notes on individuals who would be useful to interview and add to the story, and so I had progressed to acting as an informal assistant and driver for them. After the press conference, everyone had gathered in the Hotel Giotto bar to socialise over a few drinks. Among the guests were a party of junior ranks and NCOs from the RAF Regiment Queen's Colour Squadron (QCS) who would be on ceremonial duty through the following day. At around midnight, I drove David and Martin back to their hotel and agreed to pick them up early the next morning and drive them around for the day. Desmond's family (his nephews, John (accompanied by his wife, Liz) and Dave, and niece, Judy) were guests of honour, so official transport and drivers were laid on for them.

I arrived, as arranged, at the TV crew's hotel on the eastern side of Assisi's old town and waited in reception. After several minutes and no sign of them, I asked a receptionist to call up to their room. They had overslept. As I waited, I watched as a few guests in uniforms and suits ambled through reception. Clearly, they would be present at this morning's ceremonies too.

We were actually the first ones at the crash site. This ceremony was to unveil the monument to Desmond at the edge of the field where his plane came down. It had been funded and erected by the villagers. In front of it was a rectangular bed of soil with flowers laid in the pattern of a Union Jack.

I parked, then I got out and watched as the adrenaline began to kick in for David and Martin, who were checking and rechecking their equipment and running through scripts and timings. They walked down the lane to choose their vantage point for filming. The sun was already burning brightly in the cloudless sky, the temperature in the low 20s and climbing.

A couple of days before, I had found a florist in St Maria d'Angeli and, in mangled Italian, ordered a floral tribute. I had chosen a wreath of broad green leaves as the base and a mix of carnations and roses overlaying it in the colours of an RAF roundel. I planned to lay it myself privately, probably after the ceremony.

Minutes later, a couple of vehicles drew up, followed by police. Taking this as our cue to move, I took the wreath out of the boot and, helping the other two carry some camera gear, walked down the lane to the memorial where several villagers had already gathered. I stood by the roadside to watch the proceedings. Men in suits and uniforms mixed with women in either floaty, patterned summer dresses or formal funeral black.

The QCS began to line up on the wide section of white gravel laid to the side of the memorial stone. On this occasion, there was to be none of the crisp precision drill movements for which the squadron is renowned; there was little room to move in the lane due to the crowd of people now in place.

After about 15 more minutes, a small cavalcade drew up. Police motorcycle outriders escorted one limousine with the family in, with one behind for the dignitaries. As they got out and took their places, the crowd drew silent for a moment. The family stood facing the memorial. To the left of them were the QCS. In front was a podium with the Italian dignitaries gathered behind it.

Desmond is Laid to Rest

In the distance, a faint engine sound grew steadily louder, then overhead appeared a single-engined aeroplane. A Stinson Sentinel in USAAF colours flew low over the field, much as that spotter plane sent out that Sunday in 1944 would have done as it looked for Desmond. Only this time, it dipped its wings in tribute, made several passes from different directions and finally flew off towards Foligno.

Then the service began, with prayers read by the priest followed by speeches from the Italian representatives. They included Leo Venieri of RoAF, General Tofi of the Italian Army and the Mayor of Assisi, Claudio Ricci. The British dignitaries included AM Ian McNicholl (Deputy C-in-C Strike Command) and Cdr Shawn Steeds, the naval and air attaché. The sun was behind the crowd, and we all gradually shuffled forwards to try to catch as much of the remaining shade as was available within the spread of the trees in front of the memorial.

The QCS had no chance to avoid the sun's glare though. They had to remain on parade, and one of them succumbed to the heat. He was visibly pale and looked on the verge of passing out as he was escorted off parade towards the team's van. Two sharp-eyed paramedics caught him just at the moment his knees gave way. With his arms around the paramedics' shoulders, he was placed in the back of the van, out of the heat to recover.

After more speeches, the service ended, and the crowd began to mingle and disperse. At the back of the crowd, I saw a slight figure in a suit begin to make his way towards the memorial. It was Eugenio. I caught his attention and beckoned him over. Eventually, I managed to catch Dave's attention, and the hairs on the back of my neck stood up again as I introduced him to Eugenio. The two shook hands and Dave called over to John and the others, who each met Eugenio in turn. Despite the language barrier, the expression of pleasure at one's company and sincerity of thanks can be understood in any language. It seemed for Eugenio that the years had fallen away. When I had met him for the first time the previous evening, it was clear he had wanted to meet the family for so long. Sixty-two and a half years was a long time to wait. Photos of everyone were taken in front of the memorial.

As the crowd thinned out, I decided to lay my wreath, but there was no time to linger; the family were quickly ushered off to their waiting car to be taken to the next ceremony. David the reporter asked who the elderly man was. I explained it was the eyewitness I had met. By now Eugenio had left the family and was walking to his car. Sensing he might be about to lose him, David ran after him, trying to catch up and persuade him to do an interview. Eventually, we set off for the cemetery.

At the cemetery, the three of us made our way down the left side of the headstones to the area roped off for the media. We wondered why we were the only ones there. It transpired the other cars had been taking everyone to the church nearby for another ceremony to commemorate the Liberation of Assisi. The services for Desmond had been fitted around those planned for the locals to remember their liberation from the Germans. Many of the graves in this cemetery were for young Allied soldiers killed in June 1944 as they tried to push the Germans back. There were a few RAF graves here too besides that of Desmond's, and almost without exception all of them were aged in their early twenties.

The break in proceedings gave us time to catch our breath and pick our spots in the area reserved for the media from which to watch the service of rededication. David was evidently keen to have another crack at getting Eugenio on camera somehow. 'When you see him,' he said, 'keep an eye on him please and don't let him get away!' I agreed, then I stepped over the blue rope and took a couple of photos of the new headstone to mark Desmond's plot.

Before long, the congregation left the church and began to gather in the cemetery, filling up the neatly clipped grass spaces in between the headstones. Sue Raftree, who was working in the MoD's casualty investigation team, wandered over. Sue told me that almost all the same officials and the QCS were heading to Poland in the autumn to do a similar remembrance service there for the crew of an RAF bomber that had been shot down in 1944–45 and only recently recovered. Every so often, a few more bodies of missing airmen are found and commemorated like this.

As the priests took up their positions behind the large wooden lectern behind and to the side of Desmond's grave, Warren Ringham strode over wearing a busby headdress with a plume in it and carrying a trumpet. He asked if I would take a couple of photos of him as he played the Last Post over the grave, which I agreed to do.

There looked to be around 200 people gathered in the cemetery – an impressive turn out – and not just made up of military representatives.

Desmond is Laid to Rest

The family were last to arrive and stood directly in front of the grave that had been dug for the replacement coffin. The crowd again fell silent as the QCS carried Desmond's remains into this corner of a foreign field once more. They slow marched down the centre of the cemetery, turned to approach the grave from the back and placed the coffin very slowly and precisely onto the wooden slats laid over the hole. A large Union Jack was draped over the coffin, and on top of the flag were Desmond's medals and silver RAF wings in a framed mount.

The service began and was conducted by three priests in turn: Archbishop Sorrentino, Padre Canil and RAF chaplain Sqn Ldr Nick Pnematicatos. After socialising with the family and guests the night before, the chaplain gave a moving speech in celebration and remembrance of Desmond's life and sacrifice. That same evening, when we had first met the chaplain and the RAF Regiment, the flight sergeant leading the detachment, Andy Franklin-Brown, had spoken of how the regiment struck a balance between enjoying the good times and knowing when to 'turn it on' and snap into work mode to focus on the job. Given these lads were probably, on average, about as old as the Spitfire pilot they were carrying had been when he died, and they had recently been told they were going on active service to Afghanistan at the end of the year, everyone understood the need to make the most of the free time they had while they had the chance.

It was a situation I felt sure Desmond would have related to. I thought again about all I had read about him and his many squadron colleagues who he had served with. I wondered if the daring Spitfire ace laid before us now had also been one of those who had been full of beer and high spirits after the party at the Hotel Giotto in July 1944, striding through the dark and quiet streets of Assisi bellowing the songs of the Third Reich ('*Horst Wessel*' and '*Deutschland Uber Alles*'). Secretly I hoped he had.

There were prayers, a hymn (the traditional 'Abide with Me') and readings. Then the band struck up with 'God Save the Queen' followed by the Italian national anthem. Warren stepped forward to play the Last Post as Desmond's coffin was slowly and carefully lowered into the freshly dug plot by the QCS. His medals were removed from the top of the coffin and the flag folded neatly by the airmen. Both were then presented to John.

Then there was a loud rush as from the back of the cemetery, above the church, came three single-engined aircraft in close V formation flying low, trailing thick white smoke. I wished they had been Spitfires, but they were not. Nevertheless, Desmond would have approved wholeheartedly, particularly when one of the three rolled away to the left of the formation and performed a 'missing man' salute to the distinguished fighter ace beneath.

When the service ended and the congregation began to drift away, David gathered his equipment and went off with Martin to film the family's reaction to the service, instructing me to find and hold on to Eugenio.

I hovered around looking for a gentleman in a dark suit to round up. After a minute or two I spotted him and beckoned him over to where the TV crew were interviewing John. When they had finished, David suggested we take Eugenio back to the crash site so he could be interviewed there. John Purtell, the man from the British Embassy in Rome who had been at the press conference, agreed to come along and translate. Bruno came along too. We made our way back to the cars and set off in a little convoy for Castelnuovo while the family and dignitaries returned to the Hotel Giotto for a long formal lunch over wine, followed by equally long speeches.

Once again, I stood well away to one side and found it fascinating to watch David and Martin work, both in front of and behind the camera. After an hour or so their session drew to a close. I approached John Purtell, and he agreed to help me arrange a similar interview for my own research. I wanted to try to capture the new information properly, in the hope of finding out what had actually happened to Desmond's Spitfire. I also hoped I could get a clearer understanding of what Eugenio had been trying to say to me the previous evening. When filming was over, we left once more for the Hotel Giotto to relax and have a meal.

The bar area was very quiet when we arrived. All the guests were still eating a sumptuous lunch. The RAF itinerary had warned of this: 'in previous years this has lasted 2–3 hours,' the leaflet said. True to form, at around 4 p.m. the lunch ended, and the guests wandered back up to the bar. The French windows were open onto the veranda, and a cool breeze wafted in. The journalists and I had acquired chilled drinks and a large burgundy leather Chesterfield sofa each. After all the early starts and rushing about, this was a welcome chance to relax.

We discussed the meal and tributes that had been paid to Desmond. I told the family I was going to go back to the field with the translator and try to interview the eyewitnesses at length. The family also said they wanted to go along and visit it properly before they returned to England the next day. Within half an hour we all headed back down the hill to the crash site.

From the interviews I conducted with the eyewitnesses that Saturday afternoon, Bruno (whose experience was limited because he was so young and inside the farmhouse) explained, further to his recollection of the explosion, that he remembered an Army major had called at his farmhouse to ask his father for assistance digging the Spitfire out. Four people, he said, helped to excavate the ground at the time in very heavy rain.

Eugenio Pennacchi had a deeper recollection, including of the liberation. He told me when the Allied troops first arrived in 1944, their tanks came up from the south but stopped some way away from the village, thinking the people who had gathered on the outskirts to watch them were Germans. An English officer asked, 'Who are they? Are they Germans?'

Someone told him, 'No, they're Italians.'

The Germans retreated very quickly to the north because they were afraid of being encircled by the Allies.

The British, Eugenio said, brought life (and chocolate!) to the village. There were parties, and the local girls went along to them too. Eugenio used to sing in a barber shop quartet for a time and played the piano but, he said ruefully, there was a British officer who was staying in the village who played much better than he could. One of the houses in the village was commandeered as an officers' mess, with eight men living on the first floor and several more beneath. Today the house stands opposite the village shop, which also doubles as a café and mini community centre and houses a display case on its main wall with a few bits of Desmond's Spitfire. All the rural houses in and around the village were full up with refugees, so the ordinary soldiers had to sleep in tents in the fields. In all, he said, the British did not remain for very long in Castelnuovo.

After the war ended, Eugenio became an electrician and went to live in Switzerland. He said he had a good single life up to the age of 36, when he got married and raised a son and a daughter. He moved back to Castelnuovo in the 1960s. His wife predeceased him, but he remained in his house not far from the centre of Castelnuovo, where he had been sitting in the square with his friends back in 1944.

Eugenio was 18 years old at the time and was in the piazza in the centre of Castelnuovo. He was a barber by trade, so often used to cut the soldiers' hair. That afternoon, he had finished work and was relaxing with friends in the square when, at about 3.30 p.m. in the afternoon he saw an aircraft, a Spitfire, come in from the east from the direction of Foligno, heading towards Perugia. It had been performing a few aerobatics (some loops) but was then just flying straight and level at a height of about 700m. The weather was clear and sunny but with a few clouds. Suddenly he heard the engine begin to scream and the aircraft entered a dive. He did not see the pilot try to get out, and there was no parachute. The aircraft just dived straight into the ground with the engine still screaming.

Eugenio was adamant the Spitfire had not been shot down; there was no other aircraft involved (either German or British, Italian or American), there were no pieces falling off it and it did not trail smoke, manoeuvre side to side or spin as it came down. The engine made a steady, continuous sound during its flight, and he did not hear it 'pop', bang or falter. It did not try to approach horizontally as though to land, nor did it dive vertically straight down. Instead, he saw it dive at an oblique but very steep angle of approximately 70°. It just skimmed the top of an old oak tree that stood at the side of the lane before it hit the ground. There was a huge explosion and ball of fire. Straight away he ran from the piazza across the fields for about a mile or so to find where the aircraft had come down. When he arrived, he found he was first on the scene, but others arrived soon after. It was clear there was nothing they could do for the pilot and, in fact, there was not a lot to see because the bottom part of the impact hole had collapsed and closed over almost immediately. Scattered around on the ground were pieces of the wings, and they found the tail wheel and some bullet casings. He could see small patches of fire on the ground resulting from splashes of fuel but nothing larger.

The next day, an English officer dressed in civilian clothes and accompanied by other soldiers came to Eugenio's house in Castelnuovo and asked for labourers. He spoke very good Italian, but Eugenio did not hear what he said so asked his uncle, 'What do they want?' and was told in reply that they wanted help to dig the aircraft out and recover the pilot. The officer had offered to pay them too, so they agreed to go. Two days later, there were about four of them together who started the excavation. By now the weather was appalling with torrential rain. The ground was very heavy to dig because it was bare earth and already waterlogged, so the sides kept falling back into the hole as they dug the earth out. Furthermore, the hole kept filling up with water. Still, they kept going, and at about 2m down found more pieces. At this point they stopped for a rest, and someone lit a cigarette. Suddenly there was a huge bright flash of flame as the fuel that was around and seeping out of the soil ignited. Eugenio jumped out of the hole straight away, fearing another explosion. Fortunately, no one was hurt, and his friends just laughed. When he felt it was safe, Eugenio got back in the hole and started to dig again.

Soon they began to find more and more pieces but couldn't tell which bit was which due to the damage. Eventually they found the parachute, and at that point the English officer said, 'Dig slower now because you're going to find the body of a captain.' First, they found the parachute, which the local women took away to use later for dresses and clothes. They then found the pilot's body in the cockpit along with his 'dog tags' (identification tags), which the officer in charge took away with him. All the time from when the aircraft crashed to when they finished the digging, the site was guarded by British soldiers. On the original excavation, they dug the site by hand for the best part of a week. When RoAF came in 2005, they took away five big skips over the course of a couple of days.

In early 1944, the third eyewitness, Antonio Cavallucci (Bruno Cavallucci's cousin), was 13 years old. Antonio supported the family, his mother and sisters, with the wages he earned from selling vegetables in the market to the British and Allied forces in and around Castelnuovo. There were RAF, RCAF and SAAF personnel, as well as British and Indian troops all based in and around Castelnuovo. The regiments rotated through the locality every month or so, and while they were there Antonio's mother washed their clothes and traded the cleaning of laundry for chocolate. Antonio himself sold eggs, tomatoes and fruit, which he traded on for cigarettes. He used an empty 500-litre wine barrel, and the troops put their cigarettes in the barrel as payment. The soldiers traded soap in return for beef and meatballs, to replace their tinned beef and biscuits.

On that Sunday in November, Antonio was walking eastwards along the road towards the village of Castelnuovo when he heard the distinct sound of a Spitfire. The aircraft was not doing aerobatics at that point, and he heard the engine make a steady sound as normal. For some reason it then became high pitched as it went into a dive from about 3,000ft high, and Antonio saw it dive straight into the ground at a steep angle, not vertical and not horizontal. It was not on fire nor trailing smoke before it hit the ground, and it was on its own; no other aircraft were around, so he too confirmed it was not shot down. There were no Germans around there at that time, so there were no anti-aircraft guns around there at all – certainly none that were fired against the Spitfire. After the crash another aircraft from the airfield appeared, flew around and circled the area looking to see what had happened and where the crash had been.

Some time afterwards, a British Army officer, a major, came round asking for help from the villagers to dig the aircraft up and find the pilot. There was only one officer with the group of soldiers, and he had a crown on his epaulettes, so as a result of his close dealings with soldiers in the village marketplace, Antonio clearly recognised him as a major. Antonio was not one of those who helped with the dig, but there was at least one Cavallucci and another friend called Mario Falconelli who were there. He visited the site and recalled seeing lots of machine gun bullets spread all over the field after the impact. At the time the field was bare earth but has always been used to grow grain crops as it had been then: barley, wheat, sunflowers, maize.

These stories from the witnesses hold key clues as to what happened but only go so far as to help rule out possible causes rather than explain fully what actually caused the crash. Spitfire MH614 was not shot down, involved in a collision or suffered any other impact. The engine did not cut out, according to the three men on the ground, but kept running all the way down. This might then rule out contributory factors such as those that had been experienced earlier in 1944 when there were problems with contaminated fuel. The contaminated fuel caused the Merlins to cut out completely, resulting in a loss of power and a corresponding loss in engine noise as would be heard from the ground. There were no leaks, flames or smoke trailing behind the aircraft before or during its descent. The Spitfire was on its own in fairly clear weather, so Desmond had not become lost or disorientated in cloud and, therefore, bad weather can be ruled out as a contributory factor too.

The late Saturday afternoon in June was still beautifully warm and sunny, the surrounding fields sufficiently far away from the main roads and motorway that it was impossible to hear the traffic noise. A gentle breeze swept the higher branches of the trees that lined the narrow tarmac road and made the ripened ears of wheat occasionally sway gently from side to side. Nothing could be heard except for the odd birdsong, and the few people gathered about fell naturally into hushed conversation. The flowers and wreaths were still in place, but the crowds had long since gone, and the whole area was quiet and peaceful again. The sunlight gave the field a deep golden hue.

This time I ventured further into the field, having noticed earlier what appeared to be a very subtle dip in the wheat, which was only visible from the very edge of the field. Leading from the back of the memorial stone was a narrow path, only 12in wide, of flattened wheat stalks. I followed it out, realising it led to the dip itself. Leo Venieri confirmed this dip was indeed the actual place where Desmond's Spitfire had come down. The earth that had been removed to extract the remaining pieces of the plane, then replaced when everything had been salvaged, had since settled to form a gentle depression in the ground.

As I approached what had been the rim of the crater dig, I noticed a single red poppy hidden between the stems of wheat right in the centre of the dip. The only thing I knew about poppies was they grow in rough ground, which is why they had been among the first wildflowers to emerge in the fields along the Western Front after the guns had fallen silent after the armistice. Their deep red petals became emblematic of a soldier's blood that had seeped into the soil where he fell. I looked around for other poppies, but there was just one.

John, Dave and Judy were standing around the memorial stone and, as I came back to the edge of the field, I told them what I had found. I walked back to the car and left them alone for a few minutes.

Eventually Judy approached and asked me, very quietly, 'What would Desmond's final thoughts have been?'

'I don't know' was the truth, of course, but felt unhelpful. Instead, I replied, 'Well, no one can ever know the mind of a person in those circumstances, but his background doesn't give the impression he was one to resort to blind panic at all. I think he would have tried to keep control of the aircraft and bring it out of the dive.' It was the best answer I could give.

CHAPTER 29

The Knowns and Unknowns

When Desmond decided to carry out that air test, the St Egidio aerodrome was quiet. The rain of the last few days had moved away to the north, and the weather was now fair – light cloud, patches of clear sky and dry with light wind.

The fact this air test took place on a Sunday suggests the training schedule was ready to make use of the good weather forecast for the week ahead and all aircraft would be needed. So, rather than hold up the schedule, Desmond probably decided to fly the Spitfire that afternoon to ensure the aircraft was available for use. His was the only flight taking place at this time from this unit. Everything was going well until halfway through the return leg of his flight when the aircraft suddenly pitched forward and entered a steep dive from around 3,000ft from which it never recovered. Why? Why did a decorated fighter ace, who was familiar with practically every type of Spitfire flying at that point and with hundreds of hours of operational flying experience in all conditions enter an irretrievable dive from which he made no attempt to escape? It made no sense.

Tying the evidence from the records with the eyewitness testimonies rules out several possibilities.

First, Desmond was not shot down either by friendly or enemy aircraft or anti-aircraft artillery. Second, the weather was fair and, according to the eyewitnesses, the visibility good and clear, so he did not succumb to high winds, storm clouds or lightning. Nor did he fly into cloud, become disorientated and emerge too low to prevent hitting the ground.

Third, given the surrounding geography, Desmond was well clear of the nearest high ground, so poor navigation and high terrain obscured by cloud can be ruled out.

That just leaves two main areas: technical failure (which caused either a severe and irretrievable mechanical malfunction with the aeroplane, or which led to pilot incapacitation) or pilot error. These are not easy to distinguish between, given the circumstances. The lack of a detailed investigative report and the minimal evidence from the remaining parts of the Spitfire mean the final result could even be a mix of the two. Of these possibilities, pilot error seems hardest to comprehend because Desmond was such a highly experienced pilot. And yet, it is a highly likely reason for the cause of the crash.

Whether it was a technical fault or his own fault that initiated an irretrievable dive, Desmond simply ran out of luck. He had flown aircraft that had suffered technical failures and managed to fly them back to base. Notably, even when shot down, Desmond had never taken to his parachute to try to escape. This could account for his remaining in the aircraft during its final seconds of flight: his self-belief that having either suffered a severe technical fault or made a mistake, he could continue to fly the aircraft and bring it back. That said, because he was relatively low, around 2,500ft, he would have had only a few seconds to decide to either pull out of the dive altogether or bail out and use his parachute before he would have been too low to do so. I remained intrigued by the mystery and, having become deeply involved in the demise of a fighter pilot I had come to admire, I naturally wanted to find out more, but in the early stages every lead resulted in a dead end.

Then came a chance meeting with Gp Capt Iain Laing, a highly experienced Typhoon pilot who also flew Spitfires for the RAF's Battle of Britain Memorial Flight (BBMF). In fact, he piloted the Mk IX that flew in Desmond's honour for five years from 2007 to 2012, which the BBMF had painted in the original 1944 silver colour scheme. At the time of our meeting in 2016, at a ceremony to mark the family's donation of Desmond's memorabilia to the Yorkshire Air Museum at Elvington, Gp Capt Laing was Station Commander, RAF Coningsby. I asked him to describe how he found flying that type of Spitfire. In describing the aerobatic display he performed, he happened to describe the manoeuvre closest to dive-bombing which, it was said by one of the eyewitnesses, Desmond was flying when he crashed: 'You put the nose down to enter a dive at around 70° and 200 knots. Pull-out is around a thousand feet so as not to overstress the airframe, but you can expect to pull around 4g.'

In 1943–44, some Mk IXs that entered a dive of this type were prone to a phenomenon called 'wing buckling': one pilot flying this same manoeuvre managed to literally pull a wing off his Spitfire, which caused his fatal crash.[1]

Was wing buckling a cause? Pilots could enter a dive easily, but too hard a pull-out could cause them to black out and lead to airframe damage, chiefly wing buckling. A plane that is successfully recovered from this kind of manoeuvre could still be landed, but given the resulting overstress to the airframe, it would lead to the aeroplane being taken offline for repair and a one-way conversation with the CO for the unfortunate pilot – something Desmond had experienced himself having wrecked three Spitfires in his career. However, Desmond's Spitfire remained intact throughout its final manoeuvre, so although wing buckling might have occurred, it did not cause the loss of a wing.

Could it have been, for example, carburettor icing that prevented the engine from firing properly? This had been a problem in early Merlin engines when carburettor icing could lead to engine failure. Depending on the engine model and its associated components, a Merlin engine fitted with a Skinners Union float-type carburettor could have experienced such a problem under certain flying conditions. The Merlin 66 was commonly fitted to the Mk IX Spitfire and usually fitted with a Bendix-Stromberg pressure carburettor which, by enabling direct fuel injection under negative-g conditions, along with oil-heated throttles, virtually eliminated the chance of icing in the carburettor itself.[2] The RoAF team retrieved the engine block, but its condition means it is unlikely it can be examined properly. Although one eyewitness said the engine coughed and nosed over, the engine was, according to three other eyewitnesses I interviewed, confirmed to be still running when the Spitfire was in its terminal dive.

Of course, it would have been virtually impossible to tell in 1944 if engine difficulties played a part, and it will remain so now. The impact of the Spitfire with the dense brown clay was devastating. What was retrievable was not subject to the same detailed investigation as would nowadays be the case. Fighter aircraft were not equipped with the same kind of electronic instrumentation and monitoring devices they are today, nor was there the same level of interaction between military and civilian bodies to make detailed investigations and report their findings. Capt Sinclair's report of the time was not kept and has seemingly been lost forever. Unusually too, no court of inquiry was established – the last known one for 5 RFU had been held in September 1944.

I wondered what Desmond's mother, Sarah, would have made of it had she been alive today and received the news now instead of several decades ago. Back then, though heartbroken, she accepted the news. There was little else that could be done. The war and the world moved on, though Sarah, Muriel and Molly never forgot Desmond. When I asked Muriel about Desmond's time after the end of his second tour, she paused, as though looking for a reason, before replying simply to say she didn't know why he had not returned after he finished operations. Muriel was set to marry Jim in August 1944, but sadly Desmond did not return for the wedding.

Desmond had shown no sign of wanting to stand down. A few days after his second tour expired at the end of July 1944, he received notice his instructor posting to 5 RFU would be effective from 7 August. Yet his logbook shows he took a month's leave and stayed in Italy before reporting to 5 RFU on 12 September. I believe Desmond decided to stay on, perhaps with an eye to flying a third tour in Italy, or with the expectation he would be sent home around Christmas to begin his third tour in the UK. Third tours were rare, simply because the odds were increasingly stacked against pilots to survive, if stress and fatigue did not ground them first. Some exceptional and notable pilots managed it though: Guy Gibson, Charles Pickard, Leonard Cheshire and Hughie Edwards from Bomber Command; Billy Drake, Neville Duke and Eddie Edwards from Fighter Command and the DAF. Flying as a Spitfire instructor perhaps suited Desmond more at this stage, with the informality he had become accustomed to and the mix of people he was meeting from all over the world. A return to the stiff formality of an RAF squadron in the UK would not have suited him, what with all the rationing and bad weather to contend with as well. If only he hadn't stayed in Italy, I thought. But, of course, Desmond was seeing Patsy on a regular basis, and this too may have played a part in him continuing to fly there.

Whether Patsy thought they had a future together will never be known. In 2015, I found Patsy's memoir in the RAF Museum archives at Hendon. In it she mentioned Desmond's last flight. I wrote to the family. When I tracked down her son, Rob, he was retired and then volunteering as a missionary with his wife in Ethiopia. Rob had helped his mum compile her wartime memoir and photographs for donation to the RAF Museum. In his correspondence he was adamant his mum and Desmond were just friends. He advised that 'there was no documentary evidence of "Ibby" except what was in her memoirs. I think that may only have been a photo.' He also understandably pointed out that 'Mum's wartime "flame" was not a subject for discussion in her later married life. I think she limited her mention of Ibby to aeroplane incidents only.'

When I asked Rob what his mum knew about Desmond's crash, he replied, 'I heard her say more than once that he crashed doing a victory roll over the airfield (she didn't specify which) on return from a sortie. She may have had wrong info. Mum spoke of that with passion – "Silly man. He broke the very strong rule on not doing that." She felt his loss.'

This had to be hearsay because, firstly, Desmond was not over the airfield at Perugia. Secondly, the eyewitnesses from Castelnuovo village who had seen the Spitfire confirmed that, although it had completed a few loops, it was flying straight and level, in a normal attitude before it dived and crashed. There was an indication too that the pilot may have been demonstrating a dive manoeuvre. This aspect was part of the RFU's training syllabus. Indeed, Desmond routinely led his trainees out to the range on Lake Trasimeno to practise strafing and dive-bombing targets floating on the lake. So perhaps Desmond had selected a quiet area to test if the aircraft, which would be used for training the day after, could perform that particular manoeuvre.

The excavation by RoAF in 2006 was thorough, but they found no new evidence that could be determined from the examination of the remaining material. Besides, they had neither the technical skills within the team nor had expert investigators working with them, so it was not possible to do as the British Air Investigation Branch would do, for example, and reassemble all the pieces and work out how the aircraft had crashed. Especially since the wings and fuselage had long since gone.

Desmond had been in air-to-air combat with many experienced enemy pilots, been shot up, his aircraft damaged and been injured himself, but he had still always brought his aircraft in to land – albeit sometimes not where or how he intended. Add to this his number of hours and the variety of aircraft he had flown (including at least eight variants of Spitfire alone), it is clear his confidence and perhaps even complacency could be important factors here. It is tempting to think that a highly experienced pilot couldn't make a fatal mistake, but another crash at a more recent air display shows what can happen.

The Shoreham air crash happened on a beautifully clear summer's day in August 2015. No other aircraft were involved and, following months of coverage, analysis, a thorough investigation by the relevant authorities, a court trial and a public inquiry, the conclusion was the pilot had entered an aerobatic manoeuvre (a loop) at the wrong height. No matter what he had done subsequently, by continuing with the manoeuvre, he was never going to be able to pull out in time. He, too, was highly experienced, with thousands of hours as a fighter pilot, display pilot and civilian pilot. Ultimately, the evidence revealed he had been too low to pull out. He was lucky to survive a crash that could easily have killed him and very nearly did. Tragically, eleven people died when the aircraft crashed onto a road junction outside the airfield perimeter. When the details of the crash investigation – including photographs, video footage and detailed digital imagery – were released and the profile of the Hawker Hunter jet on impact was made public, it brought home to me the possibility that, unfortunately, Desmond's last dive could have been initiated at too high a speed and low an altitude to pull out from no matter what he did. From the moment his Spitfire achieved a certain speed and dive angle around 70° from the vertical, once below 1,000ft, Desmond was always going to hit the ground too steep, too hard and too fast to survive the impact. However, the RAF's own rule is that in the event of an aircraft accident, aircrew can only be found negligent unless there is absolutely no doubt whatsoever about the cause. In this case, it is not clear cut what the cause of Desmond's fatal dive was, and in truth we shall never know. Whether it was an intentional manoeuvre or not, everything in his background suggests Desmond would have stayed with the Spitfire to try to land it, whatever the likely outcome would be.

The last photo of Desmond was taken by Patsy on 6 November, two weeks before his death. The photograph chosen for Desmond's memorial stone though, taken exactly two years earlier in North Africa, was the right one because it shows him just after he had pulled off his most daring escape. He is looking directly towards the camera, laughing heartily. His battledress jacket and shirt collar are open, his hat at a jaunty angle, face unshaven. He didn't want to be locked up for the rest of the war, so he took a chance and made a run for it. That day it worked. His expression says it all: 'I'm the one that got away!'

That was his approach to life and his approach to flying. He assessed the situation and decided what he would do, even if it meant pushing his luck. On Sunday 19 November 1944, he did just that, but this time his luck ran out. Imagine if his luck had held though. What a story he would have had to tell.

THE END

Notes

Comments from Desmond's logbooks are as he wrote them at the time. Details on his postings, promotions and pay are referenced in his service records unless otherwise stated.

An Introduction

1. Winston Churchill's speech to Parliament, 4 June 1940 (Hough, R. and Richards, D., *The Battle of Britain: The Jubilee History* (Guild Publishing, 1990), p. 105.

Chapter 2

1. Interview with John Richardson, June 2015. Wilson was the only member of the family to have undertaken such a trip, which was still quite a rare thing for anyone to do at that time. A family photo showed Wilson standing proudly in Red Square in Moscow wearing a smart three-piece suit, a gold pocket watch chain fastened to his waistcoat and a trilby hat, looking very pleased to have made his pilgrimage. John added that Wilson was also a dedicated communist – a wealthy one at that – with the money and facility to travel round-the-world on his own at a time when many could not.
2. 'The New Zealand Official Year-book, 1935', www3.stats.govt.nz.
3. New Zealand Shipping Company Ltd passenger manifest, www.findmypast.co.uk c/o Barbara McCulloch.
4. crie.org.nz/research-papers/M.Abbott_H.D_OP2.3.pdf.
5. New Zealand Shipping Company Ltd passenger manifest, www.findmypast.co.uk c/o Barbara McCulloch.
6. Air Ministry Form 1406, Desmond's service record; 'RAF Training', Ken Fenton's War, www.kenfentonswar.com/raf-training.
7. Ibid.; Wragg, D., *RAF Handbook 1939–1945* (Sutton, 2007), pp. 119–21.

Chapter 3

1. Invented in America in the early 1930s, and first delivered to the RAF in 1937, the Link Trainer enabled pilots to practise manoeuvres, sorties and cross-country flights using just the instruments for reference. The primary reference instruments were the airspeed indicator, altimeter, vertical-speed indicator, horizon indicator, turn and slip indicator and directional gyro. In the cockpit, the pilot's workload is high as he has to monitor each instrument to ensure he maintains the correct speed, height, orientation and course of the aircraft during his flight (edencamp.co.uk/blog/forgottenfriday-the-link-trainer).

Chapter 4

1. Jarrold, J. and Delve, K., *Did You Survive the War?: An Ordinary Fighter Pilot's Story* (Suffolk, 2006), p. 17.
2. AIR 26/ 567, 8 SFTS Operations Record Book.
3. Ibid.

Chapter 5

1. AIR 29/ 681, 53 OTU Operations Record Book, July 1941.
2. As per Bill Whalen, son of Jimmy Whalen's cousin.
3. AIR 29/ 681, 53 OTU ORB, July 1941. Desmond records Marion's surname as Pluteause, but the ORB gives the pilot's name as Sgt Plomteaux and the date of death as 10 July not 12 July as noted by Desmond. In the early years, before the USA entered the war, several hundred young American men crossed the Atlantic to fight for Britain. A handful of rich, well-connected men like William 'Billy' Fiske managed, in full publicity, to join the RAF and fight briefly in the Battle of Britain. The majority of mercenary pilots who wanted to seek adventure or defend the motherland lacked the money and the contacts though. Their best chance was to do what Marion Plomteaux had done, which was to head for Canada to enlist in the RCAF and hope nobody thought to check more thoroughly. If they did and they were caught, then under the US Nationality Act of 1907 they faced being expatriated (stripped of their US citizenship). Anyone acting as a recruitment agent faced a $10,000 fine and lengthy imprisonment. The Canadian government, meanwhile, accepted these recruits, having openly supported the UK since the outbreak of the war and happily sent any men and materiel of the RCAF they could spare in support (Fydenchuk, P., *Immigrants of War: Americans Serving with the RAF and RCAF During WWII* (W.P.F. Publications, 2007), p. 9).

Chapter 6

1. Fydenchuk, P., *Immigrants of War: Americans Serving with the RAF and RCAF During WWII* (W.P.F. Publications, 2007), p. 9.

Chapter 7

1. Pearce, W., 'Cobb Railton Land Speed Record Car', 2020, www.oldmachinepress.com.
2. 'New Air Speed Record', *Nature* 143 (1939), pp. 756–57, available at www.nature.com.
3. The correct nomenclature for the Messerschmitt fighters and fighter-bombers was 'Bf', which stood for *Bayerische Flugzeugwerke* or (lit.) Munich Aircraft Factory, whereas 'ME' referred to the designer Willy Messerschmitt. The term 'ME 109' was most commonly used by the pilots in wartime and so is used in this text: Tidy, Sqn Ldr D.P., 'South African Aces of World War Two', *Military History Journal*, 2(2), 2007.
4. Glancy, J., *Spitfire: The Biography* (Atlantic Books, 2006), p. 96.
5. Quill, J., *Spitfire: A Test Pilot's Story* (Crecy, 1996), pp. 198–99.
6. Smith, R.C., *Hornchurch Eagles: The Life Stories of Eight of the Airfield's Distinguished WWII Fighter Pilots* (Grub Street, 2002), pp. 96–111.
7. *The London Gazette*, citation for Jack Charles' DFC, 15 July 1941.
8. AIR 27/ 512, 54 Squadron ORB.
9. Ibid.
10. 'Roadstead': an attack on enemy ships at sea by bombers (or fighter-bombers) escorted by fighters (Price, Dr A., *Aircraft of the Aces: Late Mark Spitfire Aces 1942–1945* (Osprey, 1995), p. 52).
11. Ibid.; Desmond's logbook refers.
12. Circus: an attack by a small force of bombers with powerful fighter escort intended to lure enemy fighters into the air so they could be engaged by RAF fighters (Price, *Aircraft of the Aces*, p. 52).
13. AIR 27/ 512, 54 Squadron ORB.
14. Ibid.
15. AIR 50/ 21/ 43, 54 Squadron combat reports 27 September 1941; AIR 27/ 512, 54 Squadron ORB.
16. This was Plt Off Marland of 603 Squadron (AIR 27/ 2079, 603 Squadron ORB).

Chapter 8

1. 'Rhubarb': a small-scale attack by fighters using cloud cover and surprise, with the object of destroying enemy aircraft in the air and/or on the ground and/or striking at ground targets (Price, Dr A., *Aircraft of the Aces: Late Mark Spitfire Aces 1942–1945* (Osprey, 1995), p. 52).
2. AIR 27/ 512, 54 Squadron ORB.
3. AIR 27/ 890, No. 4 Delivery Flight ORB.
4. Ibid.
5. Ibid.; AIR 27/ 512, 54 Squadron ORB.
6. Shores, C. and Ring, H., *Fighters Over the Desert* (Arco, 1969), p. 7.

Chapter 9

1. Brown, R., *Shark Squadron: The History of 112 Squadron 1917–1975* (Crecy, 1994), p. 39.
2. Thomas, N., *Kenneth 'Hawkeye' Lee DFC: Battle of Britain and Desert Air Force Fighter Ace* (Pen & Sword, 2011), p. 126.
3. Drake, B. and Shores, C., *Billy Drake, Fighter Leader: The Autobiography of Group Captain B. Drake, DSO, DFC & BAR, DFC (US)* (Grub Street, 2002), pp. 8–34.
4. AIR27/ 873, 112 Squadron ORB.
5. Holland, J., *Together We Stand: North Africa 1942–1943: Turning the Tide in the West* (HarperCollins, 2005), p. 176.
6. Brown, *Shark Squadron*, p. 67.
7. Between 1918 and 1993, Distinguished Flying Crosses were awarded to officers only. NCOs got the DFM.
8. Holland, *Together We Stand*, p. 174.

Chapter 10

1. Holland, J., *Together We Stand: North Africa 1942–1943: Turning the Tide in the West* (HarperCollins, 2005), p. 181.
2. Shores, C. and Ring, H., *Fighters Over the Desert* (Arco, 1969), p. 136.
3. AIR27/ 873, 112 Squadron ORB. Oddly, this event does not appear in *Fighters Over the Desert* by Shores and Ring. The entry for the previous day, when Desmond claimed his first confirmed victory, is present but his being shot down on 5 July is not. The date recorded for this event in Brown's *Shark Squadron: The History of 112 Squadron 1917–1975* as 7 July is also incorrect.
4. Lavigne, M. and Edwards, Wg Cdr J.F., *Kittyhawks Over the Sands: The Canadians and RCAF Americans* (Quebec: Lavigne Aviation Publications, 2002), p. 185.
5. Haskew, M.E., 'Churchill's General', *Britain at War* (Key Publishing, August 2022), p. 52.
6. Desmond had personal experience of this when he wrote: 'July 8 (operation no. 48) Tac[tical] Recce. Slight ack-ack from own troops.' It would not be the first time he was shot at by his own side.
7. AIR27/ 873, 112 Squadron ORB.
8. AIR 26/315, 239 Wing ORB, quoted in Wynn, H., *Desert Eagles* (Airlife Publishing Ltd, 2001), p. 17.
9. LH/ 9/ 24/ 20, Rommel's letters, 2–10 August 1942.
10. Drake, B. and Shores, C., *Billy Drake, Fighter Leader: The Autobiography of Group Captain B. Drake, DSO, DFC & BAR, DFC (US)* (Grub Street, 2002), p. 34 and p. 42.
11. Ibid., p. 57.
12. Watson, B.A., *Exit Rommel: The Tunisian Campaign 1942–1943* (Stackpole Books, 2007), p. 7.
13. Churchill, W.S., *The Second World War: The Hinge of Fate: Volume IV* (Reprint Society, 1953), p. 354.
14. Quoted in Bungay, S., *Alamein* (Aurum Press, 2003), p. 118.
15. Churchill, *The Second World War*, p. 376.

16 Holland, J., *Heroes: The Greatest Generation and the Second World War*, pp. 295–303; Shores C. and Ring, H., *Fighters Over the Desert*, p. 157; 'Jagdgeschwader 27', wikipedia.com – this gives the name of Clade as the section leader but identifies the ME109s as coming from V/JG 27 not II; Neillands, R., *The Desert Rats*, p. 132. In the latter account, the assertion that Gott survived but was killed attempting to return to the wrecked aircraft to rescue the others trapped inside is incorrect. James Holland interviewed Jimmy James for his account, which appears in *Heroes*, and this is the main source of material for the events surrounding Gott.

17 Brown, R., *Shark Squadron: The History of 112 Squadron 1917–1975* (Crecy, 1994), p. 70.

18 AIR 27/ 873, 112 Squadron ORB.

19 AIR 27/ 873, 112 Squadron ORB. His aircraft was reported as 'Category I damaged' – i.e. repairable by squadron fitters.

20 This was possibly Uffz König of I Gruppe who reported being in a lone duel with a Kittyhawk before being shot down (Shores and Ring, *Fighters Over the Desert*, p. 178).

Chapter 11

1 Shores, C., *Aces High, Volume 1* (Grub Street, 1994), p. 181; Shores, C., *Aces High, Volume 2* (Grub Street 1999), p. 62; Richey P., *Fighter Pilot* (Cassell, revised edition 2001), p. 35.

2 Moulson, T., *The Millionaires' Squadron: The Remarkable Story of 601 Squadron and the Flying Sword* (Pen & Sword, 2014), p. 160.

3 WO 201/ 2495 'Extract from 9th Australian Division Report on Operations El Alamein 23 Oct–5 Nov 42', National Archives.

4 The sortie details are found in AIR 27/ 2070, 601 Squadron ORB. It was not uncommon for these still relatively new 20mm cannons to jam at altitude, sometimes due to the freezing cold air in the upper atmosphere. It remained a persistent problem with this weapon, and many pilots instead preferred the 0.303in. machine guns or the superior American 0.5in. cannon fitted to the P-40 Kittyhawk. Spitfires had two firing buttons on the control column: one for the guns, one for the 20mm cannon.

5 HW 1/ 1044 National Archives.

6 Divisional strengths around mid-August 1942 were as follows: the Afrika Korps in this area now comprised the remnants of the 15th and 21st Panzer Divisions and the 90th (Light) Division (DAK). But the losses had been such that the remaining components of these divisions were now mere 'phantoms'. For example, Panzer Regiment 8, was down to just eight tanks and in the whole of 15th Panzer Division there were only six 50mm anti-tank guns. The 21st Panzer Division had thirty tanks and sixteen anti-tank guns and 400 men. (Battistelli, P.P., *Rommel's Afrika Korps* (Osprey, 2006), p. 57.)

7 Battistelli, *Rommel's Afrika Korps*, p. 19.

8 The message read:
'From Liaison Officer with Delease to Fliegerfuehrer (Air Commander Luftwaffe) on the afternoon of 6/11: You are requested to inform General Gandin, if he is with you, that Field Marshal Rommel requests his excellency Barbasetti with

General Gandin to come to a conference at Sidi Barani on the morning of 7/11 with Fliegerfuehrer, where he expects to arrive. Please let Delease know, if General Gandin has been contacted. (HW 1/ 1044 National Archives.)

9   AIR 27/ 2070, 601 Squadron ORB.
10 Henry, R., 'Armoured Command Vehicles', *Military History Journal*, 16(6), 2015, South African Military History Society, www.samilitaryhistory.org.
11 Moulson, T., *The Flying Sword: The Story of 601 Squadron* (MacDonald, 1964), pp. 143–44; AIR 27/ 2070, 601 Squadron ORB.
12 Rommel's views on the treatment and interrogation of prisoners stemmed both from his background as a child in Ulm and his education in military college. His wartime reputation for fairness dated back to the capture of St Valery in France 1940 and the surrender of what was left of the Scottish 51st Highland Division while the main British, French and other Allied units evacuated from other coastal ports up to Dunkirk in the north. The division had been re-formed around those evacuees who managed to leave on the last ship to sail for England before the town fell, and through other ports, then shipped out to North Africa in preparation for the El Alamein offensive. The Highland Division was now among the Allied formations pushing Rommel's troops back towards Libya and Tunisia. The sources for the known incidents of Rommel meeting Allied prisoners and treating them fairly are from Young, D., *Rommel: The Desert Fox*, p. 104 and pp. 129–34; von Luck, *Panzer Commander: The Memoirs of Colonel Hans von Luck* (Cassell, 1989), p. 50, pp. 107–8 and p. 128; LH 9/ 24/ 20, Rommel's personal letters (English translation), Liddell Hart Centre, p. 13; Brook, H., *True Stories of D-Day* (Usborne, 2006), pp. 23–33.
13 Moulson's report that he used a tank rut to hide in comes from the interview he had with intelligence officer Kennth Carew-Gibbs after the war. However, it is not Desmond's recollection; he doesn't mention it, just that he hid until the search died down. (Moulson, *The Flying Sword*, p. 145.)
14 AIR 27/ 2070, 601 Squadron ORB.

Chapter 12

1   Pitchfork, Air Cmde G., *Shot Down and on the Run: The RAF and Commonwealth Aircrews Who Got Home from Behind Enemy Lines 1940–45* (The National Archives, 2003), p. 176.
2   Frank Pledge's diary 7 November 1942, 250 Squadron, quoted in Lavigne, M. and Edwards, Wg Cdr J.F., *Kittyhawks Over the Sands: The Canadians and RCAF Americans* (Quebec: Lavigne Aviation Publications, 2002), p. 290.
3   Moulson, T., *The Flying Sword: The Story of 601 Squadron* (MacDonald, 1964), p. 146.
4   Brown, R., *Shark Squadron: The History of 112 Squadron 1917–1975* (Crecy, 1994), p. 85.
5   Air 27/ 2070, 601 Squadron ORB; from another account of this combat, it seems likely this particular 109 was a Messerschmitt flown by Unteroffizier Alfred Kiefer of III/JG 27 (Shores, C. and Ring, H., *Fighters Over the Desert* (Arco, 1969), p. 213).
6   Air 27/ 2070, 601 Squadron ORB.
7   Drake, B. and Shores, C., *Billy Drake, Fighter Leader: The Autobiography of Group Captain B. Drake, DSO, DFC & BAR, DFC (US)* (Grub Street, 2002), p. 55.

Notes

8   NAAFI (Navy, Army and Air Force Institutes), which runs catering supplies and facilities for the armed forces.
9   Duke, Sqn Ldr N., *Test Pilot* (Grub Street, 2003), p. 76.
10 William 'Billy' Kirkwood was married to Martha, who lived at their home in Accrington. Billy was 37 and had enlisted in the East Lancashire Regiment. He served in the 1st Battalion before being attached to the 1st Armoured Divisional Provost Company of the Corps of Military Police, serving with the rank of lieutenant. During an earlier action he had been 'mentioned in despatches' for bravery. Then, on 8 April 1943, while travelling in a vehicle when on duty in Tunisia, he was killed when the vehicle drove over a landmine, which exploded. He is buried in the CWGC military cemetery in Sfax, Tunisia (www.cwgc.org); Promotion: WO Class II William KIRKWOOD (163032) to be Lt 28 December 1940 (Supplement to the *London Gazette*, 4 February 1941).
11 Lt W.J. Kirkwood (163032) (died of wounds) (Supplement to the *London Gazette*, 6 April 1944).
12 This was Spitfire no. BR175, code letter 'C'. Air 27/ 2070, 601 Squadron ORB.
13 Glancey, J., *Spitfire: The Biography* (Atlantic Books, 2006), p. 103; March, P., *The Spitfire Story* (Sutton, 2006), p. 41.
14 Both took place on 23 January 1943.
15 Lavigne and Edwards, *Kittyhawks Over the Sands*, p. 135.
16 *London Gazette*, 12 February 1943, National Archives.
17 Moulson, T., *The Millionaires' Squadron: The Remarkable Story of 601 Squadron and the Flying Sword* (Pen & Sword, 2014), p. 160.
18 Moulson, *The Flying Sword*, p. 146.
19 'Make angels': climb to patrol height. Air 27/ 2070, 601 Squadron ORB; Shores, C., *Aces High, Volume 1* (Grub Street, 1994), pp. 499–500; Shores, C., *Aces High, Volume 2* (Grub Street, 1999), p. 158.
20 Duke, *Test Pilot*, p. 84; Air 27/ 2070, 601 Squadron ORB.
21 Brown, R., *Desert Warriors: Australian P-40 Pilots at War in the Middle East and North Africa 1941–1943* (Queensland: Banner Books, 2000), p. 249. Brown notes the Luftwaffe losses as being fifty-nine JU-52s transport, nine ME109 fighters and one ME110.
22 Interview by Conrad Wood with John Tilston, 6 September 1999, IWM Collections (www.iwm.org.uk), catalogue no. 19054, reel 2.
23 Brown, *Desert Warriors*, p. 254.
24 Duke, *Test Pilot*, p. 84.
25 A few days before, Desmond's mate, 'Babe' Whitamore, returned to 601 Squadron as B Flight commander, having completed almost three months as the commanding officer of the 244 Wing Training Flight. He was now a flight lieutenant and the holder of a DFC. Jerry Westenra stepped in to command A Flight.

Chapter 13

1   Duke, Sqn Ldr N., *Test Pilot* (Grub Street, 2003), pp. 86–88.

Chapter 14

1. Duke, Sqn Ldr N., *Test Pilot* (Grub Street, 2003), p. 73.
2. Based predominantly on his own experience, Sorley estimated the optimum time a pilot could expect to keep the target in view, as it appeared within the tiny boundaries of his gunsight. The test he carried out, firing at an old biplane fighter on a static range using eight of these machine guns, demonstrated this. From a distance of 400yds, a 2-second burst riddled the old airframe in front with bullets in many key areas and so proved the point he was trying to make. Assuming a standard rate of fire of 1,000 rounds per minute per 0.303 gun, this equates to 17 rounds per second. For a 2-second burst, this gives 34 rounds per gun, which for eight guns, equals 272 rounds (Bungay, S., *The Most Dangerous Enemy: A History of the Battle of Britain* (Aurum Press, 2001), pp. 71–72).
3. Duncan-Smith, Gp Capt W.G.G., *Spitfire into Battle* (John Murray, 2002), p. 48.
4. Ibid., p. 37.
5. Each Browning machine gun fired at a rate of 1,200 rounds per minute, giving twenty rounds per second and a total time (if carrying 1,200 rounds) of 60 seconds. However, each machine gun magazine held only 350 rounds, which meant the total firing time available was reduced from a theoretical 60 to a practical 17.5 seconds per machine gun. The manufacturers at Messerschmitt had already fitted a 20mm cannon into the nose hub of the ME109 and found it had a great effect. Each ME109 had a single machine gun fitted in each wing, and two more on the nose of the aircraft, firing through the propellor disc using an interrupter gear mechanism of a type first developed in the First World War. These features made it much easier for a pilot to aim and estimate where the bullets would arrive at.
6. 'Elvin, V.', Obituary, *The Times*, 5 June 2021, p. 79.
7. Desmond wrote this one surviving letter on an 'airgraph', a recent innovation that quickly became a favourite among Allied troops serving overseas and was the equivalent to a text message or social media post today. The Post Office sent out standard blank forms for service personnel to write on. To save space, weight and time, each letter was then photographed. A single roll of film would hold up to 1,500 letters. The films were transported back to the UK, where they were enlarged again, printed on paper and folded so the address at the top fitted into the envelope's window, then posted out to the recipient.
8. Decorated earlier in 1943 with both the Distinguished Flying Medal (awarded to NCOs) and DFC (awarded to officers), which he received a month after his promotion directly from flight sergeant to flight lieutenant, Edwards was also a distinguished Spitfire pilot with several victories to his name. By the end of his second tour, Edwards had accounted for twelve ME109s and one MC202 destroyed; a third share in a ME323 six-engined transport aircraft, along with five 109s as probables and eleven aircraft as damaged, which included nine more 109s and two FW190s (Shores, C., *Aces High, Volume 1*, pp. 248–49).
9. Lavigne, M. and Edwards, Wg Cdr J.F., *Kittyhawks Over the Sands: The Canadians and RCAF Americans* (Quebec: Lavigne Aviation Publications, 2002), p. 148.
10. Ibid., p. 136.
11. 'Edwards J.F.', Obituary, *The Daily Telegraph*, 19 May 2022.

Chapter 15

1. In *Aces High, Volume 2*, p. 115 by Shores, C., the addition to Desmond's biographical notes includes the phrase 'special flying duties from 7–23 September' before a temporary posting to Air HQ at ADEM. Desmond makes no mention of this latter posting himself, and his service record shows that his time at Aboukir finished on 25 October 1943 (which corresponds with his last flight in a Spitfire Mk XI). He was then posted to Air HQ 'P.P. op: flying' or 'pending posting' back to operations.
2. Morgan, E.B. and Shacklady, E., *Spitfire: The History* (Key Publishing, 1987), pp. 324–26.
3. March, P., *The Spitfire Story* (Sutton, 2006), p. 48.

Chapter 16

1. Author's correspondence with Gp Capt Steve Lloyd, the then Deputy Head of the MoD Air Historical Branch. See additional note below relating to the full citation for the DFC awarded in May 1944 for further details.
2. Moulson, T., *The Millionaires' Squadron: The Remarkable Story of 601 Squadron and the Flying Sword* (Pen & Sword, 2014), pp. 160–61.
   Ray had taken a huge risk in leaving his prison camp. The change in government had not been a civilised handover. In fact, there had been a coup through which Marshal Badoglio seized power. He ordered an armistice, during which time Italian soldiers, either in whole units, small groups or as individuals, decided which way they would fight. Eventually the Italians came to cooperate with the Allies and officially fight against the Germans. Yet many fascist supporters and German sympathisers continued to fight in support of the regular German Army, the Wehrmacht. Still others simply deserted and returned home in secrecy, abandoning their military service altogether to spend their days as far away from suspicious eyes as possible. The effect of this complex patchwork of allegiances in Italy was that it now made it even more difficult for any escapers and evaders to decide who to trust because loyalties lay in many different camps. There were fascists, communists, Allied supporters, resistance fighters (the *Contadini*) and the plain old ordinary citizens who may decide to help anyone, or avoid everyone altogether, depending on the circumstances. Added to that were the German forces of which the SS divisions now also formed a part. The SS had not served in North Africa, but they were very much a part of the war in Italy, and it was highly likely that they would not be as sporting to any Allied pilots they captured as the Afrika Korps had been to the likes of Desmond.
3. All background information on squadron living conditions at Foggia are from AIR 49/ 273, 601 Sqn Medical History of the War.
4. Maj Malcolm Stephen 'Bennie' Osler had been awarded the DFC in January 1942. Originally from Benoni in South Africa, for a short time before the war Osler had worked as an assistant sampler in the New Modderfontein gold mine. His nickname, 'Bennie', came from the famous Springboks rugby player of that name. At the age

of 21, Osler joined 1 Squadron SAAF as a flight commander in June 1941 flying Hurricanes in the Western Desert right through till May 1942. He returned to his native South Africa for instructor and Staff College posts before returning to the Mediterranean theatre with the rank of major to take up a post as flight commander of 145 Squadron in September 1943 (Shores, C., *Aces High, Volume 1*, p. 474; Tidy, Sqn Ldr D.P., 'South African Aces of World War Two', *Military History Journal*, 2(2), The South African Military History Society).

5   Duncan-Smith, Gp Capt W.G.G., *Spitfire into Battle* (John Murray, 2002), p. 154.
6   AIR 26/ 328, 244 Wing ORB.
7   Lance 'Wildcat' Wade was killed on 22 January 1944 when the Auster in which he was making a routine flight went into a spin and crashed near Foggia. He had been a squadron leader and commanding officer of 145 Squadron of 244 Wing throughout 1943. At the time of the accident, he was by then a wing commander with twenty-five confirmed victories, which made him the top-scoring American ace to have served in the RAF (AIR 26/ 328, 244 Wing ORB); Wilfred Duncan-Smith recalled that Lance, among others, epitomised the American Eagle pilots 'who by nature were generally tough rough adventurers out for what they could get for themselves, they were nevertheless an immensely likeable bunch of chaps' (Duncan-Smith, *Spitfire into Battle*, p. 120).
8   Desmond recorded that this took place on 15 November, but the squadron records contradict this and state the attack took place on 14 November.
9   AIR 27/ 2072, 601 Squadron ORB; AIR 26/ 328, 244 Wing ORB.
10 The newspaper name is unknown because Muriel did not keep the title or note the date of the paper, but it is likely to be a contemporary local newspaper.
11 Harvey-Bailey, A., *The Merlin in Perspective: The Combat Years* (Rolls-Royce Heritage Trust, 1995), p. 85.
12 601 Squadron received news from the Air Ministry on 1 March 1944 that Waugh had survived the crash and had been captured and taken prisoner. According to *Aces High*, Waugh was captured by the Germans and eventually ended up in Stalag Luft III in Silesia, eastern Poland. He saw out the rest of the war there before returning eventually to South Africa and taking up a religious vocation. However, his service no. is given as 103557V in the squadron ORB, rather than the no. 103637V quoted in Shores, C., *Aces High, Volume 1*, p. 620.
13 Avery, M.C. and Shores, C., *Spitfire Leader: The Story of Wg Cdr Evan 'Rosie' Mackie DSO, DFC and Bar, DFC (US), Top Scoring WWII RNZAF Fighter* (Grub Street, 1999), p. 127.
14 AIR 27/ 2072 601 Squadron ORB.
15 Zaloga, S.J., *Anzio 1944: The Beleaguered Bridgehead* (Osprey, 2005), p. 8.
16 Avery and Shores, *Spitfire Leader*, p. 127.
17 Up until very late in the First World War, British pilots did not carry parachutes. The open cockpits of their aircraft made entry and exit easier, but when a fire started in mid-air, rather than jump or burn to death, some young men had been known to put their service revolvers to their heads instead. Shortly after Desmond had shared a flight across the desert with General Gott, Gott was killed when the bomber he was in was shot down. Gott and the other passengers in the fuselage

compartment behind had survived the crash landing but were trapped and burned to death. Desmond had seen several friends shot down and always hoped they took to their parachute in time or survived a forced-landing.

18 Given the circumstances, Henderson's aircraft had relatively minor damage. It was classed as category B and sent away to be repaired at the main depot. Desmond's Spitfire though was a complete write-off, suggesting he was lucky to have got out of it in one piece.

Chapter 17

1 AC/91/8/15 601 Squadron ORB – original diary, 26 January 1944, RAF Museum Hendon.
2 Ibid., February 1944; AIR 27/ 2072, 601 Squadron ORB; AIR 26/ 328, 244 Wing ORB.
3 Ibid.
4 Goodson, Col J.A., *Tumult in the Clouds* (Arrow, 1986), p. 81.
5 Duncan-Smith, Gp Capt W.G.G., *Spitfire into Battle* (John Murray, 2002), p. 186.
6 AIR 26/ 328, 244 Wing ORB. On 23 February 1944, Mr Leach, another of Rolls-Royce's technical representatives, arrived at Marcianise to spend a few days on the ground examining things to do with the engine problems the wing had been having. It was said that the final solution to it all would be elaborate filtering measures intended to remove impurities from the petrol supplies. As a permanent solution, the Spitfires were to be retro-fitted with Streamline filters shipped over from the UK as soon as possible. In the meantime, the fiddly and time-consuming task of cleaning the Merlin plugs continued until the new filters arrived.
7 AC/91/8/15, 601 Operations Record Book – original diary, February 1944, RAF Museum Hendon; AIR 27/ 2072 601 Squadron ORB; AIR 26/ 328, 244 Wing ORB. There are subtle differences between these official accounts and the original diary. One is that the handwritten account states which section each pilot flew in, which the ORB does not. However, the correct names and titles of each pilot with their service numbers appear in the ORB, while they are omitted from the original, which lends greater personal detail to the ORB, but it then fails to mention that Black Section were attacked first by four ME109s. The ORB also states that when Desmond was attempting to rejoin his section, 'a dogfight was still in progress and F/O Ibbotson joined in attacking an ME109 from 40 degrees astern …', but it omits the detail about the fact they were at low level *and* that Desmond actually took on six 109s. Although Desmond himself implies that it was *them* who attacked *him*, rather than the other way around as it was recorded in the handwritten report.
8 AIR 27/ 2072, 601 Squadron ORB.
9 The details of this day's events are taken substantially from AC/91/8/15, 601 Squadron's original diary, March 1944, RAF Museum Hendon, with additional details from AIR 27/ 2072, 601 Squadron ORB, and Desmond's own logbook, which gives the pilots nicknames as well as verifying who else made claims that morning. Pete Pote ('Blue 2' and Desmond's wingman) and André Eid ('Blue 3')

each claimed an ME109 as destroyed. Three of those remaining Spitfires, including the newcomers, André Eid and Alan Simpson, had used up so much fuel during their fights that they had to land and refuel at Nettuno landing ground, before returning to Marcianise.

10 AIR 26/ 328, 244 Wing ORB.
11 Henderson's loss was formally posted as 'Presumed Dead' in a signal received by 601 Squadron on 16 January 1945. AIR/27/2072, 601 Squadron ORB; Shores, C. and Massimello, G., *A History of the Mediterranean Air War, 1940–1945: Volume 4 – Sicily and Italy to the fall of Rome 14 May, 1943–5 June, 1944* (Grub Street, 2018), p. 551.
12 AIR 27/ 1818, 417 Squadron ORB.
13 Ibid.
14 Pratt, S.E., 'Benchmarks: March 17, 1944: The Most Recent Eruption of Mount Vesuvius', *Earth* (2016), earthmagazine.org.
15 According to AIR 26/ 328, 244 Wing ORB, this formation actually numbered more than fifty enemy fighters.
16 AIR 27/ 2072, 601 Squadron ORB, quotes eight 109s flying as top cover. Desmond stated twelve were flying as top cover.
17 The details of this combat are taken from AIR 27/ 2072, 601 Squadron ORB; AIR 26/ 328, 244 Wing ORB; and Desmond's own logbook.

Chapter 18

1 The squadron records noted the award as follows: 'His Majesty the King has been graciously pleased to award a Bar to D.F.C. to No. 129238 F/Lt. D. Ibbotson RAFVR/GD for gallantry in flying operations while serving with the Squadron. During the WESTERN DESERT campaign while with the Squadron F/Lt. Ibbotson was awarded the D.F.C. This latter award has been well earned by this pilot and leader. F/Lt. Ibbotson is the Squadron's 'B' Flight Commander and his score to date is 11 enemy aircraft destroyed, 5 probables and 8 damaged.' The citation for Desmond's second DFC dated 23 May 1944 reads: 'Since the award of his Distinguished Flying Cross, this officer has continued to take part in operations against the enemy with outstanding courage and determination. His keenness during his first tour of duty was such that his squadron requested his return. Since then he has completed many attacks on locomotives, mechanical transport and petrol dumps. He has destroyed at least 11 enemy aircraft and damaged others.' The citation itself does not appear in the National Archives as might be expected. The 'byline' confirming the award of the second DFC appears in the *London Gazette* but not the citation. Instead, this copy of the citation text comes from the author's correspondence with Gp Capt Steve Lloyd, the then Deputy Head of the MoD Air Historical Branch, Bentley Priory of 16 January 2006.
2 Addington, S., *Reaching for the Sky: One Hundred Defining Moments from the Royal Air Force 1918–2018* (Uniform, 2018), p. 92.
3 AIR 26/ 328, 244 Wing ORB.

Notes

4 Rawlins, R., 'A WAAF's eye View of WW2, 1939–45', 2014 (unpublished).
5 Ibid.
6 AIR 2/ 15759.
7 This list is taken from Patsy's memoir 'A WAAF's eye View of WW2, 1939–45'. The order of battle for 5 Group in September 1939 was Waddington, Scampton, Hemswell and Cottesmore as listed in Falconer, J., *Bomber Command Handbook 1939–1945*, 2003, p. 271. It changed again in 1942 and 1943 but never included the airfields at Doncaster or Lindholme.
8 *London Gazette*, Tuesday 11 February 1941, p. 832.
9 Colin's Hampden (PL-H, registration AD900) was intercepted by a Luftwaffe ME110 night-fighter piloted by *Oberleutnant* Helmut Woltersdorf of II./NJG1, who was already an ace, having shot down eight enemy aircraft before this one and brought down the Hampden at 2.57 a.m. local time over Streekweg Hoogkarspel in northern Holland (Middlebrook, M., and Everitt, C., *The Bomber Command War Diaries: An Operational Reference Book, 1939–1945* (Pen & Sword, 2014), p. 154).
10 Rawlins, 'A WAAF's eye View of WW2'.
11 Zaloga, S.J., *Anzio 1944: The Beleaguered Bridgehead* (Osprey, 2005), p. 90.
12 AIR 27/ 2072, 601 Squadron ORB.
13 Duncan-Smith, Gp Capt W.G.G., *Spitfire into Battle* (John Murray, 2002), p. 193.
14 Early on the morning of 16 June at around 7.30–8 a.m. 'Mitch' Hammet had led a patrol of four Spitfire IXs up to the north and east of Perugia, where they first strafed two German soldiers in a motorcycle and side car, followed by an open-top staff car. Then further along the road they spotted a Mk IV panzer tank camouflaged with branches and hiding behind a house. Circling round to make their approach, the Spitfires edged lower to make their run-in, peppering the panzer and its house with a considerable number of accurately delivered rounds. On their way back south, back towards base, they approached Perugia airfield, where they came up against some very intense light-calibre flak. Hammet was now extremely busy looking out for targets, return fire and the other Spits. He had used up all his ammunition on another German motorcycle and side car when he spotted Sgt Lascelles flying at 200ft approaching a small village near the airfield. Hammet warned Lascelles to steer clear, then was distracted by groundfire from the airfield again which, this time, hit his own Spitfire. He radioed the other pilots to re-form and follow him home before things got any worse. Lascelles was last seen by one of the other pilots turning to join his leader flying at 500ft directly over Perugia airfield when he ran straight into another intense barrage of anti-aircraft fire from the German guns. Although Hammet was able to bring his Spitfire home, Lascelles was not seen or heard from again and was eventually listed as 'Missing – Particulars Unknown'. He had been with the squadron for only three weeks before being shot down. It was not until a few weeks later when the squadrons moved up to occupy Perugia that the missing Spitfire (No. MJ389) was found in a wood near the airfield with Lascelles' body beside it. That same day, 601's sister squadron, 417 Squadron, lost Flt Lt Ingalls when, after strafing German vehicles hidden under trees, his Spitfire was also hit by flak and crashed. His squadron also located his aircraft soon

after they arrived at Perugia. It was found a few miles north of the airfield along with the pilot's grave about 200yds away from the crash site. Members of the squadron returned to the site the day after the find to hold a graveside ceremony. Both now lie in Rivotorto military cemetery. Lascelles lies in the same row, third grave along from Desmond's: VIII, H, 1 and VIII, H, 3 respectively.

15 Carver, Field Marshal Lord, *Imperial War Museum Book of the War in Italy 1943–1945: A Vital Contribution to Victory in Europe* (Pan Books, 2002), pp. 211–16.
16 Rawlins, 'A WAAF's eye View of WW2'.
17 Ibid.
18 Ibid.
19 Desmond borrowed Seafire LR645. It was the only time he flew one. The Fleet Air Arm pilots were received from No. 4 Naval Fighter Wing, led by Lt Cdr Baldwin DSC, who was serving on the aircraft carrier *Attacker*. The pilots had been sent over to Fabrico on a short attachment to a fighter-bomber wing to gain operational experience and were divided out among the other squadrons. Baldwin himself was the guest of 601 Squadron and brought with him Lt Heywood of 807 Squadron from the carrier *Hunter*, Lt Neilson and Sub Lt Fry both of 809 Squadron from the carrier *Stalker* as well as four Seafires (navalised versions of Spitfire VBs) and seven groundcrew (AIR 26/ 328, 244 Wing ORB; AIR 27/ 2072, 601 Squadron ORB).
20 Rawlins, 'A WAAF's eye View of WW2'.
21 Ibid.
22 AIR 26/ 328, 244 Wing ORB. Horst Wessel, a Nazi Party (NASDAP) activist, who in the early days of the party composed 'The Flag', which was to become the signature tune of the NASDAP. Wessel himself was killed during one of the early and often violent *Putsches*, or political rallies, thus ensuring his name became synonymous with the anthem.

Chapter 19

1 Desmond Ibbotson's official service record, RAF PMS Gloucester.
2 AIR 29/ 587/ 2, 5 RFU ORB.
3 Extracted from the logbook of student Plt Off Eric Clive Masters (SAAF), who joined D Flight, 5 RFU and flew Kittyhawks between 6 and 18 September 1944 prior to joining 260 Squadron at the end of that month (RAF Museum).
4 Also convened on 15 September 1944 was the official court of inquiry into a fatal accident involving the Spitfire VB of one of the students, 2nd Lt Waters (SAAF), who had crashed on 11 September 1944. This was usual following a fatality but, in Desmond's case, there is no record of a court of inquiry being convened in either the 5 RFU or wing records after his accident on 19 November.
5 On 8 October 1944 one of the 5 RFU student pilots, Sgt Law, was practising bombing runs on Lake Trasimeno. As he finished one run, his Spitfire (no. ER214) crashed into the lake. Law was killed instantly. The engineering officer, Fg Off James, drove out to the scene, but there was very little of the aircraft to be seen

and the pilot's body was never recovered. A week later, on 15 October, Sgt Fox accidentally dived into the lake in his Spitfire (no. ER730) while carrying out strafing runs. Again, Fg Off James attended the scene to recover some of the debris. Small pieces of wreckage including the pilot's helmet, a battledress sleeve and an Air Force blue sock were retrieved, but although the lake was dragged at the spot marked by an oil patch on the surface of the water, the body of Sgt Fox was also never found (AIR 29/ 587/ 2, 5 RFU ORB).

Chapter 20

1 AIR 29/ 587/ 2, 5 RFU ORB.
2 *Air Ministry Pilot's Notes for Spitfire IX, XI & XVI (Merlin 61, 63, 66, 70 or 266 engine)*, 3rd edition, 1947 (Republished by Crecy, 2004), p. 21.

Chapter 21

1 Following each crash in October, the attendance of the engineering officer, Fg Off James (promoted to flight lieutenant on 29 October 1944) at the scene was noted along with details of what he managed to retrieve. Yet there is no record either in 5 RFU's ORB or 11 Squadron SAAF ORB of him attending the scene of Demond's crash.
2 AIR 29/ 587/ 2, 5 RFU ORB.
3 AMCS Signal x16/22 referenced in Desmond Ibbotson's official service record, RAF Form 543, RAF PMS Gloucester.
4 Ibid.
5 AIR 29/ 587/ 2, 5 RFU ORB.
6 AIR 23/ 8298, Control and Disposition of Tactical Air Force Units in Italy, 15 November 1944.
7 AIR 29/ 587/ 2, 5 RFU ORB.
8 At the beginning of November, 11 Squadron SAAF was regularly receiving orders to move to a new base only for the orders to be cancelled a few days later, so it stayed at Perugia. Part of the squadron was sent to Florence on 12 November, but this was cancelled indefinitely on 15 November.
9 This is thought to be a planned move to the airfield at Peretola, where the remainder of 8 Wing SAAF were based.

Chapter 22

1 British Film Institute review, www.screenonline.org.uk.
2 Holland, J., *Royal Air Force: The Official Story* (Welbeck, 2018), pp. 162–63; Duke, Sqn Ldr N., *Test Pilot* (Grub Street, 2003), pp. 166–67.

Chapter 25

1. The translation by Marco Maiani of the story of the excavation undertaken by RoAF comes from their book written in 2009 containing details of all their excavations to that date, including a chapter on Desmond's find. That chapter is précised here. Since then, they have gone on to find several more remains of aircrew who participated in this theatre of war, at sites across Italy (Iezzi, E., *Cacciatori d'Aerei* (Walberti, 2009), pp.183–203).
2. A Pro Loco is a civic membership association of volunteers that works with schools, local businesses and institutions in order to project ways to enhance the town and provide assistance to visitors.

Chapter 27

1. www.cwgc.org.
2. Since renamed the Joint Casualty and Compassionate Centre Commemorations team based at Innsworth House, Imjin Barracks, near Gloucester.

Chapter 29

1. Morgan E.B. and Shacklady, E., *Spitfire: The History* (Key Publishing, 1987), pp. 316–18.
2. Harvey-Bailey, A., *The Merlin in Perspective: The Combat Years* (Rolls-Royce Heritage Trust, 1995), pp. 45–46 and Appendix VI, p. 136.

Glossary

AA	Anti-aircraft artillery – also called 'ack ack'.
Ace	The informal title for a pilot who has shot down at least five enemy aircraft confirmed.
ACM	Air Chief Marshal.
AOC	Air Officer Commanding an RAF group.
AM	Air Marshal.
Armed Reconaissance	A reconnaissance mission prepared to attack any targets encountered.
AVM	Air Vice-Marshal.
Bandit	An aircraft positively identified as enemy or hostile.
Bar	The award of the same medal more than once.
Buzz	To fly very low over a target or object.
CFI	Chief Flying Instructor.
C-in-C	Commander in Chief.
CO	Commanding Officer.
Circus	A daylight formation of fighters escorting bombers.
Crash-landing	Situation when a pilot experiences a loss of engine power and/or control before or during landing.
DAF	Desert Air Force.
DAK	Deutsches Afrika Korps, or Africa Corps.
DF	Delivery flight.
DFC	Distinguished Flying Cross. Awarded only to commissioned officers. When suffixed by *, it signifies that a Bar to the medal has been awarded.
DFM	Distinguished Flying Medal. Equivalent to the DFC but only awarded to non-commissioned officers.
DSO	Distinguished Service Order.
E/a	Enemy aircraft.
ELG	Emergency landing ground.
Flak	Anti-aircraft fire, from the German *Fliegerabwehrkanonen*.

Fg Off	Flying Officer.
Flt Lt	Flight Lieutenant.
Flt Sgt	Flight Sergeant.
Forced-landing	Situation when a pilot experiences a significant problem mid-air and has to land quickly.
FW190	Focke-Wulf 190.
GHQ	Group Headquarters (RAF) or General Headquarters (Army).
Glycol	Aircraft engine coolant.
Gp Capt	Group Captain.
ITW	Initial Training Wing.
JG	*Jagdgeschwader* – (German) Fighter Wing.
JU-52	Triple-engine transport aircraft, nicknamed '*Tante Ju*' (Aunty Ju).
JU-86	High-altitude reconnaissance variant of the JU-88 with a pressurised cockpit.
JU-87	Junkers 87 dive-bomber. Also known as 'Stuka' from the German title *Sturzkampfflugzeug*.
JU-88	Junkers 88 twin-engined medium-range bomber.
KIA	Killed in action.
LAC	Leading Aircraftman.
LG	Landing ground. Also, an ALG – advanced landing ground. Usually a rough-and-ready airstrip, not always a fully equipped airfield.
LMG	Light machine gun.
Lt	Lieutenant or, if German, *Leutnant*.
Lt Gen	Lieutenant General.
MAAF	Mediterranean Allied Air Forces.
MC202	Macchi Castoldi. Named after the designer Mario Castoldi, the chief engineer of Aeronautica Macchi, the Italian aircraft manufacturer. The MC202 was officially called Folgore or Thunderbolt.
MIA	Missing in action.
MoD	Ministry of Defence (or MOD).
MT	Motorised transport.
MU	Maintenance unit.
NCO	Non-commissioned Officer.
Op	Operation – a formation of aircraft sent out to carry out a specific task or mission.
ORB	Operations record book. A daily diary of events kept by all RAF units.
OTU	Operational training unit.
Plt Off	Pilot Officer.
PoW	Prisoner of War.
PT	Physical Training.
RAAF	Royal Australian Air Force.
RAFVR	Royal Air Force Volunteer Reserve.
Recce	Reconnaissance.
RFU	Refresher Flying Unit.
Rhubarbs	Small-scale freelance fighter/fighter-bomber strikes against targets of opportunity.

Glossary

RCAF	Royal Canadian Air Force.
RNZAF	Royal New Zealand Air Force.
Roadsteads	Low-level attacks on enemy shipping.
RT	Radio-Telephone, by voice not Morse.
SAC	Senior Aircraftman.
SAAF	South African Air Force.
Sgt	Sergeant.
Section Officer	WAAF rank equivalent to flying officer in the RAF.
Sortie	A flight made by one or more aircraft.
Sqn Ldr	Squadron Leader.
Strafe/Straffe	An attack from the air with machine guns and/or cannon.
Uffz	*Unteroffizier*.
WAAF	Women's Auxiliary Air Force.
Wg Cdr	Wing Commander.

Bibliography

National Archive Sources

AIR 2/ 15759.
AIR 23/ 8298, Control and Disposition of Tactical Air Force Units in Italy, 15 November 1944.
AIR 26/ 315, 239 Wing Operations Record Book.
AIR 26/ 328, 244 Wing Operations Record Book.
AIR 26/ 567, 8 SFTS Operations Record Book.
AIR 27/ 512, 54 Squadron Operations Record Book.
AIR 27/ 873, 112 Squadron Operations Record Book.
AIR 27/ 890, No. 4 Delivery Flight Operations Record Book.
AIR 27/ 1818, 417 Squadron Operations Record Book.
AIR 27/ 2070, 601 Squadron Operations Record Book.
AIR 27/ 2072, 601 Squadron Operations Record Book.
AIR 27/ 2079 603 Squadron Operations Record Book.
AIR 27/ 2110 611 Squadron Operations Record Book.
AIR 29/ 587/ 2, 5 RFU Operations Record Book.
AIR 29/ 681 53 OTU Operations Record Book, 1941.
AIR 49/ 126 239 Wing Medical History Reports, May 1944.
AIR 49/ 273, 601 Squadron Medical History of the War.
AIR 50/ 21/ 43, 54 Squadron Combat Reports, 27 September 1941.

HW 1/ 1031, file for the prime minister's correspondence containing British intercepts of German signals.
HW 1/ 1044.
HW 1/ 1059.
HW 1/ 1066.

London Gazette, 15 July 1941.
London Gazette, 12 February 1943.
Supplement to the *London Gazette*, 4 February 1941.
Supplement to the *London Gazette*, 6 April 1944.

WO 201/ 2495 'Extract from 9th Australian Division Report on Operations El Alamein 23rd Oct–5th Nov 42'.

RAF Museum Sources

AC/91/8/15, 601 Operations Record Book – original diary, February 1944, RAF Museum Hendon.
Rawlins, R., 'A WAAF's eye View of WW2, 1939–45', 2014 (unpublished).

Imperial War Museum Sources

AL 834/ 1/ 1-2, DAK war diary translated by Dawson.
Catalogue No. 19054, Interview with John Tilston, 6 September 1999.

Liddell Hart Centre Sources

LH 9/24/20, Rommel's letters (English translation).
Nelson, Sqn Ldr T.R. 'A Desert Landing' (*KLM Pilots Association Magazine*, 1948).

Published Sources

Air Ministry Pilot's Notes for Spitfire IX, XI & XVI (Merlin 61, 63, 66, 70 or 266 engine), 3rd edition, 1947 (Republished by Crecy, 2004).
Addington, S., *Reaching for the Sky: One Hundred Defining Moments from the Royal Air Force 1918–2018* (Uniform, 2018).
Avery, M.C. and Shores, C., *Spitfire Leader: The Story of Wg Cdr Evan 'Rosie' Mackie DSO, DFC and Bar, DFC (US), Top Scoring WWII RNZAF Fighter* (Grub Street, 1999).
Battistelli, P.P., *Rommel's Afrika Korps* (Osprey, 2006).
Brook, H., *True Stories of D-Day* (Usborne, 2006).
Brown, R., *Shark Squadron: The History of 112 Squadron 1917–1975* (Crecy Books, 1994).
Brown, R., *Desert Warriors: Australian P-40 Pilots at War in the Middle East and North Africa 1941–1943* (Queensland: Banner Books, 2000).
Bungay, S., *Alamein* (Aurum Press, 2003).
Bungay, S., *The Most Dangerous Enemy: A History of the Battle of Britain* (Aurum Press, 2001).
Carver, Field Marshal Lord, *Imperial War Museum Book of the War in Italy 1943–1945: A Vital Contribution to Victory in Europe* (Pan Books, 2002).
Churchill, W.S., *The Second World War: The Hinge of Fate: Volume IV* (Reprint Society, 1953).
Davidson, M. and Taylor, J., *Spitfire Ace: Flying the Battle of Britain* (Channel 4 Books, 2003).
Drake, B. and Shores, C., *Billy Drake, Fighter Leader: The Autobiography of Group Captain B. Drake, DSO, DFC & BAR, DFC (US)* (Grub Street, 2002).

Bibliography

Duke, N., *Test Pilot* (Grub Street, 2003).
Duncan-Smith, Gp Capt W.G.G., *Spitfire into Battle* (John Murray, 2002).
'Edwards J.F.', Obituary, *The Daily Telegraph*, 19 May 2022.
'Elvin, V.', Obituary, *The Times*, 5 June 2021.
Falconer, J., *Bomber Command Handbook 1939–1945* (Sutton, 2003).
Ford, K., *El Alamein 1942: The Turning of the Tide* (Osprey, 2005).
Fraser, D., *Knight's Cross: A Life of Field Marshal Erwin Rommel* (HarperCollins, 1993).
Fydenchuk, P., *Immigrants of War: Americans Serving with the RAF and RCAF During World War II* (California: W.P.F. Publications, 2007).
Glancey, J., *Spitfire: The Biography* (Atlantic Books, 2006).
Goodson, Col J.A., *Tumult in the Clouds* (Arrow, 1986).
Harvey-Bailey, A., *The Merlin in Perspective: The Combat Years* (Rolls-Royce Heritage Trust, 1995).
Haskew, M.E., 'Churchill's General', *Britain at War*, Key Publishing, August 2022.
Holland, J., *Together We Stand: North Africa 1942–1943: Turning the Tide in the West* (HarperCollins, 2005).
Holland, J., *Heroes: The Greatest Generation and the Second World War* (Harper Perennial, 2007).
Holland, J., *Royal Air Force: The Official Story* (Welbeck, 2018).
Holmes, R., *In the Footsteps of Churchill* (BBC Books, 2005).
Hough, R. and Richards, D., *The Battle of Britain: The Jubilee History* (Guild Publishing, 1990).
Iezzi, E., *Cacciatori d'Aerei* (Walberti, 2009).
Jarrold, J. and Delve, K., *Did You Survive the War?: An Ordinary Fighter Pilot's Story* (Suffolk, 2006).
Johnson, AVM J.E., *Full Circle: The Story of Air Fighting* (Cassell, 1964).
Johnson, AVM J.E., *Wing Leader* (Goodall, 2000).
Kaplan, P., *Fighter Aces of the Luftwaffe in World War II* (Pen & Sword, 2007).
Kingcome, B., *A Willingness to Die: Memories from Fighter Command* (Tempus, 2006).
Lavigne, M. and Edwards, Wg Cdr J.F., *Kittyhawks Over the Sands: The Canadians and RCAF Americans* (Quebec: Lavigne Aviation Publications, 2002).
March, P., *The Spitfire Story* (Sutton, 2006).
Middlebrook, M. and Everitt, C., *The Bomber Command War Diaries: An Operational Reference Book, 1939–1945* (Pen & Sword, 2014).
Morgan E.B. and Shacklady, E., *Spitfire: The History* (Key Publishing, 1987).
Moulson, T., *The Flying Sword: The Story of 601 Squadron* (MacDonald, 1964).
Moulson, T., *The Millionaires' Squadron: The Remarkable Story of 601 Squadron and the Flying Sword* (Pen & Sword, 2014).
Neillands, R., *The Desert Rats: 7th Armoured Division 1940–45* (Weidenfeld and Nicolson, 1991).
Pitchfork, Air Cmde G., *Shot Down and on the Run: The RAF and Commonwealth Aircrews Who Got Home from Behind Enemy Lines, 1940–1945* (The National Archives, 2003).
Price, Dr A., *Late Mark Spitfire Aces 1942–45* (Osprey, 1995).
Price, Dr A., *Spitfire Mark V Aces 1941–45* (Osprey, 1998).
Quill, J.K., *Spitfire: A Test Pilot's Story* (Crecy, 2005).
Richey P., *Fighter Pilot* (Cassell, revised edition, 2001).
Rolls, Flt Lt B., *Spitfire Attack* (William Kimber, 1987).

Sarkar, D., *Spitfire!: Courage and Sacrifice* (Victory Books, 2006).
Shores, C. and Massimello, G., *A History of the Mediterranean Air War, 1940–1945: Volume 4 – Sicily and Italy to the Fall of Rome 14 May 1943–5 June 1944* (Grub Street, 2018).
Shores, C. and Williams C., *Aces High, Volume 1: A Tribute to the Most Notable Fighter Pilots of the British and Commonwealth Forces of WWII* (Grub Street, 1994).
Shores, C., *Aces High, Volume 2: A Further Tribute to the Most Notable Fighter Pilots of the British and Commonwealth Forces of WWII* (Grub Street, 1999).
Shores, C. and Ring, H., *Fighters Over the Desert: The Air Battles in the Western Desert, June 1940 to December 1942* (Arco, 1969).
Smith, R.C., *Hornchurch Eagles: The Life Stories of Eight of the Airfield's Distinguished WWII Fighter Pilots* (Grub Street, 2002).
Thomas, H., *Spirit of the Blue: Peter Ayerst – A Fighter Pilot's Story* (Sutton, 2005).
Thomas, N., *Kenneth 'Hawkeye' Lee DFC: Battle of Britain and Desert Air Force Fighter Ace* (Pen & Sword, 2011).
von Luck, H., *Panzer Commander: The Memoirs of Colonel Hans von Luck* (Cassell, 1989).
Watson, B.A., *Exit Rommel: The Tunisian Campaign, 1942–1943* (Stackpole Books, 2007).
Wellum, G., *First Light* (Penguin, 2003).
Wragg, D., *RAF Handbook 1939–1945* (Sutton, 2007).
Wynn, H., *Desert Eagles* (Airlife Publishing Ltd, 2001).
Young, D., *Rommel: The Desert Fox* (HarperCollins, 1953).
Zaloga, S.J., *Anzio 1944: The Beleaguered Bridgehead* (Osprey, 2005).

Published Internet Sources

BFI Screenonline, www.screenonline.org.uk.
Abbot, M., The Origins of Technical Education in New Zealand, crie.org.nz/research-papers/M.Abbott_H.D_OP2.3.pdf.
Henry, R., 'Armoured Command Vehicles', *Military History Journal*, 16(6) (2015), South African Military History Society, viewed at www.samilitaryhistory.org.
'Illustrated War Diary of Flight Sgt. (late Flying Officer) Brian M. Thompson Distinguished Flying Medal' (2006), viewed at www.3sqnraafasn.net/subpages/thompson.
'Jagdgeschwader 27', www.wikipedia.com.
'New Air Speed Record', *Nature*, 143 (1939), pp. 756–57, viewed at www.nature.com.
New Zealand Shipping Company Ltd passenger manifest, from www.findmypast.co.uk c/o Barbara McCulloch.
Pearce, W., 'Cobb Railton Land Speed Record Car', 2020, www.oldmachinepress.com.
Pratt, S.E., 'Benchmarks: March 17, 1944: The Most Recent Eruption of Mount Vesuvius', *Earth* (2016), viewed at earthmagazine.org.
'RAF Training', Ken Fenton's War, www.kenfentonswar.com/raf-training.
The Commonwealth Graves Commission, www.cwgc.org.
'The New Zealand Official Year-book, 1935', www3.stats.govt.nz.
The Union of Pro Loco Associations, www.ichngoforum.org.
Tidy, Sqn Ldr D.P., 'South African Aces of World War Two', *Military History Journal*, 2 (2) (2007), The South African Military History Society, viewed at www.samilitaryhistory.org.
www.bundeswehr.de/de/.

Index

Aberdeen, Scotland 39, 73
Aberfan, South Wales 46
Abyssinia (Ethiopia) 30, 90
Accrington, Lancashire 138
Afrika Korps, v 85, 94, 95, 96, 108, 115,
      116, 117, 120, 121, 124, 133, 134,
      136, 149, 232
   Officers
      Buchholz, *Generalmajor* 136
      Streich, Lt General 121
   Units
      15th Panzer Division 108, 297
      5th Light Division 121
Ahrenfeldt, Helen 93
Air Ministry 57, 67, 142, 199, 228, 229,
      241, 265, 302
Albert, Park, New Zealand 29, 78
Albuquerque, New Mexico 47
Aldershot, Hampshire 199
Alkmaar, Holland (German Naval
      Hospital) 230
Allison aero engines 183
American aircraft
   Consolidated B-24 Liberator 106, 130
   Martin 187 Baltimore 108, 215
   North American B-25 Mitchell 185
   North American P-51 Mustang 182,
      183, 213
   Stinson Sentinel 275
   Tomahawk 91, 113, 141
   Warhawk 91

American 'Eagle' Squadrons 50
Amsterdam, Holland 230
Associated Equipment Company 85, 120
Atlantic Wall 175
Auckland, New Zealand 29, 31, 78
Australia 75, 76, 196, 240, 263
Australian War Museum 172
Aviation Candidates Selection Board 33

Babbacombe 33
Barbasetti, His Excellency, General Curio
      (Head of Delease, the Delegation
      of the Italian Supreme Command
      in North Africa) 117
Barbini, Bruno 258
Barnstaple, Devon 47
Barras, Joan 147, 228
Bartolini, Dr Giorgio 259
Basilica of St Francis *see* Italy, Basilica di
      St Francesco, Assisi
Battle of Britain Memorial Flight 160, 286
Beaton, Cecil 99, 207
Beirut, Lebanon 104
Bendix-Stromberg supercharger 170, 287
Benelux (Belgium, Netherlands,
      Luxembourg) 32
Berlin, Germany 116, 117, 183
Binyon, Laurence (Poem 'For the Fallen')
      21
Blackpool 33, 201
Bletchley Park, Buckinghamshire 117

Boscini Vitali, Mario 257
Boverton, Llantrisant, South Wales 47
Brazil 198
Bremen, Germany 200, 201
Britain, Battle of 32, 33, 43, 44, 47, 54, 57, 58, 59, 64, 66, 68, 96, 110, 165, 188, 231, 294
British Army
   Commanders
      Auchinleck, General Sir Claude 'The Auk' 100, 106, 113
      Brooke, General Sir Alan 106
      Gott, General William Henry Ewart 'Strafer' 101, 102, 106, 107, 117, 297, 302
      Leese, General Oliver 209
      Montgomery, Lt General Bernard Law 106, 107, 113, 114, 115, 116, 125, 209
   Units
      11th Hussars 127
      1st Guards Motorised Infantry Brigade 203
      4th Armoured Brigade 95
      61st Motorised Infantry Brigade 203
      7th Armoured Division 100, 101
      8th Army 96, 102, 106, 107, 127, 129, 209
      The East Lancashire Regiment 128, 270, 299
      The Gurkha Regiment 131
      XIII Corps 101
British Flying Training Scheme 38
British Newspapers
   Aeroplane magazine 92
   London Gazette 131, 197, 304
   Sunday Despatch 59
   The War Illustrated 74, 145
Brough, East Yorkshire 34, 35

C&C *see* Codes and Ciphers
Caithness, Scotland 73, 82
Camberley, Surrey 198
Cambridge 34, 45
Canil, Padre 277

Cardiff, South Wales 46
Castletown, Scotland 73, 74, 82, 196
Cavallero, Marshal of Italy, Ugo 112
Cavallucci, Bruno 11, 156, 252, 258, 281
Cavallucci (family) 229
Cavallucci, Domenico 258
Chief Flying Instructor (CFI) 41, 43, 84, 92, 93, 212, 240
Churchill, Winston 16, 75, 86, 95, 100, 106, 107, 130, 167, 174
   speech, 1940 16
Cicogna, Mario 258
Cobb, John (world land speed record holder) 55
Coccumella *see* Italy, Hotel Cocumella, Sorrento
Codes and Ciphers 199
Colwinston, South Wales 47
Commonwealth War Graves Commission 236
Crete, Greece 75, 149
Cromarty, Scotland 39
Cunningham, John 'Cats Eyes' (test pilot) 233
Cyril Stubbs & Co. Ltd 31

Daba *see* El Daba
Dalmonte, Uliano 258
Dario 17, 18, 20, 21
D-Day 175, 202
De Lazzari, Father Francesco 155, 260
Derry, John (test pilot) 233
Desert Air Force (DAF) 89, 94, 95, 96, 97, 98, 100, 110, 116, 139, 141, 166, 167, 172, 175, 182, 190, 210, 288
   Training Flight 89, 191, 212
Devon 33, 47
Distinguished Flying Cross 43, 296, 304
Distinguished Flying Medal 43, 300
Distinguished Service Order 135
Dover, Kent 58
Dover Straits 58
Duncan, Air Corporal G.L. (8 Sqn SAAF) 261
Dundee, Scotland 39

Index

Dungeness, Kent 67
Dunnet Bay, Scotland 73

Edinburgh, Scotland 39, 64, 72
Elvin, Violetta 146
Elvington, North Yorkshire 286
Empire Air Training Scheme 38
Esso, petrol 170
Ethiopia 30, 90, 289

Falconelli, Mario 282
Far East 76, 90, 91, 165, 197, 236
Farnborough, Hampshire 199, 233
Ferroni, Carlo 257
First Aid Nursing Yeomanry 199
First World War 30, 32, 33, 58, 101, 114, 128, 199, 270, 300, 303
Folkestone, Kent 58, 63, 72
France 16, 32, 33, 43, 58, 59, 60, 61, 62, 63, 64, 68, 76, 89, 90, 92, 93, 94, 111, 135, 136, 149, 154, 164, 170, 175, 196, 200, 270, 298
   Arras 61
   Bethune 61
   Dunkirk 32, 58, 60, 64, 298
   Gravelines 65
   Le Mans 93
   Le Touquet 66
   Lens 61
   Lille 60
   Marquise 64
   Mazingarbe 61, 62, 64, 66, 67
   Neuf Berquin 60
   Normandy 175, 202
   Paris 93
   Pas-de-Calais 61
France, Battle of 111, 135, 198
Franco, General Francisco 30
Frankfurt, Germany 230
Franklin-Brown, Flt Sgt Andy 277
French aircraft
   Dewoitine D.520 149

Gandaberunda, Hindu double-headed eagle 49

Gandin, General Antonio 117
Genzano, *see* Italy, Genzano di Roma
German Condor Legion 56
Germany 30, 32, 55, 56, 67, 166, 230
Goodwood *see* Westhampnett, Chichester, West Sussex
Grangemouth, Scotland 73, 75
Gravesend, Kent 58

Hampdens *see* Handley-Page Hampden
Harewood, West Yorkshire 29, 30, 31, 35, 42, 51, 52, 53, 65, 77, 78, 79, 81, 105, 107, 169, 228, 231, 249, 255, 265
Harrogate Grammar School 30, 31
Hendon, London 11, 289, 303
Hirst, David, Yorkshire TV reporter 10, 159, 269, 273
Hitler, Adolph 30, 76, 94, 95, 100, 112, 115, 116, 175, 202
Holland 201, 230, 305

Ibbotson, Ada 30, 77, 79
Ibbotson, Horace 29, 30, 31, 52, 76, 77, 79, 236
Ibbotson, Molly 9, 29, 129, 145, 233, 234, 235, 236, 238, 265, 288
Ibbotson, Muriel 9, 16, 19, 20, 29, 31, 33, 52, 53, 74, 76, 77, 78, 88, 128, 129, 145, 147, 163, 169, 172, 176, 207, 211, 228, 233, 234, 235, 238, 239, 240, 241, 243, 250, 262, 263, 264, 265, 266, 267, 271, 288, 302
Italy
   Basilica di St Francesco, 216, 220, 227, 236, 237, 264, 272
   Genzano-di-Roma 185
   Hotel Coccumella, Sorrento 206, 211
   Mount Vesuvius 184, 191, 195, 196
   Perugia 10, 11, 155, 203, 208, 209, 211, 213, 214, 215, 216, 217, 221, 222, 227, 228, 265, 271, 280, 289, 305, 306, 307
   Pisa 203, 229

Poggiomarino 191
Pompeii 191
Pontedera 229
Popoli 173
Porto Civitanova 172, 212
Ravenna 155, 258
Rignano 209
Rimini 203
Rome 11, 16, 18, 155, 168, 174, 175, 176, 185, 186, 190, 192, 196, 201, 202, 203, 204, 211, 266, 278
Salerno, landings at 9, 16, 239
Sangro (river) 164, 167, 169
Siena 211, 214
Sorrento 206, 212, 248
Spoleto 203
St Egidio (airfield) 11, 203, 217, 271, 285
St Maria degli Angeli 21, 155, 207, 222, 249, 259, 260, 272, 274
Straits of Messina 164, 174
Terni 167, 168, 169
Tevere (river) 220
The Vatican, Rome 202
Tollo 169
Tuscany 214, 264
Umbria 11, 15, 22, 214, 238, 258, 264
Venafro 197, 204, 205, 246
IWGC *see* Commonwealth War Graves Commission

Jamaica 50
Jensen, Patsy 9, 12, 196, 197, 198, 199, 200, 201, 202, 203, 204, 205, 206, 207, 208, 209, 211, 212, 213, 214, 216, 220, 229, 230, 232, 235, 237, 238, 241, 245, 246, 247, 248, 249, 289, 291, 305
Jersey, Channel Island 93
Junkers *see* Luftwaffe aircraft

Kesselring, Generalfeldmarschall 112, 117
Kirkwood, Lt William John 128, 299
Kitties/ Kitty *see* Curtiss P-40 Kittyhawk

Klopper, South African General 95
Knaresborough Grammar School 33

Leeds, West Yorkshire 31, 33, 44
Lincoln, Lincolnshire 199
Little Hulton, Bolton, Lancashire 49
London, England 11, 30, 31, 33, 43, 55, 58, 110, 120, 165, 200, 201, 228
Luftwaffe 30, 33, 39, 56, 58, 62, 65, 68, 69, 89, 97, 102, 110, 117, 133, 134, 137, 138, 149, 150, 151, 167, 176, 181, 182, 186, 190, 196, 203, 297, 299
Luftwaffe aircraft
Fieseler Storch 117, 125
Focke-Wulf FW190 135, 137, 149, 181, 182, 186, 188, 189, 192, 300
Heinkel 56
Heinkel HE-111 125, 130
Junkers JU-52 112, 136, 299
Junkers JU-86R 149
Junkers JU-87 Stuka 89, 100, 109, 118, 119, 125, 129, 130, 131, 139
Junkers, JU-88 73, 118, 133, 139, 149, 151
Luftwaffe Messerschmitt, types
ME109 (Bf) 56, 57, 60, 62, 63, 67, 68, 106, 107, 108, 109, 110, 113, 114, 118, 126, 127, 132, 133, 134, 135, 137, 139, 154, 167, 181, 186, 187, 188, 189, 192, 193, 194, 295, 297, 299, 300, 303, 304
ME109E 56, 57, 66, 102
ME109F 56, 100, 108, 115, 132
ME109R 56
ME323 136
Luftwaffe squadrons
II/ JG27 106, 108
III/ JG27 109
V/JG27 297, 298
III/ JG53 109
I/NJG 1 305

M/T *see* Motorised Transport
MAAF HQ *see* Mediterranean Allied Air Forces

Index

Maiani, Marco 11, 162, 257, 308
Malizia, Luigi 257
Malta 75, 76, 110, 129, 135
Manston, Kent 43, 62
Marcross, South Wales 47
Mark IX *see* Spitfire Mk IX
Martin, Yorkshire TV cameraman 10, 17, 18, 20, 159, 273, 274, 278
McKie, Wilson 30
Mediterranean Allied Air Forces 195, 197, 201, 202, 204, 206, 228, 247
Merthyr Vale *see* Vale of Merthyr, South Wales
Messina Straits *see* Italy, Straits of Messina
Middle East 75, 76, 84, 100, 106, 140, 149, 150, 230
Mills, John 232
Montrose, Scotland 38, 39, 41, 42
Moscow, Russia 146, 293
motorised transport (MT) 96, 101, 102, 138, 166
Mussolini, Benito 99, 126, 154

National Archives, The, Kew, London 11, 263, 304
New Zealand 29, 30, 31, 32, 36, 78, 91, 108, 133, 165, 173
Non-Commissioned Officers (NCOs) 33, 51, 171, 273, 296, 300
North Africa
  Aboukir, Egypt 147, 148, 149, 150, 151, 152, 153, 154, 271, 301
  Abu Sueir, Egypt 140, 141
  Aghiela, Libya 126
  Alam Halfa, Egypt 113
  Alexandria, Egypt 76, 93, 98, 99, 128, 139, 148
  Algeria 124
  Ben Gardene, Libya 131
  Bou Goubrine, Tunisia 88, 134
  Bou Grara, Tunisia 88, 134
  Cairo, Egypt 76, 96, 98, 99, 100, 104, 106, 107, 110, 124, 128, 131, 134, 139, 141, 148, 167
  Cap Bon, Tunisia 136, 138
  Casablanca, Morocco 130, 135
  Castel Benito, Libya 130, 131
  Derna, Libya 99
  Egypt 17, 75, 76, 90, 95, 115, 117, 126, 128, 129, 139, 140, 141, 142, 146, 148, 212, 230
  El Adem, Libya 126, 131
  El Alamein, Egypt 99, 101, 104, 105, 109, 110, 114, 117, 123, 150, 167, 170, 190, 298
  El Assa, Libya 131
  El Ballah, Egypt 142, 144, 146, 147
  El Daba, Egypt 97
  El Hamma, Tunisia 134
  El Hasseiate, Libya 126
  Gabes, Tunisia 132, 134
  Gambut, Egypt 83, 84, 92, 125, 126
  Gazala, Libya 110, 125, 126
  Hamraiet, Libya 129
  Hazbub, Libya 131
  La Marsa, Tunisia 201
  Libya 16, 75, 83, 84, 93, 95, 99, 125, 129, 298
  Marble Arch (memorial), Libya 126, 127
  Mareth, Libya 132, 133, 134
  Marturba, Egypt 126
  Medenine, Tunisia 132, 133, 134
  Mersa Matruh, Egypt 85, 86, 116, 117, 119, 122, 131
  Mishiefa, Egypt 125
  Morocco 124
  Nagrah, Egypt 127
  Qattara Depression, Egypt 99, 101, 112
  Sfax, Tunisia 134, 135, 299
  Sidi Barrani, Egypt 117, 118, 122
  Sidi Haneish, Egypt 97
  Sidi Rezegh, Libya 95
  Sousse, Tunisia 134, 136
  Suez Canal, Egypt 90, 100, 110, 141, 142, 151
  Tobruk, Libya 76, 95, 100, 103, 106, 125, 134
  Tripoli, Libya 126, 127, 129, 135, 139
  Tunis, Tunisia 135, 136, 139, 201

Tunisia 16, 88, 125, 129, 134, 138, 140, 149, 154, 163, 165, 174, 190, 298, 299
Western Desert 75, 86, 103, 124, 131, 167, 302, 304
Zt Msus, Libya 126
North Sea 39, 51, 58
Northern Ireland 74
Norway 32, 39

Ostend, Belgium 67
Ottawa-Hull Bridge 51

Panama 31
Panama Canal 31
Pantelleria (Italian Island) 138
Pennacchi, Eugenio 11, 26, 157, 159, 275, 276, 278, 279, 280, 281
Pernambuco, Brazil 200
Pilots
  American
    Scudday, Plt Off. Fred 50
    Warner, Plt Off. J. 50
  RAAF
    Hammet, Flg Off. Mitch 212, 305
    Radcliffe, Flt Lt Alan J. 191, 212
    Simpson, Flt Sgt Alan 188, 190, 304
  RAF
    Aitken, Sgt 63
    Armitage, Sqn Ldr Dennis Lockhart 49, 50
    Bader, Wg Cdr Douglas 165
    Bax, Sgt 63
    Brady, Sgt 73
    Bruce, Flg Off. 100
    Brunton, Flg Off. 91
    Charles, Flt Lt Edward Francis John 'Jack' 59, 69
    Cheshire VC DSO DFC, Gp Capt. Leonard 288
    Clowes DFM, Flt Lt Arthur Victor 'Darky' 43, 111
    Colyer, Sgt 167, 169, 176
    Coulson, Sgt 215

Cuddon, Plt Off. Brian A.F. 'Compo' 84, 127
Davidson, Flg Off. 192
Drake DFC, Billy 10, 43, 48, 84, 92, 102, 104, 107, 109, 110, 111, 127, 288
Draper, Sgt 64
Duke DFC, Sqn Ldr Neville 62, 130, 135, 136, 139, 140, 141, 142, 197, 233, 288
Duncan-Smith, Wg Cdr Wilfred G.G. 165, 202, 244, 302
Dundas, Wg Cdr Hugh 'Cocky' 198, 207
Edwards VC DFC, Gp Capt. Hughie Idwal 288
Eid, Flt Sgt Andre 181, 188, 190, 243, 303, 304
Evans, Plt Off. 62, 63
Fenton, Sgt 67
Fox, Sgt 215, 307
Garton DFC, Flt Lt Geoff 97, 103, 140
George, Sgt 167, 176, 178
Gibson VC DSO DFC, Wg Cdr Guy, 288
Gleed, Wg Cdr Ian Richard 'Widge' 135, 165
Greaves, Sgt 100
Gregory, Flt Sgt 217
Guthrie, Sgt 69
Harris, Plt Off. 'Streak' 61, 63
Henderson, Flt Lt W.R. 'Hindoo' 173, 181, 188, 190, 304
Henderson, Sgt 176, 177, 178, 182, 183, 184, 303
Hewlett, Sgt 36
Holton, Sgt 192, 193
Houghton, Sqn Ldr 99, 124
Ingram, Flt Lt Bruce 114, 118
Jarrold, Flt Lt Jerry 38
Knoll, Sgt George 'Felix' (Polish) 93
Lacey, Sqn Ldr James Harry 'Ginger' 33
Law, Sgt 215, 306

Index

Leitch, Flt Lt 214
Llewellyn, Plt Off. Donald E. 118, 119, 137
McDonald, Sgt 70, 71, 72
McGahey, Sgt Frederick, George Thomas 47
Mitchell, LAC P. 39
Moore, Sgt 167
Mottram DFC, Flt Lt Roy 43, 59, 60
Nelson, LAC 40
Nicholls, Sqn Ldr John Hamilton 190
Nichols, Flg Off. 40, 41
Orton, Sqn Ldr Newell 'Fanny' 59, 64, 111
Overton, Sgt 64
Overton, Wg Cdr Charles 213
Parker, Flt Sgt 182
Pavlu, Flt Sgt (Czech) 63
Pickard DSO DFC, Wg Cdr P. Charles 288
Pook, Sgt 59
Preece, Sgt 65
Rawlins DFC, Sqn Ldr Colin Guy Champion 199, 200, 229
Ross, Sgt 176, 177
Ryder, Wg Cdr Edgar 47
Samuel, Flg Off. 126
Saunders, Sgt W. 47
Scott-Malden DFM, Sqn Ldr David 'Scotty' 64, 69
Skalski, Sqn Ldr Stanislaw 165
Smith, Sqn Ldr Hiram 59
Stapleton, Wg Cdr Eric 59, 61, 62, 63
Steele, Sgt 126
Taylor DFC, Sqn Ldr John Stuart 132, 133
Thomas, Sqn Ldr E.H. 59
Tilston, Sgt John 'Tilly' 243, 247
Toller, Sgt 114
Wade, Sqn Ldr Lance 'Wildcat' 166, 244, 302
Walker, 'Jimmy' 83, 84, 100
Whitamore, Flg Off. William Michael 'Babe' 83, 100, 111, 113, 118, 165

RCAF
Crichton, Flg Off Joseph 'Big Joe' Michael S. 85
Edwards DFM DFC, Flt Lt James Francis 'Stocky' 138, 139, 263
Gilboe, Nelson 139
Goldberg, Sgt Louis 'Curly' 35
Hay, Flt Lt William B. (later Sqn Ldr) 170, 180, 205, 218, 232
Manuel, Sgt Gerald 'Jerrie' Fenwick 35
Plomteaux, Sgt Marion Arthur 36
Sherk, Ray, Sgt (later Plt Off) 31, 36, 37, 39, 98, 108, 148
Thomas, Flg Off 'Tommy' 36, 177, 178
Turner, Sqn Ldr Stan 150, 180
Whalen, Plt Off James 'Jimmy' 39, 42
Yarnell, Flt Lt Cyril 'Cy' 164, 165, 166, 170, 174, 175, 180, 181, 182, 200

RNZAF
Mackie, Sqn Ldr Evan 'Rosie' 150, 160
Morrison, Sgt J.H. 95
Westenra, Flt Lt Gerry 73, 151

SAAF
Bartleman, Lt A. 105
Bennetts, Lt 105, 106
Doveton, 2nd Lt G.D. 211
Gasson, Lt Johnny 194
Hall, Capt R.K. 205
Meaker, Capt F.J.M. 177, 181, 182
Osler DFC, Major 'Bennie' 150, 154, 155, 158, 159, 160, 163, 164, 166, 168, 169, 176, 179, 205
Pote, Lt Pete 170, 177, 181, 182
Saville DFC*, Capt Eric Cowley 'Danny' 93
Sharpe, Lt J.E. 177
Sinclair, Capt C. 219, 220, 262

Waugh, Capt Lawrence Robertson Stuart 159, 160, 179
Wearne, Lt 164, 166
Pisa Nick, 242, 245
Pitcairn Island 20
Poland 71, 251
Pope Pius XII 194
Poperinghe, Belgium 50
PoWs *see* Prisoners of War
Pratt and Whitney (aero engines) 71
Prisoners of War 31, 60, 109
Pudney, John 222
Purtell, John, FCO official 253

QCS *see* Queen's Colour Squadron
Queen's Colour Squadron, RAF Regiment 251
Quill, Jeffrey, Supermarine test pilot 46

Raftree, Sue 246, 251
Ramsgate, Kent 48
Rangitane (Merchant Vessel) 21
Rangitata (Merchant Vessel) 20
Rattigan, Terrence 222
Rawlins, Delphine 189
Recife, Brazil 191
Reggia Aeronautica, Italian Air Force 122, 153
Ricci, Claudio 250
Richards, Anthony (Observer) 225
Richardson, Jim 203, 230
Ringham, Warren 251
Rio de Janeiro, Brazil 191
Rivotorto, Military Cemetery 11, 235, 237, 238, 248
Rochester, Kent 48
Rochford, Essex 48
Rolls Royce, inspector, Harker, Ronald 'Ronnie' 172
Rolls Royce (company) 29, 172
Rolls Royce engine types
  Griffon, 45
  Merlin, 29, 172
  Merlin 45, 45
  Merlin 61, 145
  Merlin 66, 156, 157, 182, 212, 262

Romagna Air Finders (RoAF) 12, 234, 235, 242, 250, 257, 264
Rome, British Embassy 8, 253
Rommel, Generalfeldmarschall, Erwin 11, 77, 78, 83, 84, 87, 88, 90, 95, 99, 100, 101, 102, 103, 104, 105, 108, 109, 112, 113, 116, 124, 243
Roosevelt, President Franklin D. 90, 104, 119
Rosyth, Scotland 28
Royal Air Force
  Aircraft
    Armstrong-Whitworth Whitley 19
    AVRO Lancaster 81
    AVRO Manchester 191
    Blenheim 51, 52, 55, 56, 58, 59
    Curtiss P-40 Kittyhawk 71
    Harvard 40, 73, 134, 201, 207
    de Havilland Tiger Moth DH-82A 24, 25, 27, 38, 74
    de Havilland DH-98 Mosquito 153, 188, 196
    de Havilland DH-110 225
    Dominie 66, 68
    Douglas Boston 208
    Douglas DC-3 Dakota 193, 204
    Handley-Page Halifax 81
    Handley-Page Hampden 191, 220
    Hurricane 23, 27, 28, 29, 32, 45, 49, 51, 57, 59, 60, 71, 73, 87, 97, 118, 119, 133, 134, 135, 136
    Miles Master 27, 32
    Short Stirling 81
    Supermarine, Spitfire types
      Mk IA 38, 45, 46, 80, 145
      Mk IIB 32, 45, 67
      Mk IV 45
      Mk V 44, 45, 46, 47, 118, 135, 144, 145, 151, 152, 205, 213
      Mk VB 44, 127
      Mk VC 98
      Mk VIII 151, 152, 156, 157, 159, 173, 186
      Mk IX 122, 127, 140, 143, 144, 146, 152, 157, 198, 211, 261, 262

Index

Mk LF IXe 211
Mk XI 145, 146
Taylorcraft Auster 151, 187, 188, 196, 197, 198, 217
Vickers Wellington 80

Airfields and bases
- Biggin Hill, Kent 48, 53, 66
- Boscombe Down, Wiltshire 46, 141, 142, 145
- Chivenor, Devon 36
- Coltishall, Nofolk 54
- Digby, Lincolnshire 190
- Doncaster, South Yorkshire 190
- Drem, Scotland 65
- Duxford, Cambridgeshire 76, 172
- Finingley, South Yorkshire 190
- Grantham, Lincolnshire 190, 192, 200
- Hawkinge, Kent 54, 65
- Headington, Oxfordshire 190
- Hemswell, Lincolnshire 190, 191
- High Wycombe, Buckinghamshire 189
- Hornchurch, Essex 43, 44, 47, 48, 49, 51, 52, 54, 55, 56, 59, 64, 65, 66, 69, 88, 98
- Kirkwall, Orkney Islands 192
- Lindholme, South Yorkshire 190
- Leconfield, East Yorkshire 22, 37, 38, 39, 40, 41, 42
- Llandow, South Wales 35, 36, 37, 74
- Lympne, Kent 59, 64, 65
- Montrose, Scotland 30, 31
- Northolt, Middlesex 150
- North Weald 23
- No. 1 Receiving Wing, Babbacombe, Torquay 23
- No. 2 Initial Training Wing, Cambridge 24
- No. 3 Recruit Centre, Padgate, Warrington 23
- No. 4 Elementary Flying Training School, Brough, East Yorkshire 24
- No. 9 Recruit Centre, Blackpool 22
- Redcar, North Yorkshire 192
- Scampton, Lincolnshire 190
- Tangmere, Chichester 75
- Waddington, Lincolnshire 190
- Weeton, Blackpool, Lancashire 192

Branches
- Administrative and Special Duties 190

Commanders
- Broadhurst, Air Vice Marshal, Harry 'Broady' 48, 49, 52, 125, 126, 151, 188
- Coningham, Air Chief Marshal, Arthur 'Mary' 79, 188
- Douglas, Air Chief Marshal Sir Sholto 130, 188
- Dowding, Air Chief Marshal Sir Hugh 60, 133
- Elmhirst, Air Commodore Tommy 81
- Kingcome, Gp Capt Brian 125, 126, 150, 180, 187, 188
- Leigh-Mallory, Air Vice Marshal Trafford 55

Commands
- Fighter Command 35, 47, 133, 263
- Bomber Command 22, 60, 189, 190, 263

Flying Training Units
- Elementary Flying Training 24, 28
- Operational Training Units 28
- 5 Refresher Flying Unit 180, 203
- 53 Operational Training Unit, Heston, Middlesex 31, 32, 34, 35, 63
- 61 Operational Training Unit 35
- 73 Operational Training Unit 131

Groups
- 5 Group 190
- 14 Group 69

Maintenance Unit 33, 139, 140
Museum 263

Officers
- Aston, Reverend Sqn Ldr 194
- James, Flg Off (Engineering Officer 5 RFU) 39, 92, 138, 209
- Carew-Gibbs, Plt Off Kenneth 105
- Dickson, Air Vice Marshal 202

Laing, Gp Capt Iain 261
McNicholl, Air Marshal Ian 250
Pnematicatos (RAF Chaplain), Sqn Ldr Nick 252
Sorley, Sqn Ldr Ralph 133, 134
Thomas, Sqn Ldr 'Doc' (601 Squadron Medical Officer) 194
Simulator, Link Trainer 26, 29
Squadrons
  No. 1 (F-Fighter) squadron 75
  54 Sqn 43, 44, 47, 49, 52, 53, 55, 56, 57, 59, 61, 62, 65, 66, 67, 68, 69, 156, 186
  56 Sqn 23
  65 Sqn 46
  91 Sqn 32
  92 Sqn 49, 96, 119, 124, 126, 129, 150, 160
  93 Sqn 151
  112 Sqn 73, 74, 92, 98, 129, 131
  124 Sqn 66
  128 Sqn 74
  129 Sqn 37, 38, 39, 40, 98
  144 Sqn 191
  145 Sqn 96, 129, 150, 151, 180, 188
  242 Sqn 51
  250 Sqn 129
  260 Sqn 100
  266 Sqn 38, 39
  601 Sqn 96, 97, 98, 101, 102, 104, 105, 111, 113, 119, 122, 124, 127, 128, 129, 146, 148, 149, 150, 151, 155, 163, 168, 170, 173, 176, 179, 180, 181, 185, 200, 204, 205, 211, 219, 239, 243
  603 Sqn 49, 50, 54, 56
  611 Sqn 49, 53, 54, 65,
Volunteer Reserve 23, 30
Wings
  131 Polish Wing 150
  239 Wing 74, 87, 89, 90, 92, 115, 129, 206
  244 Wing 96, 126, 129, 150, 152, 160, 171, 187, 188, 194, 199, 201
  324 Wing 151, 171

Royal Army Medical Corps 18
Royal Army Service Corps 113
Royal Artillery 48
Royal Australian Air Force
  Squadrons
    3 Sqn 74, 93, 129
    450 Sqn 74
    450 Sqn 93, 129
Royal Auxiliary Air Force 30, 96
Royal Canadian Air Force 36, 205
  Squadrons
    401 Sqn 148
    417 Sqn 150, 171, 180
Royal Flying Corps 22, 198
Royal Military Academy Sandhurst 117
Royal Military Police 117, 200, 203
Royal Naval Air Service 22
Russia 72, 137, 138

Seddon, LAC John Henry (RAF Regiment) 238
Seddon Memorial Technical College 20
Shoreham, West Sussex 265
Sicily 124, 126, 127, 128, 129, 141, 146, 149, 161
Sorrentino, Archbishop 252
South Africa 191, 205
South African Air Force
  Squadrons
    5 SAAF Sqn 100
    11 SAAF Sqn 206, 219
  Wings
    7 (SAAF) Wing 208
South African Army Units
  6th South African Armoured Division 197
Spanish Civil War 19, 45
Stalag Luft III, near Sagan 220
Steeds, Shawn, Commander, Royal Navy, British Naval and Air Attaché 10, 250
Stuka *see* Junkers JU-87 Stuka
Swindon, Wiltshire 33
Switzerland 193, 255

Index

'The Flag', Horst Wessel 8
The Millionaires *see* 601 Sqn
Tofi, General 250
Torquay 23

ULTRA, Bletchley Park, Buckinghamshire 104
United States Army Air Force (USAAF) 39, 249
  Groups
    79th Bomb Group 128
    340th Bomb Group 181
University of British Columbia 40
Uzbekistan 138

Vale of Merthyr, South Wales 35
Vancouver, British Columbia 39, 41
Venieri, Leo 9, 235, 238, 250, 258

WAAFs *see* Women's Auxiliary Air Force
Wakefield, West Yorkshire 138
Ware, Fabian 246
Warrington 23
Wehrmacht 19, 138, 202
Western Desert (North Africa) 71, 88, 112, 120
Westhampnett, Chichester, West Sussex 43
Wetherby, West Yorkshire 23
Winchester, Hampshire 33
Women's Auxiliary Air Force 185, 190

Yorkshire Air Museum 226, 261

Zibetti, Alderman Emiliano 236